HORROR IN HADDONFIELD

HORROR IN HADDONFIELD

THE UNTOLD STORIES OF HALLOWEEN

ANDREW GREVAS

TUCKER
DS
PRESS

Horror in Haddonfield: The Untold Stories of Halloween

Cover design by Matthew O'Connell
Edited by David Bushman
Book designed by Scott Ryan

Published in the USA by Tucker DS Press
Columbus, Ohio

Contact Information
Email: TuckerDSPress@gmail.com
Website: TuckerDSPress.com
Twitter: @FMPBooks
Instagram: @Fayettevillemafiapress

This book is dedicated to Debra Hill, Donald Pleasence, and Moustapha Akkad.

A memorial plaque for Moustapha Akkad. Image courtesy of Ivan Bukta

CONTENTS

THE *HALLOWEEN* FILMS:

Halloween (1978): Written by John Carpenter and Debra Hill. Directed by John Carpenter.

Halloween II (1981): Written by John Carpenter and Debra Hill. Directed by Rick Rosenthal.

Halloween III: Season of the Witch (1983): Written and directed by Tommy Lee Wallace.

Halloween 4: The Return of Michael Myers (1988): Written by Dhani Lipsius, Larry Rattner, & Benjamin Ruffner and Alan B. McElroy. Directed by Dwight Little.

Halloween 5: The Revenge of Michael Myers (1989): Written by Michael Jacobs & Dominique Othenin-Girard and Shem Bitterman. Directed by Dominique Othenin-Girard.

Halloween: The Curse of Michael Myers (1995): Written by Daniel Farrands. Directed by Joe Chappelle.

Halloween H20: 20 Years Later (1998): Written by Robert Zappia and Matt Greenberg. Directed by Steve Miner.

Halloween: Resurrection (2002): Written by Larry Brand and Sean Hood. Directed by Rick Rosenthal.

Rob Zombie's *Halloween* (2007): Written and directed by Rob Zombie.

Rob Zombie's *Halloween II* (2009): Written and directed by Rob Zombie.

Halloween (2018): Written by Jeff Fradley, Danny McBride & David Gordon Green. Directed by David Gordon Green.

Halloween Kills (2021): Written by Scott Teems, Danny McBride & David Gordon Green. Directed by David Gordon Green.

Halloween Ends (2022) Written by Paul Brad Logan, Chris Bernier, Danny McBride & David Gordon Green. Directed by David Gordon Green.

-CHAPTER 1-
WELCOME TO HADDONFIELD

The Shape. Michael Myers. Even the bogeyman. It doesn't matter what we call him. He's all of these things. He's the evil that lurks in the darkness and the sounds we can't explain. Michael shows us that even in the suburbs, we should listen to that little voice in the back of our head that warns us to turn around. Yes, something or someone may in fact be watching. Nowhere is safe. Evil is everywhere. Evil has always been everywhere.

The Shape is a fictionalized iteration of real-world evil. In the period of time in which he was created, that meant serial killers like Ted Bundy, John Wayne Gacy, the Zodiac Killer, Son of Sam, and the Hillside Strangler who dominated headlines, striking fear in families and communities alike. Hijackings. Bombings. Jim Jones and the Peoples Temple. In the decade that preceded the release of the first *Halloween* film, John Kennedy, Robert Kennedy, and Martin Luther King Jr. had all been gunned down; the images still played in our heads. While we often idealize the 1960s and 1970s, make no mistake about how violent that period of time was. The Shape was the violence and fear we saw on our living room TVs each night. He was the danger parents warned their children about. He was the bogeyman, and the bogeyman has always been real.

Over the course of the thirteen films in the *Halloween* franchise, the

School exterior. Image courtesy of Ivan Bukta

goalposts have often moved. What once was a simple scary story about a man in a mask who killed babysitters widened in scope considerably. We got the mythology behind the mask. We got more family members who may or may not have had the same desire to kill. We got to see a world where Michael Myers didn't exist. We got origin stories, ancient cults, copycats, and Busta Rhymes with mad karate kicks. Even with all the world-building and story resets, one thing has remained undoubtedly true: people love to fear Michael Myers. When there was no Michael in *Halloween III: Season of the Witch*, fans revolted. When *Halloween Ends* told the story of a young, traumatized man attempting to first learn from and then replace Michael Myers, fans revolted. Arguments over the thirteenth film and whether it's good or not are a staple of Facebook fan groups, and those debates don't seem to be ending anytime soon.

The question is why? Why can't there be a film about other creepy things that happen on Halloween night? Why can't Michael Myers ride off into the sunset only to have someone new become the Shape? Viewers have an intrinsic fascination with Michael that's understandable. He predates other popular horror franchise icons of the era, such as Jason Voorhees and Freddy Krueger. He's inherently creepier than most on-screen villains, largely due to his silence. He doesn't make us laugh. He doesn't want anything from his victims except their death. Anyone in his proximity is in danger Michael.

A fascinating duality exists here. As his twin designations— the Shape and Michael Myers—suggest, he is both otherworldly and of this world. The first film tells us he is a young boy who kills his older sister. That same film (and certainly the sequels) shows us he has to be something more than human. Later sequels try to explain the root cause, but Michael remains an enigma who walks the line between man and monster. He's both the seemingly benign neighbor who snaps one day and the demon that makes things go bump in the night. As long as he remains unexplainable, he will be intriguing.

Since 1978, the Shape has been a part of our culture. Teenagers have slumber parties, eating popcorn and gasping as they watch evil descend on Haddonfield. Those teenagers grow up to have kids who have slumber parties and watch Michael track his younger sister, Laurie, down twenty years later. And those teenagers grow up to have kids who don't have to wait for home video to see Michael wreak his havoc on Haddonfield in David Gordon Green's trilogy. Times have changed, but Michael Myers is consistent. For more than four decades now, audiences have been watching Michael on big screens and small, in living rooms, at drive-ins, in movie theaters. Michael Myers has become folklore, and that's why we reject anyone else as the Shape. Michael, the Shape, the bogeyman—it doesn't matter what we call him. He has weaved himself into our lives and refuses to let go. Real-world evil has in some terrifying ways evolved since *Halloween* came out in 1978, but on screen, evil in the personification of Michael looks the same, and there's some odd comfort in that. With all due apologies to Anthony Michael Hall and the angry mobs of people from Haddonfield, evil isn't dying tonight, or any night. Evil has always been here and is here to stay.

The darkness personifies is directly opposed by the town of

Haddonfield itself. The birthplace of this monster is his greatest foe, with the townspeople frequently standing side by side to stare down this murderous entity. Horror permeates Haddonfield, but in perhaps the greatest metaphor of all, this fictional town represents the human spirit. We confront heinous acts but somehow find the strength to move forward. We as communities lift each other up during the worst of times. Horror films, and in particular slasher films, aren't always simple morality tales in which virgins die and drugs are bad. At their best, they're dramatized versions of the daunting challenges humans experience every day.

For this book, I set out to document as many stories from those close to the franchise as possible. *Halloween* has become a complicated saga over the years, with various timelines and eras, not to mention the multitude of performers and behind-the-scenes teams involved. This book is designed for you to be able to jump around and read out of order, which is pretty on brand for this franchise and its splintered narrative. Hopefully it can bridge some gaps as well for fans both new and old, casual and passionate. At its core, this book is my love letter to this story, to the people who brought it to life, and to the town itself.

Welcome to Haddonfield.

The Myers house. Photo courtesy of Ivan Bukta

-CHAPTER 2-

THE CARPENTER ERA

The first three *Halloween* films aren't a trilogy by any stretch of the imagination, but they do represent an era. If you've seen any of the countless documentaries that exist on 1978's *Halloween*, you are familiar with the story: young film students get together and make a movie. It's the romantic side of Hollywood, with artists who happened to be friends working closely together, each performing multiple jobs and having the kind of freedom they likely would long to experience again for the rest of their careers, after making what would become a low-budget classic. Director John Carpenter and cowriter/producer Debra Hill weren't setting out to create a blockbuster film franchise. They were just trying to make a scary movie. As it turned out, they did both.

Halloween grossed over $70 million dollars on a budget of $300,000. It's at or near the top of almost every horror-flick "best of" list you can find. It has spawned twelve sequels to date and countless imitators and was even added to the National Film Registry in 2006. On the surface, the film operates as a story about teenagers being stalked and killed on Halloween night; on a deeper level, it subverts the notion of idyllic suburbia. *Halloween* examines the power of myths and urban legends that grow stronger over the generations and asks viewers to decide if Michael is man or myth. It's accessible, yet fascinating to analyze.

John Carpenter's *Halloween* gets credit for kicking off the wave of slasher films that dominated the horror genre in the 1980s, despite in some ways being more of a Hitchcockian thriller itself in the way it created terror and suspense without a profusion of blood. Perhaps other filmmakers witnessed the success of *Halloween* and suspected a cinematic trend was unfolding but felt they could compete only by upping the ante with more sex and violence. *Halloween II*, released in 1981, actually follows that formula, resulting in a sequel that feels stylistically different from its predecessor. Still, from a narrative point of view, *Halloween II* is a continuation of the original movie, even taking place on the same night as Michael Myers extends his killing spree to the hospital where Laurie Strode is recovering from earlier events. Our killer is done with the foreplay; it's time for an evening of mayhem to reach its climax.

It did feel like a complete story had been told over the course of these first two films. Michael Myers and Loomis were presumed dead as a result of a fire, and Laurie had gotten her happy ending by escaping, with a cute boy at her side to boot [in the version released for television at least]. Horror franchises weren't the norm back then the way they are now, when we simply assume the villain will come back for another sequel. *Halloween* created the template for these horror film series and had the unenviable task of trying to keep this cash cow alive without a real blueprint to draw from. Thought about in these terms, it makes sense that Carpenter and Hill originally thought to continue the series with films about other, unrelated Halloween-night frights, but as it turned out, audiences just weren't ready to move on from Michael Myers.

Halloween III: Season of the Witch might be a beloved cult classic now, but the *Invasion of the Body Snatchers*-inspired film was given the black-sheep treatment for over two decades. Of course fans were disappointed that Michael Myers wasn't back. An expectation had been created that he was synonymous with this franchise. Still, *Season of the Witch* created a compelling mythology of its own that could have propelled the series forward. The story was rich and layered, more narratively substantial than many other horror films of the time. Perhaps there's an alternate universe where the filmmakers figured out a way to acknowledge Michael just enough in *Season of the Witch* to satisfy fans while still passing the torch to this new concept. But not in this universe.

Season of the Witch is a good film, but it exists completely on its own, in a world in which the 1978 *Halloween* is merely a movie that airs on TV. Michael Myers is nothing more than a fictional character. This well-written, compelling film is typically treated as merely a footnote in the history of the franchise. While many fans have clamored in recent years for more *Season of the Witch*-type stories, it seems unlikely to happen on the big screen. However, the long-rumored *Halloween* anthology TV series would be a perfect vehicle for more non-Michael Myers centric stories.

After *Halloween III*, there was a long hiatus between films, and many of the key players behind the scenes did not return for the fourth installment. The group of friends who had done the impossible, turning a small indie film project into a cinematic classic, had gone their separate ways after failing in their attempt to move the franchise in a new direction.

Years later, many scholars, critics, and fans alike have changed their tune on *Halloween III: Season of the Witch*. We can now look back on the Carpenter Era of *Halloween* as one of extraordinary creativity and world building, navigating uncharted seas and producing three truly exceptional horror films that gave birth to the longest-running slasher franchise of all time. A new guard would then come in and propel the series forward, but the ingenuity of the Carpenter Era will hold a special place in the hearts and minds of horror (and slasher) fans forever.

Interview: Dean Cundey (Director of Photography, *Halloween*, *Halloween II*, *Halloween III*)

Andrew Grevas: The first *Halloween* film has this reputation, this very romantic story of young filmmakers having a great time making a fun movie. Is that a fair characteristic of your experience?

Dean Cundey: Yeah, I think so. Everybody involved loved the idea of working in film. I had been out of film school for a little while working on a lot of low-budget films, action-adventure films. And then *Halloween* showed up, and there was a different feeling about it. It was being made . . . I hate to say out of love, but everybody was involved for their own personal reasons, as opposed to just making a car-crash movie or something like that. There was an awful lot of thought, involvement, and inspiration here.

AG: Artistically speaking, what influences did you have before the first *Halloween* film?

Dean Cundey: That's interesting, because *Halloween* was really sort of a different take on the genre. I had been interested in films since I was a kid. My mother would drop us off at the theater on Saturdays, and we would see Disney films, but also films where giant tarantulas attacked people, and stuff like that. There was a certain amount of suspense and so-called horror, I guess, in the films I had seen starting when I was a kid. What to me was interesting is that as opposed to a giant tarantula, the threat came from something that was possible. There was potential for this crazy guy with a knife to be possible. It involved a lot more inspiration and creativity in order to really do it effectively.

AG: When shooting the film, were you kind of drawing on those childhood inspirations at all? It was one of the first films where you really didn't know what was behind your shoulder, that type of feeling. I was curious about that inspiration.

Dean Cundey: Film has always been progressing, since it was first invented. People look for something new to do with it and have since Georges Méliès was making *A Trip to the Moon*. There was always this idea that you could do something on film that would emotionally involve an audience. I think all of the films I had watched sort of built on that. You get the sense of how film tells the story and how it affects you and so forth. If you remember that or draw on that, it adds to the next one. Now we've learned how to use computers to make goofy movies. It's always building on what went before it. Even if you don't consciously think about it until later, when you're actually involved in the film business, you're always absorbing things that scare you. I was scared because that thing jumped out from the shadows.

AG: I wanted to ask about your memories of working with both John

Carpenter and Debra Hill.

Dean Cundey: At the time it was probably one of the most rewarding and engaging involvements that I had been a part of. There was a complete sense of care by both of them. Debra I'd been working with for a couple of years, doing a low-budget movie. She was a script supervisor. Instead of just making notes and so forth, she would say to me would it be effective if the camera did this or that or the guy did something or whatever? She was involved with the filmmaking—the storytelling—more than her job entailed. She's the one who introduced me to John. They had written the movie together. When I was introduced to John and we had conversations, it was evident to me that he was also an involved filmmaker, someone who wasn't there just to record the action and actors talking. He wanted to do something that definitely affected the audience. Working with both of them was almost an eye-opening experience about how you really could become involved with creating a film.

AG: One of my favorite experiences so far working on this book is hearing Debra Hill stories, so I appreciate you telling me those anecdotes.

Dean Cundey: I always appreciated her honesty, involvement, and her dedication. Unlike some people that you work with on films, there was no sense that she was in it for the money or that she was in it for the fame. She was genuinely interested in making a good film and film storytelling, and I think she did through her sadly short career.

AG: When you think back about the first *Halloween* film and when you think about your work specifically, which shot sticks out to you the most?

Dean Cundey: John and I were talking the other day, and we both have talked about the fact that we wanted to use the very wide-screen, anamorphic format in order to create a bigger canvas and more lurking space in the frame, where you could be both hiding and revealing the suspense. To me, that was incredibly rewarding, because it wasn't just like using the camera to record the action or the dialogue performances. It was consciously being used to create visual tension and visual storytelling. There are certain shots that come to my mind with the film, things like Jamie Lee [Curtis, playing Laurie Strode], having been chased and terrorized, leaning against the wall, and gradually the face of Michael Myers becomes evident in the closet next to her. What has been pointed out to me a couple of times is the shot where Jamie Lee Curtis is leaning against the door frame in the bedroom, after Michael Myers has apparently been defeated, and he slowly sits up behind her. We did not change the focus back to him. We left him sort of out of focus, and she was sharp in the foreground. That to me was sort of the real use of the frame and how to emotionally affect an audience with it. It wasn't there just to say, "Oh look, there's a guy behind her," and you pull focus to him. You keep him this nebulous, terrifying figure. Those are two of the shots that I sort of always remember as being indicative of the technique that we were trying to accomplish. I'm sure there are others. We very consciously constructed the suspense and the reveals and so forth.

AG: The scene where you slowly see his face that you were describing first is perhaps my favorite scene in cinema history.

Dean Cundey: It was John's inspiration and my figuring out how to actually do it. That speaks to the collaboration that should be done on a film.

AG: Compared to other directors that you've worked with, what was your relationship like with John in terms of technique, artistry, and collaboration?

Dean Cundey: Well, I have to say that it's one of my most enjoyable experiences, partly because it was one of my first experiences with a very camera-aware director, one who wanted to use the frame to tell the story, as opposed to just capture action. Our relationship I've always thought of as being one of mutual respect and also collaboration, inspiration, and adding to each other's vision. When you think about it, all of what we do starts out only as something in somebody's brain. When they imagine the story and then they write the script, most of the time it's not about anything other than imagination and emotion.

I think that was one of my greatest satisfactions in working with John, that he was all about creating the emotion and the effect as opposed to capturing images.

AG: You would go on to work with two other directors for the second and third films, Rick Rosenthal and Tommy Lee Wallace. What was the dynamic like with both of those directors?

Dean Cundey: Well, Tommy Lee Wallace, on the third *Halloween* film, I had of course worked with him ever since the original *Halloween*. I realized he was also interested in individual storytelling. Rick Rosenthal, I had never met him prior. I was requested by Debra and John to work on *Halloween II* to carry through the visual style. I think Rick was actually pretty good at following through with that style. Every director likes to put their own mark on it, but he was quite flexible and followed my suggestions as far as maintaining the style and the visual storytelling.

AG: The second film is unique in the fact that a majority of it takes place in the hospital. What was that like for you, and how did it impact your style of work?

Dean Cundey: Well, it's interesting because *Halloween II*, as I understand it, was an afterthought almost. The original film, in the first week, not a lot of people came and saw it. Then of course it became a huge success and is still called a great story and was a great initial entrance into the film world for a lot of us. To me, it was really a great experience to realize that the stuff that had come from somebody's mind, an actual visual representation of somebody's thoughts and imaginations. I really enjoyed the fact that we were able to take just some thoughts and turn them into an actual film. There was a bit of time between the first one and the second one, and the second one had not been thought of at the beginning as being viable. So it was a lot of fun to get it to work, to find the thread of continuation, and then visually keep it going.

The fact that most of it takes place in the hospital was interesting because we knew it had to be dark in order to be suspenseful. So we used this essentially abandoned hospital, one that was not working at the time, and we were able to do whatever we felt like doing as far as the storytelling. There were not any sort of limitations on what we would be able to do in the physical space that we had. I think that was really sort of a great thing, because there was no concern about these conditions, like having to be out by a certain time or we can't go down there because that's the operating area or any of the limitations that could have been put on us. So we were able to invent our own hospital world. I had thought that it would be interesting if for some reason that goes dark and there's sketchy lights to make it suspenseful, because that's kind of what we wanted to do. So I invented, with air quotes around the term, these safety lights in the hallway of the hospital. The safety lights were two very small motion picture lights attached to a box that looked like it was part of the lighting system of the hospital for their battery-operated safety lights, or whatever. So that gave us control over lighting, lighting patterns, lighting quantity, all kinds of things like that. That enabled us to really create the mood that we wanted, because the idea was that suspense takes place in the dark more effectively. So we tried to do that, and I can't remember how many of these lighting units we had, but we would put them up in the corners of the hallways so that we would be able to control the light and paint the story—paint the drama, you might say.

AG: The other noticeable change in the second film was the amount of gore, which seemed to be in direct contrast to the first film, where the gore and the violence was very minimal.

Dean Cundey: Well, it was two pronged. I really appreciated the fact that we got such a great, suspenseful reaction out of the first one and we didn't use any blood. Blood to me always sort of draws attention—"Oh, look, there's spurting blood"—as opposed to your involvement with the actual action of a knife stabbing someone. You can imagine the rest of it and the blood squirting. I think it was interesting that the first film had no blood, but with the second film, there was this feeling that of course you have to have blood by the people who were subsequently taking over the show. I think it was a little disappointing that you sort of emotionally cling to this idea that the blood itself is the terror. That idea still holds, that you have to have blood in order for there to be terror. I don't think that's true. Maybe once in a while, when it seems logical or effective, but most of the time the action carries the drama, the horror, and so forth. I think sometimes it becomes almost intrusive. We did get a little bit more intrusive, and then subsequently the genre became more and more so. I'm very proud of the fact that the first film created all of this suspense and terror without the blood because you knew the effect of that knife. I think that sometimes the blood and the obvious stuff like that really just sort of draws you out of the action. Suddenly you're aware of a splash of red.

AG: It's interesting that the first film is very much a *Psycho*-type thriller in a lot of ways, and then the second film was more of a byproduct of the slasher films that were coming out at the time. Then the third film moves in the science fiction direction. I find it incredibly interesting that each of the first three films in this franchise have their own identity in a lot of ways, and I wanted to kind of follow up and get your thoughts on that.

Dean Cundey: I think that's a good observation. We were in some ways pioneering the slasher film, or the suspense horror film. With each one, everybody had to add what they thought was the next level of horror so that people would be afraid. When we made the third film, there was a conscious effort and decision that it would really just be about the tradition, the suspense of *Halloween* itself, as opposed to Michael Myers. It was thought that each subsequent film, if there were more, and they thought by that point, on the third one, that there would be more, that it would be somehow tied to the tradition of Halloween itself. Each film could then explore a different aspect and not be stuck with Michael Myers. But when it was discovered that during the third film people were saying, "But where's Michael Myers?" there was a conscious effort to return to him as a thread, and it's obviously been the continuous thread ever since. It seems to be the thing that the audience expects or wants out of the franchise. I'm pleased, I guess, but still saddened that the subsequent films all followed the same thing, variations on Michael Myers chasing after people. It would have been interesting to see how you could twist and turn the tradition of Halloween into suspenseful, thriller movies, each one being different.

AG: I was curious if that was ever a discussion point, ideas for films beyond *Season of the Witch* that could have been in that same vein. Did you ever get to that point where you guys were speaking creatively about ideas or plans for the future?

Dean Cundey: There were no concrete ideas or plans. What was talked about was "Let's find different takes on Halloween and how it can be woven together." It was kind of sad that it didn't continue like that. We had talked about while making *Halloween III* the fact that there was all of this tradition that Halloween had behind it, the tradition of Samhain, so it was unfortunate that we didn't have a chance to try other Halloween versions, and I don't know why nobody has really done that. This is a movie about Halloween, and somebody would read it and say, "Where's Michael Myers?" People have tried making horror films about almost every holiday now because that's what *Halloween* started.

AG: The third film would mark your departure, Tommy Lee Wallace's departure, and then John and Debra were severely limited after the third film. Is that a coincidence, or perhaps that the original crew felt like they had done enough for this particular franchise and didn't want to continue on with multiple Michael Myers iterations?

Dean Cundey: I think there's a certain amount of truth to that. If you look at a lot of sequels, you find that the original creators are not on it. *Romancing the Stone*, for instance, was a combined effort of Bob Zemeckis and mine working together for the first time along with various creative folks. When they got to the sequel, Bob said he didn't think he wanted to do a sequel. I'd say with a secret amount of satisfaction that the sequel didn't measure up both storywise and visually.

AG: Now, the third *Halloween* film obviously was the biggest departure. It visually looks different, it felt different, and it was a significantly different movie. What were your thoughts about the script? I know you liked the idea of moving in a different direction, but what did you think about this particular story?

Dean Cundey: I thought it was interesting, to examine something about Halloween that we weren't really aware of as kids. We always put on these supposedly scary costumes and went around and scared people into giving us candy, even though obviously people were not scared. I was very pleased with the idea of it being different. One of my guidelines as a cinematographer is that each film should speak on its own, have its own style that best tells the story, with the best visual storytelling with the camera, and all of that. I know it was a conscious effort to not be an artificially terrifying movie but was to sort of explain the tradition of Halloween or at least one version of it, to tell it in a way that was effective for that particular mood, style, and storyline. I think it was a conscious effort on my part and certainly on Tommy Lee's part to do something that was not going to be construed as a rip-off or anything. It had to stand on its own.

AG: I recently spoke with Stacey Nelkin, one of the stars of *Halloween III*, and she described Tommy Lee Wallace as being like jazz music. She said that he was free-flowing and kept using the phrase "jazz music" when she was describing his directorial style. Does that hold true for you as well, or would you describe the style as being different?

Dean Cundey: Yeah, I can see her analogy there. I guess if you wanna talk about jazz, it's sort of music that's a little more free-flowing according to emotional reactions, and depending on what your style of jazz is, the music itself is finding its own way. I think that's a good description of Tommy Lee. He was open to suggestions and open to inspiration. He didn't come with rigid thoughts. He would react to the opportunities given to him both in performances and also in the visuals as well as in the production design. I can see jazz music.

AG: Any particular shots or scenes from your personal work that really stick out to you as favorites from the third film?

Dean Cundey: I know that there's a scene where there's the large glowing rock. The question was how to make that work. Of course we didn't have CGI work in those days. All of the visual effects had to be optical and manual. If we went through the optical, the shots get grainier and more contrasty, and they are obviously artificial shots.

I wanted to try to avoid that, so I developed this little system where we covered the rock with reflective Scotchlite paper. Then, I had built in my garage a partial mirror that went in front of the camera at an angle. You could reflect light straight down the axis of the lens apparently into the Scotchlite, which is the most effective way to get the Scotchlite to work, the reflective stuff on the freeway when your headlights hit it. It doesn't work as effectively if the light is off to one side, so I developed this sort of one-off thing that I used a couple of times subsequently, but mainly for this one shot that made the giant rock glow mysteriously and magically. I take a certain amount of satisfaction in developing that technique and the fact that it worked, although it's not like one of those jaw-dropping things. It's sort of like people say, "Oh, look, the rock is glowing," which is what they should do, because it's all about the story.

AG: Were there ever any attempts to get you to work on additional *Halloween* films, beyond the third?

Dean Cundey: Not really. I think when it was taken over and John was no longer hands on involved with them, everybody put together their own team, for their own vision. I felt we had done what I could do, what I enjoyed doing with the stories and the films, so I was never disappointed by the fact that I was never called back to work on any of the other films. I'm not sure I would have been thrilled, because we had done what we could do to create the franchise. After that it became a little odd, I thought. You know, the Michael Myers mask that we used was there to give him no personality, to make him an enigmatic figure. I was disappointed when the mask itself started getting terror effects and decaying, dead looks, stuff that was not part of the original tension but also not part of what happens with a rubber mask. So there was this conscious effort to impose on the films a new sense of terror. I've never regretted not being able to do anything subsequently.

AG: In conclusion, did you have any additional stories or anecdotes you perhaps wanted to share?

Dean Cundey: I always remember this, and I've mentioned it a few times. John graduated from [University of Southern California] film school, and when we made *Halloween*, John was invited to show it to the film department at a special screening in the auditorium and their screening room. Myself, Debra, John, Tommy Lee, and maybe someone else went there for a Q + A after the movie. They screened it for this audience of probably fifty or sixty students and film people. Afterward, we sat up on the stage, and they were asking questions. One student stood up and said, "I have to ask you, 'Why in the world would you make this movie?'" We kind of looked at each other, knowing that first of all, it was a creative film job. Secondly, and I think it was Debra who finally said, "Frankly, we wanted to do this in a way that was more than what was expected and had some style. We wanted to make a film that would maybe become a classic." The student said, "Wait a second, do you think this movie could become a classic?" She said, "Well, we hope so." He said, "That's the most ridiculous thing I have ever heard, this film becoming a classic." Then he walked out. I've always said to myself, Well, what did he miss? And two, Where is he today? This was like three or four weeks after it opened and had suddenly become a viable film.

Interview: Sandy Johnson (Judith Myers, *Halloween*)

AG: How did you land the role? What was the process like?

Sandy Johnson: I was called to an interview through the *Playboy* agency. It took place in one of the locations where they were actually shooting other scenes from *Halloween* in another part of the house. John Carpenter, Debra Hill, and others were there. I read several different parts and screamed upon request. The next day I received a call from my agent that said I had been cast as Judith Myers.

AG: A lot has been said about the close-knit, family-like feeling while making the movie. Was that your experience?

Sandy Johnson: Yes, it has been that way on all my films. Everyone wants all involved to be successful and to create a great film. It is a ton of fun and a very bonding experience.

AG: What kind of discussions did you have with John Carpenter about the role prior to filming?

Sandy Johnson: We talked about the general atmosphere of both shots, of course staging, and the emotional aspects of each scene. We discussed logistics such as how to fall safely and timing for the blood release.

AG: The first scene of *Halloween* really sets the tone for not just this movie, but twelve subsequent sequels and really the slasher genre as a whole. What does that mean to you personally, being the first victim and kicking off this impressive chain of events that truly changed the history of film?

Sandy Johnson: I am so proud to be part of the *Halloween* franchise. Being in the first few minutes of the first *Halloween* movie and not only the first kill but also the only kill of the young Michael Myers is so cool. The impact of the film worldwide never ceases to astound me. I enjoy the stories and memories of what my scene meant to the fans. I am grateful and blessed to have been selected to play Judith Myers.

AG: Tell me about filming your death scene. This is before CGI and on a small-budget film. How many takes did you have to do? How difficult was it to film your death scene?

Sandy Johnson: Although it was a complex shot due to the new Panaglide camera, utilizing a stand-in for the young Michael, and other logistics related to shooting on location rather than a studio, we did it in two takes.

The scene downstairs was fun and flirty, while the shooting upstairs was actually pretty scary. Being an actual old house, it was dark, and when they were coming up to kill me, the stairs creaked. Sitting there alone, unlike in a studio, I could hear them coming to kill me.

AG: Sex scenes and nudity in film are obviously handled quite differently than they used to be. What was the experience of filming your death scene topless like for a young actress? In many ways, it shaped theories about Michael's killings at least partly being sexually motivated and feels very important to the narrative.

Sandy Johnson: One of the reasons I was selected for the role was because I had appeared in *Playboy* and had made other films involving nudity. I was comfortable being nude, and everyone I worked with put me at ease. It was low-budget but not unprofessional. The death scene was actually quite private as compared to a set. I do think that Michael was triggered by sexual activity, and that aspect is crucial to his character.

AG: Memories of both John Carpenter and Debra Hill?

Sandy Johnson: I remember the great direction given by John and Debra. They set me at ease and worked their magic. They were very focused and did a great job of acting out for us what they wanted. They worked so well together. They made their vision very clear for us.

AG: Were there ever any discussions about bringing you back for a cameo in one of the sequels prior to your appearance in *Halloween* (2018)?

Sandy Johnson: I don't actually know, because I had moved away by the time they started making sequels. They did not locate me again until just before *Halloween* (2018), in which I did appear.

AG: Over the last few years, you've been more active with the fan community. What's that been like for you?

Sandy Johnson: It has been one of the biggest highlights of my life. The fans are amazing, kind and loving, plus so much fun. They have welcomed me into the horror community family as if I had always been there. Getting to know *Halloween* fans through social media and conventions has been amazing. I have made so many friends and reconnected with cast members. I have traveled to Germany, the UK, and Canada to meet with foreign fans, which was outrageously fun. I miss the seasons where there aren't cons, because I don't get to visit with fans. I hope to get invited to many more conventions so I can meet fans in new places. In addition, I am working on getting back into acting. I have done a few virtual cameos and my first on-set film in forty-five years, *The Executioner*. I am now preparing to do more on-set shoots. My website has also given me an additional way to connect with fans. I enjoy making collectibles for it, such as the bloody Judith Myers hairbrush and spattered young Michael Mask. *Halloween* has enriched my life in countless ways. I am truly blessed.

Interview: Lance Guest (Jimmy, *Halloween II*)

AG: What was the casting process like for *Halloween II*?

Lance Guest: I answered this exact same question for a book about a year ago. It's not a bad story, but if I repeat myself too much, I will sound like those segments on the John Oliver show where everyone says exactly the same sound bite over and over and over again, as if they were coached. It's hilarious—when it's not me. So since there is only one answer, I will have to state it a little differently. It was February 1981, and it was for 8:30 a.m., forty-five minutes away in a small indie film office in Burbank. I had been auditioning for about three months and actually working for one. I'd booked three small parts in TV shows, the first being *Lou Grant*. I had a screen test for the lead character in a film called *Split Image* during the previous December, for which I'd have to sign a three-picture deal with Polygram before even doing the test. That also took place on the same day as a final exam at UCLA, which I had been attending. I decided to withdraw from school after finals, as I was getting way too many auditions to really justify going. My dad would help me out with rent as long as I was going to school, but once I was out, so was he. I had also just finished a three-month run of a great play called *Transgressor* out in Hollywood and had additionally booked my first paying gig, as an understudy for an off-Broadway import rock musical as the rhythm guitar player in the band, which also included several supporting parts. I say all this because it was a bit of a whirlwind three months.

I'm pretty much a morning person as a rule, but I was a little bleary, pulling up at eight thirty and trying to find the very small production office. I had seen a tape of the first *Halloween* and remembered a very serious and introverted Laurie Strode and that it seemed to be the film version of all the nightmare babysitter stories that made the rounds of middle school sleepovers. Walking in, I recognized Mary Gail Artz [casting director for *Halloween II*], Debra Hill, Rick Rosenthal, and if John Carpenter was there, it would be the only time I remember seeing him. He's kinda hard to miss with all that cool long white hair, but I don't remember seeing him during production. Standing in front of me, cheery, chipper with her now trademark close-cropped blonde hair, along with her big-as-the-state-of-Montana personality, was Jamie Lee Curtis. "You're adorable!"

Then she says to the others: "He's adorable!" She walks up to me, pulls the front of my sweater up (I was rocking the crewneck-sweater-and-plaid-flannel-shirt combo, as my character was described as a "college boy"), and sticks her head under my sweater. Resurfacing, she flashes me a quick smile. "Ready to do this?"

I don't remember which scene we read. It might've been the one with the epic "They should've handled him more carefully" line, or maybe just one of the many involving a Coke—I don't know. As the very serious actor I wanted to be, I spent countless hours staying in character, writing up backstories, justifying all the things required of me—which were, basically, running, slipping in blood, NOT dropping the gurney, and having a crush on Jamie Lee Curtis. In hindsight, none of it really required much work.

AG: Tell me about the shoot. The hospital location has become iconic among fans. What was it like to film in the building? What other locations did you shoot at? How long were you filming?

Lance Guest: I think we worked at two different hospitals at least. One was up the 405 off of Nordhoff, and the other was in Long Beach, I think. Wherever it was, it was near the airport and required a lot of takes, as jets would come every forty-five seconds or so. A lot of people have commented that there didn't seem to be any other patients in the hospital, which was true in reality but not really in the reality of the film.

AG: Your character, Jimmy, was really the only character that was close with Laurie Strode in this film. Memories of working with Jamie

Lee Curtis?

Lance Guest: She was so dynamic and spirited that she really came alive when the camera stopped, as poor, terrorized Laurie was as far from her as she could be. It would be as if Robin Williams was playing Travis Bickle and then cut is called. I think she used to sing "Sex & Drugs & Rock & Roll" when the camera wasn't rolling.

AG: When you think back on filming *Halloween II*, what day of work on set sticks out most to you today?

Lance Guest: I think it was the day that I slipped in the blood, because the setup originally called for an amount of blood that wouldn't normally fit inside a human body, like a small sea of blood. I was never sure what the original vision was. I just remember arriving at the set, where there was an eight-by-eight square frame made out of two-by-six lumber with a plastic/vinyl liner to make a small pool into which was poured thinned-out, red liquid that would SPLASH like a wave, kind of like in *The Shining*. Someone showed up, I think it was Rick, who said, "This is crazy. Nobody has that much blood." It looked like about ten to fifteen gallons of blood. My memory might be faulty as to who it was. I remember the stunt fall took three different angles, of which I was in two. I remember not wanting to screw up my close-up where I have to fall into frame on my head. I remember Dick Warlock [stunt coordinator/Michael Myers for *Halloween II*] making sure everyone was safe, but that they couldn't put a very soft cushion under my head because the shot was so close that you could tell it was a cushion. I just needed to be a couple of inches out of frame when I dropped, but I must not have thought of that and dropped from a full sitting position. I hit the thin Masonite on top of a thin layer of Styrofoam, which was on top of the concrete floor and rang my bell, as it were. It was probably my fault. I wanted it to look real, and I was twenty.

AG: Did John or Debra have a story presence on set? What was it like working with them, if you did?

Lance Guest: I saw Debra every day. She was nice to me. I remember being part of a late-night meeting in a motor home. I don't remember what the topic was, but I was thrilled to be included. It was my first feature film experience, so everything was memorable. I knew John was pretty famous, and I really enjoyed his movies, especially *Escape from New York* and *Christine*, which I auditioned for. But I was never in the editing room, and I don't remember him being on set. He was a mystery. Debra was tough and serious. And that her hometown was Haddonfield, New Jersey.

AG: What was it like to make a sequel to a film as beloved as *Halloween*? What sense of pressure, if any, was felt to live up to the original?

Lance Guest: It was my first film job, so I was less concerned about preserving any legacy, since it was only three years in the past. It was a direct-cut sequel, so we were mostly concerned with simply matching the tone and basic feel. I think it was successful. Rick did a good job. I wasn't responsible for directing the film, so I didn't feel any pressure to "measure up." I just had to be the best Jimmy I could.

AG: Any additional on-set memories you care to share?

Lance Guest: I had been trained as a theater actor, and there is a pretty high energy pace to the film, at least for my character, so my entrances were always ME CHARGING IN. Often I would overshoot my mark, repeatedly, until Rick had to say, "Lance, I really want you to be in the film, but you're makin' it tough on me." Dick Warlock, the stunt coordinator, was also Michael Myers most of the time, which was ironic, since he would be the least evil character I can imagine, besides Nick Castle, who was Michael in the first movie. Both superfriendly, hilarious guys. Nick and John Carpenter are friends, went to film school together, and it was in the editing room of *Halloween 2* that Nick saw me running through the halls and thought I might be right for his upcoming project, *The Last Starfighter*. I didn't find this out for about twenty years.

AG: Let's talk about deleted scenes. In the television version of the film, your character survived and was seen again with Laurie at the end. What else do you recall filming that never made the screen?

Lance Guest: Honestly, it's been forty-three years, and I don't remember any additional scenes, but that's what happens when you see a completed movie more times than you actually film it. You forget what was shot and then cut out. That said, I absolutely remember the ending AS WRITTEN and shot! I was totally surprised when my first movie came out opening night and I was NOT sitting up in the ambulance at the end. Wait . . . what about me making it to the end? That's showbiz.

Later I figured that Jamie had been doing this character for three years now, and I had heard that she may not want to keep going on (she had done three or four other horror movies, and she was only a year or two older than me). So the audience had been on this ride with her, and since this may be the last time they would see Laurie, she should have the last frame to herself. I mean, honestly, who the fuck was I?

Years later, however, in the official TV version, I am very much alive at the end, and the scene plays as written and shot. It was after *Starfighter* came out, so maybe some decision was made regarding that. I never got the story. I haven't seen that scene much, so I'm not sure exactly what I say, but I believe both versions, alive and dead, still exist. And as they say . . . it's good to be anywhere.

AG: The cast and crew from the *Halloween* movies seem to have a strong connection to the fans. In the years since *Halloween II*, what has that fan connection been like for you?

Lance Guest: I've never really been much of a horror fan at all and was pleasantly surprised twenty-five years later when I found out that there were conventions for these things and that the fans are very loyal and excited to meet us. Very rarely would I show up for an audition in LA or NY and the filmmakers would reference *Halloween*. I started meeting the fans beginning in about 2006, and the response to our little sequel was, for the most part, extremely positive. I never would've thought that when the reviews came out at its release. So it's really nice to hear that our work is appreciated. Plus, the people are actually really pretty normal. Not being a horror fan myself, I would have had my doubts.

I did meet a fan once who started weeping uncontrollably. She kept saying this was so unlike her, but she couldn't stop. I tried everything. I told her I was starstruck by meeting Bob Odenkirk in Trader Joe's once . . . recently. Nothing worked. She finally had to walk away, returning about a half hour later, completely composed. She apologized, and we had a normal conversation, and I could tell she was quite intelligent and interesting.

AG: Was there ever any talk about bringing your character back for future sequels?

Lance Guest: I did get a *Halloween* script once, but that would happen a lot. I would get scripts all of the time on other projects. Sometimes they said it was a go, they had their money; sometimes they were just feeling the interest out. They would get my address, and a script would show up. But unless it was given to me by my agent or someone I knew personally, I could never assume it was a go. I have worked on auditions, gotten very far, gotten cast—twice for the best script I'd ever been up for—only to find out the film wouldn't be made and often were never really green lit to begin with.

I have learned that there is a character named Jamie Lloyd in a later sequel [the character was introduced in *Halloween 4*], and everyone asks if she is supposed to be my daughter, since Jimmy's last name is Lloyd. I have no answer to that.

One of the positive aspects of this being my first film experience was that the actors and the director were a pretty tight group, and we all got along pretty well. I was the youngest in the main cast and really enjoyed hearing all the NY actor stories from Leo Rossi [Budd Scarlotti], who knew a lot of the guys I was currently watching, since I liked the movies that were five to ten years old at that time. I'm one of those people that think the seventies were the golden age of film, when a lot of the experimental filmmaking techniques first made their mark, and the subjects and acting were more unusual. Leo had some great stories, besides being a really great guy. I hadn't seen a lot of them when they came out, so I had to catch them at the revival houses in my late teens and early twenties. It was a different world, before Blockbuster and Netflix.

Interview: Tom Atkins (Dr. Daniel Challis, *Halloween III*)

AG: What was the casting process like for this film?

Tom Atkins: I was offered the role by Tommy Lee Wallace, along with the blessing of John Carpenter and Debra Hill. I didn't have to audition. I had already done *The Fog* with all three of them. Nancy Loomis was invited to play my wife. She was Tommy's wife and also had been in *The Fog* and *Halloween*. They were casting for the Ellie role, and Tommy called me one day and said they were down to three finalists and asked if I would come in and read with three girls. I believe John and Debra were in the room, and the moment Stacey [Nelkin] left the room after we read together, we all looked at each other and said, "Yep, she's the one." There was chemistry, something that happened between us. I'm thrilled that she was able to be in the film and she was a pure delight to work with. I still see Stacey, Tommy, John once or twice a year. Stacey is aging much more beautifully than any of us guys.

AG: Memories of John Carpenter and Debra Hill?

Tom Atkins: Debra was pretty much in the background, and we didn't socialize too much. John was a pleasure to work with on *The Fog*, but I barely saw him while we were filming *Halloween III*. I think the score was all Alan Howarth [composer]. I don't believe John had any input in the music end of things for this film.

AG: The film notoriously had three versions of the script. When you were cast, where were they at in relation to the rewrites? Any thoughts on previous iterations of the script that you know of?

Tom Atkins: I only know the final script we shot. I have no idea what the previous screenplays were like. I've heard snippets of stories, but that's really it.

AG: Your role in this film had you do a little bit of everything—action hero, beer drinker, had you in love scenes and not only saving lives as a doctor but also trying to save the world. What was the filming experience like for you?

Tom Atkins: I wasn't an alcoholic. Dan Challis was fond of beer and women. I like to think I was an ace trauma surgeon. Filming was a joy. One of my favorite scenes was shot in the Buccaneer Lounge in Sierra Madre. It backs onto the square where the pods were distributed from in the fifties film *Invasion of the Body Snatchers*. Every five years we have a horror convention in Pasadena and have a "Beers with Atkins" event at the Buccaneer. I love that place. It hasn't changed in fifty years. The church from the ending of *The Fog* is also in Sierra Madre. I don't really expect this to happen, but if for some weird reason I found myself moving back to California, I would move to Sierra Madre.
I do remember that we got very tired of hearing the "two more days to Halloween" song. It played behind or over almost every scene we shot. At least it felt that way.

I also loved shooting the scenes that involved the Kupfer family. Ralph Strait was a dear friend of mine from working together in a theater production of *[The Resistible Rise of] Arturo Ui* by Bertolt Brecht in Williamstown, Massachusetts. It was directed by Peter Hunt. Ralph and I had a wonderful time doing that play and having drinks at Sardi's in New York when we were both in the Apple. He was a good actor, a good friend, and I miss him.
It was also a treat having Garn Stephens, my wife at the time, on the set. Her character died a terrible death in the motel room next door to me and Ellie. That was also a little weird on a personal note. I don't think Garn had to audition for the role. I think she was invited by Tommy and John to play the role of Marge. Sadly, Garn passed away last year.

I think I had walking pneumonia on the nights we had to shoot Dan Challis running around the town, climbing ladders, running across roofs, down alleyways, climbing in and out of windows. You can see me carrying a handkerchief in those scenes.

AG: The film started off as being panned and is now more than a cult classic; it's universally loved. Thoughts on the evolving reputation?

Tom Atkins: I think all of us are thrilled at the following *Halloween*

III has developed. It is stunning to me. We all thought it was a pretty good horror film when we made it, a good stand-alone film. Time has proven that to be true. I go to horror movie conventions around the country, and I am always knocked out by the increasing popularity of a film we made so long ago. The merchandising of the film is astounding to me.

AG: Were there ever any discussions about bringing you or your character back for additional *Halloween* films?

Tom Atkins: Not really, no. Fred Dekker has talked about doing another version of *Night of the Creeps*, but I don't think Tommy or John has ever entertained the idea of another *Halloween III*. Plus, John's original intent was to do an anthology of *Halloween* movies, but the producers wanted more Michael Myers *Halloween* movies.

AG: What was Tommy Lee Wallace like as a director?

Tom Atkins: Tommy was a joy to work with on *Halloween III*. He and John had been friends forever. He did special effects for John on *The Fog*, and those were pre-CGI effects. He also had hands-on experience in almost every aspect of making films. He was savvy and keen. I think he wrote a wonderful screenplay, and I'm forever grateful to him for the role of Dan Challis.

AG: All these years later, how do you feel about the film?

Tom Atkins: I love *Halloween III*. May it live long and thrive in the hearts of our beloved horror fans.

Interview: Stacey Nelkin (Ellie, *Halloween III*)

AG: To start things off, I wanted to ask about the casting process and what that was like for you.

Stacey Nelkin: It was kind of a dream process for me with that film, unlike most other projects. It was very last minute. They had been searching and searching for somebody to play Ellie. I knew the man who was already the makeup artist for the film. I had worked with him doing *The Last Convertible*. My then boyfriend/fiancé was living at his home while he was in the middle of a separation. And this guy, Ron Walters, who was an amazing makeup artist, kept talking to me about this project because he was already signed on to do the makeup, and he kept telling me about it. And I was really not interested, because I myself don't like to watch horror movies. I was traumatized by seeing *The Exorcist* when I was thirteen—literally couldn't sleep for like three weeks. Finally, I called my agent. I said, "Okay, can you just get me a copy of the script?" And I read the script, and I loved the character. I went, "Okay, I could do this," because I could just see the humor, the spunk. I just liked the character of Ellie. So I went in to read, and at this point, as I said, they'd been looking for a really long time, and I went in and I read with Tom [Atkins]. I was walking into my apartment; the phone was ringing, and it was my agent saying, "Well, you got the job, and you're starting like in two days." It was something crazy like that whirlwind, and things like that never happened, where you get the job literally that day, especially for a lead in the film. You know, usually there's a lot more stuff going on. It was a really smooth, swift process.

AG: It does sound like it. You never hear about that kind of turnaround. So with you not being a horror movie fan, had you seen either of the prior two films?

Stacey Nelkin: It must have been before, maybe when Ron was talking to me about it, I somehow got to watch the first *Halloween*, and it scared the crap out of me. This script for *Halloween III* was so different, and so I like that it wasn't just gratuitous girls taking their tops off, gratuitous toplessness, and some guy coming in and terrorizing people. It had a little more story and thought behind it; it was more sci-fi. So I liked it better. It resonated more with me.

AG: So the fact that Michael Myers would not be continuing in this film really wasn't a concern to you?

Stacey Nelkin: Oh no, not only was it not a concern, it was an asset.

AG: The film notoriously had three versions of the script. I wanted to see if you were around for any of the two previous incarnations, or by the time you were cast in the film, was it the version of the script that we would eventually see filmed?

Stacey Nelkin: Oh, that's a great question, Andrew. I'm not sure. I know that when we were on set, up near Eureka, we were shooting on location. We were playing around a lot with dialogue, but there was no major change. So I probably came after they had already made the big changes. And I know Tommy Lee [Wallace, the director], when we go to these conventions, has talked about that a lot, that the initial ending was even darker. And so yeah, he changed the script a little bit.

AG: So when you say you were playing around with dialogue, was it kind of an improv atmosphere?

Stacey Nelkin: Yeah, it really was. And then Tommy Lee would put that into the script, and we pretty much adhere to it because it just makes it easier, especially if you're shooting a film. It's one thing on stage, but when the camera needs to follow you for this line and get the close-up here, and you need to have a little more previous idea of what you're gonna be doing, just to block the cameras around you—so we would take the time before we got in front of the cameras, and then we would nail it down. Then Tommy Lee would talk to the cinematographer, and we would do it like that.

AG: What was it like to work with Tommy Lee Wallace? This was his first time directing a film.

Stacey Nelkin: Because he's a musician, he's very loose. He's very easy to work with and very sensitive in a good way, not demanding. I've worked with directors where if you deviate one word, you're going back. He was great. I think that's because his background is really as a musician, where there's just a little more spontaneity, and he's really working in sync with his actors and actresses.

AG: Were John Carpenter or Debra Hill present on set for the film?

Stacey Nelkin: Debra was around all the time. Debra was an amazing woman. She was so generous and funny and sweet. We'd girl talk a lot, and she was really amazing. She was a huge, huge presence and a big part of the movie. She was on set almost all the time.

AG: What were her contributions to the film? Everybody knows that she was such a presence. But I feel like a lot of times it's not properly articulated exactly what she brought to the table and more just that she was this driving force.

Stacey Nelkin: She was really warm, fun, and funny, and it just creates a different atmosphere that you're dealing with. So you're having happy people; you're having a better outcome all around.

AG: You and Tom Atkins had great chemistry in this movie. It almost seemed like you'd known each other for twenty years. What was it like working with him?

Stacey Nelkin: He was a gentleman. He was terrific. I mean, he really was. I think one of our first scenes was the bedroom scene, the love scene in the motel, and he was just such a gentleman, so easygoing. He was fun, with a great, acerbic sense of humor. He made the whole thing very easy for me, because when you're taking off your top, and that was the first and only time I did that, it's a little daunting. Shooting those scenes is never easy or natural. Then you're getting directions like "Kiss her a third of an inch higher to the left," and it's so crazy. He was great. Doing all these conventions all these years later since the movie really took off, we get to hang out, and I get to see him every year. We spend more time lately doing these conventions than on the set even. He's a generous, sweet, funny, and very talented man.

AG: How long was the filming for this movie?

Stacey Nelkin: It was six or eight weeks, something like that. I don't think it was more than that.

AG: How many locations did you film in?

Stacey Nelkin: Some of it we did on a set in Burbank. I think it was somewhere in the Valley. And then we were up on location in Loleta. It was a little haunted and a little creepy. We had a day shooting the bar scene, so there were various locations around Burbank and things like that. But a good chunk of it was done up by Eureka.

AG: I wanted to pick your brain on some memories that you had from filming the movie.

Stacey Nelkin: Well, I know to get myself in a kind of a spooky kind of scared anxious mood, which is never that hard for me anyway. I was reading *In Cold Blood*, the Truman Capote book. I remember that. One of my bigger memories was doing that love scene. It was freezing cold in the mornings in Northern California. This is before they have those spray tans. Now they spray you with body makeup with a hose. Back then, they would have these cold sponges, and the makeup artist would literally go over every inch of your body. It was so cold. It was an early-morning call, and I was nervous enough about having to take my top off. That was just one of those things you do because you gotta do it, right? The crazy stuff we do when we're an actress. You just surrender, like, "This is what you need me to do."

The other really cool scene to shoot was when my head comes off. We did that on the soundstage. In those days, before all the green screen and all of the fake stuff, they had to use a lot more creativity. They had to come up with these ways to do these things on their own, before all the digital stuff. The set builders built this platform that they covered with grass, and the platform was like a foot and a half high, high enough that a slender body could fit under it. They put two holes like six feet apart, and they covered it with grass. I'm underneath, and my head is popping up like a Whac-A-Mole from one of the holes while my body double is six feet away, wearing the identical outfit I've been wearing for what felt like years at that point. But it was probably at least a week or two of wearing literally the same wardrobe because it was the end scene. It was so freaky, just this literally out-of-body experience, because here's my body and she was exactly my size, six feet away. But wait, where's my body? Which I couldn't see because it was under the platform. Little things like that are just part of the magic of moviemaking, and that is really cool.

AG: It really makes you appreciate the pre-CGI special effects. It's amazing to hear you recount that, and today it would be a totally different experience. The magic is partly lost. So the film comes out, and the reviews are mixed. Tommy Lee Wallace has many quotes out there just talking about being hurt by it. But there were many people who did enjoy the film right away. I think sometimes that narrative is lost. Are you familiar with Roger Ebert's review?

Stacey Nelkin: Sure I am. He was very nice to me, I believe.

AG: Yes, he was, he called you the saving grace, actually. "She has one of those rich voices that makes you wish she had more to say and then a better role." So not complimentary toward the film, but very complimentary toward you. How did the reaction to the film impact you?

Stacey Nelkin: At the time, I was kind of on a roll, let's say. I went from that movie, which was one of those movies I never talked about because it came out and went in and out of the theaters in ten days, maybe two weeks, I went and I did *Yellow Beard* and *Get Crazy,* and I had a succession of things that were going to be bigger, or so I thought at the time. Little do we know. So it was just one of those movies I never really talked about because, as I said, I'm not a big horror fan. What I love is there's this whole subculture of people who love horror movies, and I love that because they've made our movie this cult classic. It's just so interesting, because people are so fascinating to me. There's this whole subculture of people who love it. I was always kind of more geared toward comedies because I like to laugh. I did the film and I didn't expect much of it, and nothing came of it until about twenty years later when Sean Clark [her agent] was searching for me, saying he wanted me to go to do these horror conventions. I'm like, "What people know about our movie now?" It's amazing, because now there's this new generation of people, young kids who are like eighteen, twenty, maybe up to twenty-five, who love the movie and say it's their favorite of all the *Halloween* movies, whereas their parents' generation, in the beginning of these conventions for years, they would kind of sheepishly say, "You know, *Halloween III* really was my favorite." So it's fascinating to see these young people are just unabashed lovers of the movie. That's what they saw, and they made their own decision. There was no being inundated with Michael Myers, and they got to choose, and they love it. Ours was the bastard child of the movies. Nobody talked about our movie, and then they went on to make all the other sequels. It's kind of an interesting phenomenon.

I think it's a better made film. I think it's more interesting. I think it makes people think more, as opposed to all of these horror films that are just about, as I said, gratuitous sex and, you know, just trying to scare you. There was an actual story to it, and the sci-fi element that makes it just a little more interesting. It gives it an extra dimension. Something I did want to share that I find really interesting when watching it lately: when you go to these conventions, sometimes they want you to watch the movie with them, and I've done that. The film certainly was made in a different era, and so there's so many things in the movie—nonchalant actions and behaviors that today you would look at and go, "Oh my God, he'd be arrested for that," like Tom patting the nurse on the butt and being such a bad dad. There was so much political incorrectness in it by today's standards. You could say the same watching 1940s movies, like how the women were not supposed to work or whatever. It gives it a little bit of that too because you can look at it through that lens of what it was like in the 1980s. It informs you about what life was like then.

-CHAPTER 3-
THE JAMIE LLOYD ERA

After *Halloween III: Season of the Witch*, it would have been fair to assume the franchise was dead. John Carpenter and Debra Hill had attempted to defy the Hollywood machine by making the third film the start of a new direction. Fans revolted. They had grown accustomed to the masked babysitter killer. He was the villainous face of the franchise, establishing a trend that Freddy Krueger and Jason Voorhees would both follow. Sure, fans loved Laurie Strode, but her absence wasn't a deal-breaker. Michael's was. In a move that was almost as shocking as removing Michael from the second sequel, Moustapha Akkad, a producer of the first three *Halloween* films, assumed full creative control of the franchise, buying out both John Carpenter and Debra Hill, and decided that for the tenth anniversary of *Halloween*, it was time to return to Haddonfield.

That decision to revive the franchise turned out to be the right call; we're still talking about the series today, and we're now up to thirteen *Halloween* films. For longtime *Halloween* fans, there's a lot of nostalgia associated with the Jamie Lloyd Era—*Halloween* four, five, and six. Fans in their forties and fifties today experienced these films at a pivotal age, as kids with friends or as teenagers on dates. This is their era of *Halloween*, and Danielle Harris, who portrayed Jamie Lloyd, is every bit as important to them as Jamie Lee Curtis is to fans of the earlier films. They identified with this young child being stalked by her bogeyman uncle or the teenagers defending her. There are a lot of fiercely loyal fans of the "Jamie Lloyd Era," and that dedication only intensified when these films were later retconned out of the overall narrative.

Enough can't be said about how tight the script for *Halloween 4: The Return of Michael Myers* is. One story beat feeds right into the next, which then feeds into the next. It's arguably the most logical *Halloween* film; every detail makes sense. In the wake of the divisive third film, *Halloween 4* was facing enormous pressure. It's a no-frills, stripped-down story centering on strong characters and relatable scenarios. Harris and Ellie Cornell (Rachel) captured the hearts and imaginations of filmgoers, and even to this day, the fourth *Halloween* film remains a favorite among many fans.

The fifth and sixth films are more divisive. There's a lot to admire about both films, although some of the criticism isn't undeserved. The overarching mythology spanning the three films in the Jamie Lloyd Era is one reason fans remain devoted to this section of the franchise. *Halloween 4* had one of the most memorable endings of any film in the series. Jamie's assumption of the family curse was an idea with huge potential. Loomis's emotional response as Jamie turns to violent rage at such a young age, like her Uncle Michael before her, triggered an equally emotional response from audiences. Loomis was our most trusted character in this narrative, and audience members reacted to his distress. *Halloween 5: The Revenge of Michael Myers* opted not to journey down this dark path, taking the concept of the curse in a different direction, which later dictated how *Halloween: The Curse of Michael Myers* writer Daniel Farrands would unfold his story. Even though the Curse of Thorn was largely an accidental creation, fan investment was undiminished. One thing about horror fans that's often misunderstood: they love continuity in their long-running franchises.

Halloween: The Curse of Michael Myers feels like an ending. Loomis dies off-screen. Jamie Lloyd is killed. There's a payoff to the cult story. Narratively speaking, the story had to pivot after this, though I don't think anyone foresaw these three films being retconned out. There is a strange kinship among *Season of the Witch*, *Halloween: The Curse of Michael Myers*, and *Halloween Ends*, each the third film of its era. All three represent change. *Halloween: Season of the Witch* is a drastic switch, from a universe with Michael to one without; *Halloween: The*

Curse of Michael Myers gives us an origin story and wraps up numerous plotlines; *Ends* also concludes storylines while showing us that evil exists in different forms.

Films four through six absolutely benefit from the creation of the Jamie Lloyd character. Replacing Jamie Lee Curtis was almost an impossible task, but Danielle Harris has become the other face of the franchise. This is a fact that Dimension Films, the horror and sci-fi branch of the Weinstein brothers' company, didn't seem to understand when the studio recast her role for the sixth film. However, all of those fans who stand in line to meet Danielle Harris at horror conventions to this day do get it. Most slasher franchises have to replace their leading lady at some point and then cycle through multiple replacements, typically discarding them after one film. The *Halloween* franchise didn't have to do that. Of the thirteen films in the series, only two don't feature either Jamie Lee Curtis or Danielle Harris: *Season of the Witch* and *Halloween: The Curse of Michael Myers*. Granted Harris played a different character in two of her four films, but it still speaks to the impact she has had on *Halloween*.

Of course, the Jamie Lloyd Era had its share of off-screen controversy. Fans are well-versed in many of those stories, and it certainly adds to the lore of these films. Those stories are best told by those who lived them.

Interview: Dwight Little (Director, *Halloween 4: The Return of Michael Myers*)

AG: How did you become involved with *Halloween 4*?

Dwight Little: I had just done a movie in India, a little B movie called *Bloodstone*, and Moustapha Akkad, who was sort of the godfather of this whole thing, was a director in his own right. He had been shooting in Northern Africa and different places, and he was interested in India. There was a cattle call for *Halloween 4*—in other words, the word got out in Hollywood that they were looking for a director. I presume this is when John and Debra sort of cut ties with doing *Halloween 4* and went their own way. Moustapha bought out all the rights to it and decided to proceed on his own. My reel got to their company. This is a very odd story. When he found out that I had been shooting in India, he was supercurious because he wanted to shoot there. I kind of went in under a false flag operation. I was there to be interviewed, but I had a writing partner named Alan McElroy, and he was a huge *Halloween* fan. He and I put together a pitch for *Halloween 4*, unaware of any of the previous treatments, outlines, or drafts. I just pitched him *Halloween 4* in the room. I said, "I know we're here to talk about India, but I just wanna pitch you my take." I pitched him Michael's escape and hunting down his little niece and pretty much all the big beats of the story. I didn't hear from them for the longest time, and then they came back to my manager and said, "They wanna talk about this further, but they're really worried about the time. I'm sure you've heard that there is a writers' strike at the end of March." So we had to very quickly get a draft out. Alan was just very quick.

AG:. It's been said that there were many drafts of a script for this film. I was curious if you had heard about any other scripts prior to you and Alan coming in.

Dwight Little: My manager knew Ramsey Thomas, who was Moustapha's chief lieutenant, I guess, his number two. He saw this reel that I have, this director's reel, and he brought it to their attention. I do remember being sent a treatment or an outline. There are two other credited writers on the movie with Alan. It was what I would call "teenagers getting horny and getting killed." That was my summary. I honestly was not interested on any level. I was already struggling with the idea of doing *Halloween 4*, because a fourth film after ten years seemed like a suicide mission. No one knew if there was life left in this, because *Season of the Witch* had been disappointing and had left this weird taste. Then of course Michael was dead after *Halloween 2*, and Loomis was apparently dead. The whole franchise was almost forgotten about. So I do remember seeing something that I dismissed, but I never saw a script. Alan and I knew we wanted to make an escaped-convict movie. We were really looking to do almost what you'd think of as a police procedural, with Loomis as the detective and Michael as an escaped convict. Certainly we brought in all the horror elements. We fashioned the movie so that it would grow organically. The only way we can get him out of this ward is a prison transfer. Then the only way we can free him is for him to attack the attendants. Then the only way to give him overalls is for him to kill the gas station attendant. Then he's got to shut down the phone lines, or it's not believable. Then he's gotta kill Bucky, so we shut down the power. Then he's gotta take the mask from the drugstore so that he has a mask—which is why the mask looks different from other masks, because it was a commercial mask, something a kid could buy. That was the concept of it.

AG: Jamie Lloyd does lean into the supernatural, or perhaps mystical, though.

Dwight Little: That gives us that ending. We kept asking ourselves, *What is Michael? How supernatural is Michael?* We finally decided to just say it, and there's a scene in the police station where Beau Starr asks, "What are we dealing with?" Loomis says he's just "evil on two legs." We felt like that covers everything. Either he's a psychotic demon or he's just Jeffrey Dahmer. "Evil on two legs" kind of covers a lot of ground. Then, of course, in the end we cross over into soul transfer, or however you wanna explain it.

AG: Was it a soul transfer? Was it something that was in the bloodline perhaps? What was your take on that?

Dwight Little: Well, both. I think that the bloodline passes and that Michael passes on his psychosis into his closest living relative. His inner demon is transferred over. We were definitely going for that at the end. I think it was pretty effective, because people didn't quite see it coming.

AG: Not at all. It truly is shocking.

Dwight Little: You go down the hallway, and you see the mask come down. You're wondering, Whose POV is that? But you don't have time to ask the questions before it's revealed that it's little Jamie at the top of the stairs. So it works out pretty handily in terms of time, because just when you're thinking, Now wait a minute, you're there already.

I was talking to Donald Pleasence, who I got along with overall very well. We're having a bit of a gentleman's disagreement about how to play that scene at the bottom of the stairs. He thought that it's such a huge moment, that his job as an actor is to go underneath it. He said if he leaned into it, it's gonna be a joke. People are gonna laugh at him, and they're going to laugh at the moment. I just wanna let it be about the shock of seeing what happened. I told him, "I totally understand that point of view, but if we see Loomis dissolve, then the audience will realize how psychotic this moment truly is." Loomis is always more or less in control of his emotions. He does kind of get excited in the police station earlier, though. I said, "Look, let's do a take and then let it fly for one take, and then in the cutting room, I will have you in and we'll look at all of them and see which one works better," which is an old director's trick of course. He's smart enough to know that he was being tricked, and he got talked into it, basically. When he did it, everybody in that crew and everybody on that location, we were just shocked because we knew that was the end of the movie because Loomis falls apart. So I do take credit for that, because I really fought for him to give that performance. I do think it made a singular difference as to how we feel about her at the top of the stairs.

AG: Absolutely. Loomis is true north in these films. We can trust him; we can follow him. And to see him fall apart tells you that we are in a really bad predicament to end this film.

Dwight Little: That's right. There's a long story about me not being involved with *Halloween 5*, which Moustapha asked me to be involved in multiple times. I just felt like we had done it and we had done it well, and there was a chance that a sequel would not be as good because sometimes lightning doesn't strike twice. I was very worried about that with my own career ambition. In retrospect, I wish I had done *Halloween 5* with Alan. I have not watched all of *Halloween 5*, and it's just because I feel so possessive over those characters. I had heard many times about what they were doing with *Halloween 5*, and I didn't like it.

AG: It's a sharp left turn.

Dwight Little: Michael was buried down in that well. There were so many things that were set up. Rachel was still alive. Meeker was still alive. That was the answer to why *Halloween 4* is different, and I think it is different. Our regional concept was different in making this police procedural. I think it feels different because we had a point of view, and we approached it from that point of view.

AG: It also stands out in the fact that the first three films are from a previous regime. John Carpenter, Debra Hill, Tommy Lee Wallace, Dean Cundey—several people who were around for those first three films were now no longer a part of this franchise.

Dwight Little: It was a bitter divorce, from what I understand. I'm like the new husband. I didn't have anything to do with it.

AG: Did they have any involvement? John, Debra, or any of them?

Dwight Little: I've never met John or even spoken to him. Never met Debra, never met any of them. The only ones that I had dealings with were Moustapha Akkad and Ramsey Thomas. Malek Akkad [son of Moustapha and his eventual successor] was just really young. He was in school. I don't know whether Ramsey Thomas was a bit involved with John. I assume that he was, but I've never reached out to John, and he's never reached out to me, and then that's fine with me. I respect the first *Halloween* to the ends of the earth, and I think in some ways *Halloween 4* does pay a lot of homage to the first *Halloween*.

AG: Just to kind of circle back to the ending real quick, was that always the payoff?

Dwight Little: Always. It's in the original script.

AG: Did you absolutely view Michael as being dead, and Jamie was carrying the torch moving forward?

Dwight Little: Well, yes, but to be fair, Alan and I assumed that he would have somehow come back from underneath that well. If it was a stand-alone movie, yeah, he was dead. Jamie now carried the torch of whatever demon was inside Michael, and in that sense, it is, I think, kind of a stand-alone movie.

AG: We also have to acknowledge the wonderful Danielle Harris. This was a career-making performance for her as a very young actress, and you got to essentially discover her.

Dwight Little: I did. I tried to find both her and Rachel here in Los Angeles. I just read and read and read these kid actors and teen actors. The only experience little kids have is either school theater or commercials. It's all kind of fake in some way. I said to Moustapha, "Listen, I can't find her," and he kind of looked at me, puffing on his pipe. He said, "There's millions of people in Los Angeles, and you can't find this one girl?" I said, "I want you to indulge me and let me go to New York and take a look over there. Before we say yes to one of these candidates, let me go to New York." Very few indie producers would do this, but he said, "Yeah, go and have a look around." We got a casting director out there in New York, and we started to see people, and Danielle was, I think, about the third one in the door. She was considerably older than the character, which helped us in terms of her sophistication and on set. She was very young, but she wasn't as young as the character. She came to the door, and I didn't even feel like I was going to have to read her. I did, of course, but it's like you just kind of know. She has these eyes, what I call movie eyes, that the camera just loves, and she was everything I had hoped for. Then we had the same struggle finding Rachel. I don't remember reading Ellie in New York. She must have been on tape, but we had a candidate in Los Angeles who was actually a known actress. We had tape on Ellie Cornell. I had responded strongly to whatever I saw, which I don't think was very much. I talked Moustapha into paying for a screen test, and this was not on a cell phone. This is like movie cameras and a stage and lighting and temporary sets, 35 mm film, which then we projected onto a big screen at the Raleigh stages. It was an old-fashioned screen test. We looked at both actresses, and on the big screen, Ellie just had it. She was very pretty, but she wasn't Southern California model pretty, if you know what I mean. She looked like she could be from Haddonfield. There's something about her that seemed authentic to that town. I think by the time we had Danielle and Ellie, we had the heartbeat of the movie with those two.

AG: I think that's another reason why your film stands out so much, because of those two actresses. Ellie really draws upon the Jamie Lee Curtis characteristic of the wholesome girl next door girl you can trust, and Danielle was just so enchanting.

Dwight Little: The bond that grows between them is very authentic. Rachel fights like a tiger at the end. She's fearless.

AG: One thing that I wanted to ask about is the trajectory after your film. We talked about the fifth film. By the time the seventh rolls around, there is a retcon of sorts where the stories that you and a few other filmmakers told just no longer exist in the modern timeline. How did you feel about that?

Dwight Little: Well, I checked out, to be very honest with you. I checked out once I turned down *Halloween 5*. I don't know the series. I just saw it in a hotel not too long ago, *Halloween Kills*. All I saw was Michael. He was walking through walls, and he was knocking shit down, and he looked like Terminator. I just turned it off. People are more than entitled to do what they have to do. I really checked out. I just wasn't really interested.

AG: Well, there are a couple of noticeable homages to your film in the David Gordon Green trilogy, *Halloween Kills* being the first one. Your idea of the townspeople, the guys in Haddonfield that are driving around the truck with their shotguns, that is essentially recreated in *Halloween Kills*, where the town is coming together, and it very much felt like your film.

Dwight Little: Alan told me about that one. He called me and said they stole our shit. I said, "Well, Alan, they own it; they can do whatever they want."

AG: Then, in *Halloween Ends*, what you were trying to do with Jamie with the transfer—it's not a direct copy, but it's very close, with a young man named Corey who accidentally kills a child. He's a good kid. It's an accident, and he didn't intend any harm to the child. But soon after, Michael is grooming him, essentially, and it's comparable enough to what you were doing.

Dwight Little: Malek is very knowledgeable about all of the films, and I'm sure that they had looked at why *Halloween 4* was somewhat successful. Now, we have to understand that part four was not a beloved movie when it came out. It did well at the box office, and it was kind of a hit. It was very successful financially. If you went to a theater and saw it, you could tell that the movie was working. This was before the internet, but it was not good with the critics and the fanboys. People were just not happy with the movie. Over the last thirty-five years, the consensus among the fans has really changed, I guess because it's lived on through television and it's been reissued on Blu-ray and DVD. People don't just like it; people really love it. It's a real fan favorite. I'm not sure what changed. I think times have changed, maybe.

AG: Were there ever any attempts to get you to come back for any of the subsequent films?

Dwight Little: Moustapha really wanted me for *Halloween 5*. "Please do it, please do it, please do it." At that time, I was already moving on to other things. I wouldn't mind trying again. I sort of stepped into it the other day. I said casually we should do *Halloween 4: Part Two*. Someone got a hold of that quote, and it just blew up. It sort of just took off on its own. It's funny, but it would be fun to do.

AG: When you think back on this film, what's the first memory that comes to mind from working on it?

Dwight Little: There's a lot. Working with the girls. I was older obviously, but I felt that they were both like the little sisters I never had, and I just enjoyed working with them so much. Working scenes with Donald Pleasence. I was actually kind of a fanboy. Here's a guy from *The Great Escape* and the Bond movies. I was very starstruck almost by the size of his talents. I was pretty young at the time, working with him. I also just had this great crew with me. My friend Peter Collister was shooting it. My other friend Denis Stewart was the first AD, and we had the whole tone of it set by Moustapha. Most producers are out to if not sabotage you, browbeat you in some way—to be more on time, save more money, do it their way, change things, new pages. Most producers are difficult. Moustapha was always smart. He was a very good director himself, but he was supportive instead of confrontational. He would come to set, and he would see what was going on. He would ask, "What can I do? How can I improve this situation? What do you need?" It was such a shock to have a producer like that. Usually it's like, "Cut this scene and get back on schedule," very confrontational, and he was the opposite.

In the six weeks that we shot, I think four of those weeks were all night shoots. So you get to the point with the cast and the crew where you're the only people alive. You go to work at five in the afternoon, and you don't wrap until seven the next morning. When you're going back to your hotel, the rest of the world is waking up and going to work, so you're almost in this alternate reality. You get very bonded with the people that you see all night.

Interview: Alan McElroy (Writer, *Halloween 4: The Return of Michael Myers*)

AG: Let's start at the beginning.

Alan McElroy: Dwight and I had been working on a project together. We were trying to develop an action movie called *Legion* at that time. He got the job on *Halloween 4*, and they had I think it was three scripts that just weren't working. But they already had a release date and a start date, and they didn't have a script. So Dwight came to me with the scripts and said, "We need a story." I loved *Halloween*. I loved *Halloween* from the time I was in college, and seeing *Halloween II* was one of the most fun experiences I had when I was a sophomore in college and went with a group of friends to see it. I loved the franchise. I was excited about the chance to dive in and bring the Shape back to life, but there was a Writers Guild strike coming. It was 1988, and it was coming up in like two weeks. I only had that amount of time to write the script. So I sat down, and we broke a story very quickly, and I wrote the whole script in like eleven days, turned it over to them, and that's kind of how it all came to be.

AG: What was writing at that pace like for you?

Alan McElroy: I was young back then, so I could write really fast. It's crazy when I think back on it. I used to write a lot faster. Now if I were just working on a script, the rough draft might take me three weeks. The fastest script I ever wrote, which never got made, I wrote in four days. I would just bury myself in the work and live the script while I was writing it. So eleven days wasn't that hard for me because I was so into it and I loved it so much. It really wasn't stressful. I didn't feel the pressure of the strike coming because I was into the story, and I just wrote it at the pace I would have written anything at that time.

AG: You referenced these three other scripts. Dwight was very point-blank with me that he does not remember liking any of the other scripts and credits everything good to you. What do you remember keeping from those previous scripts, and which ideas were yours exclusively?

Alan McElroy: Basically, the three scripts got tossed. I loved the story so much, and I knew the mythology probably better than Dwight did because I had loved it so much and I'm such a genre fan, and I was definitely a fan of John Carpenter and everything about *Halloween*. So I really wanted to craft something that would bring the Shape back, and that to me was the story to tell. It's hard for me to take credit for everything, but I mean that was it, top to bottom. The one thing that we kept from one of the scripts was the scene with the multiple Michael Myers. When the sheriff pulls up, and there's one and then there's another one, then another one—that was from one of the scripts. I can't remember which one, but I definitely remember keeping it. Everything else I just came up with out of my love of the genre and what I wanted to see on-screen.

AG: Did you view the Shape as a supernatural entity? Or was he a man?

Alan McElroy: I viewed the Shape as an entity, an entity that inhabited Michael Myers, an entity that had probably been inhabiting people down through time. That's one of the reasons why when you cross paths with Jackson P. Sayer, you know that he's also been pursuing forces like this. I think it was *Halloween II* where Loomis mentioned

Samhain, and I just viewed this as a force that had entered Michael, and Dr, Loomis could see it. That's why he spent those years making sure this does not leave, that it is contained within the shell of what was Michael Myers. That's where it should stay, and he was trying to sort of contain it there. That's why at the end of the movie, I wanted it to sort of move on, into Jamie. I definitely viewed it as supernatural.

AG: Was the conclusion of the film an idea that you had very early on writing or was it something that kind of organically came to you throughout writing the script?

Alan McElroy: It was my idea right from the start. That's exactly what I wanted. I wanted this ending to be like the beginning of the first film in a sense. What happened to little Michael that he went home and committed this murder? What force had touched him and entered him and caused this to happen? I wanted it to be something that was passed on, and you see that happen here. Michael Myers passed that entity on to Jamie.

AG: Dwight Little used the phrase "soul transfer." Is that how you would also phrase it?

Alan McElroy: I wouldn't call it that, but that's an interesting term for it coming from Dwight. The Shape was moving, and it needs a body for what it wants to carry out. So it moved from one to the other. Something we talked about was that it's something that exists within the family line and goes back and is sort of connected via blood through all these people.

AG: A family curse perhaps?

Alan McElroy: Yes.

AG: Something else that's really interesting about your film is that everything is very logical. One beat leads to the next, and there's no logic gaps in this film. The audience never has to suspend their belief, which makes it stand out from a lot of other genre films at the time.

Alan McElroy: I think it's probably because I also had written action movies, and I understood the pacing of action. But I really wanted it to be logical. I feel that any good horror movie that's really gonna be scary needs to be logical. Everything that people do needs to be the right move, and yet still, the kill happens or the evil is overcoming them. If all of the characters are doing things that are incredibly smart and they still can't overcome what's coming against them, that's incredibly terrifying. That's why movies where you see characters doing things that are really stupid, illogical, or that don't make any sense—it takes you out of the movie because you think to yourself, *I wouldn't make that mistake*. But if you see characters being smart and situations being realistic, then it's terrifying. I really tried to maintain that kind of mindset. I'm hoping that's part of the staying power of *Halloween 4*, that people recognize that the characters are doing the smart thing. There's a sequence in there when Ellie sees something down an alleyway, and she turns and runs because that's what you should do. You don't stand there and say, "Hi, who are you?" and walk up to the fence. You get the heck out of there. That's what I wanted to show people, that these characters are doing the smart thing but are dealing with something that is unnatural, and it will continue to come after you.

AG: One last question on the ending of the film. Did you envision Michael as absolutely being dead? In your writer's mind, would Jamie be taking the mantle moving forward? Would it be a story about her and this family curse or did you always kind of assume, well, *Anybody that comes after me will find a way to resurrect Michael.*

Alan McElroy: I wanted it to be about her. I wanted the Shape because to me it's a story about the Shape, and the Shape isn't dependent on the body of Michael Myers. It is an entity that moves through people. I wanted it to enter Jamie, and now we've moved on and the curse has continued. That is the horror for Loomis at the end. It's happening again; it's repeating again. That's why he just pulled a gun. He wants to just blow her away right in that moment because he can't imagine having to go through this again with another child that's gonna grow up and be the embodiment of evil that he sees behind those dead eyes. For me, Michael was gonna be gone, and Jamie was going to be the new vessel for the Shape.

AG: It's almost as if you provided an answer to the problems that came about in *Halloween III*, where the story was trying to move away from Michael Myers. You offered a solution to the problem from the previous film, moving away from Michael Myers. Now the Shape can look different; evil can look different. You can see a path where the future of this franchise could have looked completely different.

Alan McElroy: Moustapha came back to Dwight and I and asked us to do *Halloween 5*. But we were moving on to do this action movie together called *Rapid Fire*. Also, we were developing something else with Fox called *Tears of the Sun*, which actually became a different movie, also called *Tears of the Sun*. We were moving on, so we said, "No, we can't come back," and we both lament the fact that we didn't come back to do *Halloween 5* now. We both look back on that and think we should have carried on with the franchise and taken it in a sort of new direction.

AG: How do you feel about the direction of the franchise as a whole after your film?

Alan McElroy: I lost interest. I saw *Halloween 5*. I don't even know what I would have envisioned, but the direction it took was not something that I found at all compelling. What's very interesting is that Moustapha would always ask when we were going to come back and do another *Halloween*. But by that point, it had gone so far into left field that I wasn't interested. It's so funny because when they did *Halloween H20*, Moustapha lifted certain things from *Halloween 4* and repeated them, things that we didn't shoot, like there was a sequence where Jamie was going to be chased in this school. We shot in the school, but we didn't have time to do the thing we wanted, which is where she was gonna be in a classroom and Michael was gonna come into that classroom and she was gonna be hiding at her desk. He'd be searching for her in that room and stabbing down through these desks trying to reach her. Moustapha took that sequence and used it in *Halloween H20*.

AG: I wanted to ask a follow-up about Moustapha. I wanted to see if you had any personal memories that you wanted to share of him.

Front of high school. Image courtesy of Ivan Bukta

Alan McElroy: His voice was always so great. He would call, and just that voice of his, it was so distinct. "Alan, you come back and do another *Halloween*?" It was almost like Arnold Schwarzenegger in a way. The other thing I always remember is when he got to the scene where Loomis meets the preacher in the truck and that whole sequence. There are moments in screenplays when I'm writing and that script really comes alive, and now it's on a dead run where I'm just writing what's happening and what I'm seeing, and it's all kind of unfolding in a very real way. That sequence was that moment for me. When Moustapha read that scene, he said, "Oh, yes, that's a very writer scene." That always sticks out to me.

I've tried to get Malek to do a spin-off about the young version of that preacher, go back and do a period piece, like in the 1950s, when the song "Mr. Sandman" is actually on the radio, have him be a young preacher who comes to a small town, and it's going to be his first church, and he encounters what is essentially the Shape. But he won't do it. I just would love to tell the story of this young preacher who realizes he has come face-to-face with true evil. I would love a chance to do that.

AG: Could you ever envision yourself writing another story set in Haddonfield?

Alan McElroy: Oh, yeah. I've actually pitched to Blumhouse the idea of doing a TV series called *Haddonfield*. We've only told one story in this town, but there are other stories in Haddonfield and other things that have happened in this town. Does it sit on the ley lines of supernatural forces so that there are other things going on? It's almost like what Stephen King does with Derry or with Castle Rock. To do this in Haddonfield I think would be kind of cool.

AG: I wanted to ask about Donald Pleasence. It was the first film without Jamie Lee Curtis but with Michael. You had this really strong, youthful cast, which was counterbalanced by Donald Pleasence, who was in effect the star of the show at this point. What was it like to work with him?

Alan McElroy: He was fantastic. We were on the writers' strike, so I was able to actually go and spend two weeks on set. I didn't do any writing or anything like that, but I was there just to be a guest, to just sit next to Donald Pleasence and talk to him and have him tell me stories. He had been in so many movies that I grew up watching. He played Dr. Michaels in *Fantastic Voyage*. He was a good guy. He was a nice man. He loved the script. He really complimented the script a lot. He thought the script was very smart, and I really appreciated that he loved the script. It was just great to sit with someone who was a cinematic legend. Every single day, it was just a true gift and a blessing for me to be able to sit there and spend time with him.

AG: When you look back on your experience from writing this film in eleven days to its legacy all these years later, what stands out to you the most? How would you define your *Halloween* experience?

Alan McElroy: It has been a true blessing. I was twenty-seven at the time. I had written two TV movies, but this was something that I wrote in eleven days with purity from my heart and poured it on the page. Other than budget restrictions and constraints, what I wrote is what ended up on the screen. Other than the remake of *Wrong Turn*, that has never happened, so the purity of that—one draft, getting it down, them going off and shooting it, then being able to go on set, watch it come into fruition—it's probably the purest and most joyful experience that I've had in film. I've been doing this for many, many years, and it was my first experience, and my first experience still stands out as the best and probably the most blessed experience. I really take it as such a blessing that I got a chance to do that and enjoy it and now look back on it and that it just carries forward with such a legacy that it has.

A few years ago, Universal Studios created a horror attraction for *Halloween 4* for Halloween Horror Nights. They recreated the garage and those moments, and to step into my own story and see it brought to life as an attraction at Universal Studios was mind-blowing and, again, a blessing. Part of the joy of what I get to do for a living is to make things up and create stories. I love it, and I really sort of pray and am thankful and grateful every day that I get to do this for a living. It's been fantastic. *Halloween 4* has been something that I can always look back on with pride and joy. The fact that fans still ask me about this movie I think says a lot. Writing is a tough business. You get rewritten, and things never end up the way you wrote it, and it becomes unrecognizable when it gets to the screen. But this was something that I can say, "Those are my lines. Those are my words. Those are the characters I created." I cherish that to this day.

Interview: Ellie Cornell (Rachel, *Halloween 4* and *5*)

AG: Let's start with the casting process. I've heard this story from Dwight Little's perspective, but I'd like to hear your recollection of how this role came to be.

Ellie Cornell: Here's what's kind of funny about Dwight's perspective on the casting: he came out with a book maybe like a year ago about his directing journey, and of course I ordered a copy on Amazon. I couldn't wait because I've always been a huge fan of his, and he talked about the casting of *Halloween 4*. I had no idea that I was not the first choice, or rather that he had to fight for his decision to cast me because I guess Moustapha Akkad and the producers out in LA wanted someone a little bit more glam and less girl next door. I thought that was so cool and humbling. I went in on a Friday. I was very new to the LA acting scene. I had come from a Shakespeare training camp called

Shakespeare and Company that Bill Murray helped me discover. My agent in New York sent me to Los Angeles for pilot season. Pilot season back in the day was when you would just go on interview after interview for that time of year where they're casting series and stuff like that. I went out and read for *Halloween*. They called me back on a Friday for a screen test, and it was my first official screen test. To be honest, it wasn't that scary. I was always game for auditions because you just know it's part of the gig. Alan McElroy, who wrote *Halloween 4*, and Dwight were there. I know Alan liked my vocal quality. I kinda remember that. I read for it on a Friday, and I waited all weekend, and then they gave me the role on Monday.

At that time, there was also *Friday the 13th* and *Nightmare on Elm Street*. There were these really strong series, and it was really cool to be cast in something that was so iconic. There's a gazillion horror films that get made, but there are so few that are not just recognized but also respected. I think what Jamie Lee Curtis and John Carpenter created from the start was next level compared to what was being made at the time. And in my perspective, what I really liked about the role of Rachel Carruthers is that it continued on that trajectory. Even Kathleen Kinmont [Kelly Meeker] is the flirty, yum-yum girl, but she was still so likable. Even though I threw coffee on her because she stole Brady away, you still liked her, and she was the sheriff's daughter, and there's something about Alan's writing that really made fully developed characters that the audience could get behind. Otherwise it's like, "Oh, who cares? Kill them off," and that's not that exciting. What I have found over the years is that horror fans are really intelligent. They're smart. They don't like having things dumbed down to them. That's just my perspective from the people that I've met and the details they notice. If you try to pull one over on them, they'll call you out on it. I loved *Halloween 4*. I think it gave the fans what they wanted after *Halloween* and *Halloween II*. *Halloween III* was off the map, right? That was a totally different animal. I think what we came back with for *Halloween 4* was what the fans wanted.

AG: What was that like as a young actress? Knowing that just ten years prior, they had created this iconic movie. I believe by this point *Halloween* was the largest-grossing independent film of all time. Then a successful sequel, and then it went off the map, like you said, in the third film. Now you guys are coming in with this opportunity to revive it to the glory that I had ten years ago. Did you feel that pressure?

Ellie Cornell: I took it as a huge responsibility, and I actually had seen *Halloween III*. I don't know; it was just an odd bird. I don't know how else to describe it. It wasn't good or bad. It was just off the plotline. There's nothing to grab onto continuity-wise. I really liked the script for *Halloween 4*. I have a good nose for a story. When I read the script, I really liked it, and I was superpsyched to get offered a role. It was never like, I can do it, but I'm gonna close my eyes and hold my nose. Nothing I've ever played has made me feel that way, but let's be honest: there's a lot of stories out there that are not as strong, but this was a strong story. I loved Rachel's protective nature towards Jamie, and I thought that was a refreshing perspective. People weren't really doing movies about protecting their younger sibling, you know what I mean? It was a cool, fresh perspective that I thought would be really fun to play. Man, did we have a blast.

AG: From most accounts, a majority of this shoot was at night with a fairly young cast. How did the night shoots impact a younger group of actors early in their careers?

Ellie Cornell: Well, I have to credit Dwight. I feel like he was fully aware of how young we were, and not just young in years, but there was a naivete about it, and he was very careful to kind of keep his eye on us. I always felt like he encouraged us to get our sleep. There was something very cohesive about it. It was like a little community. Donald Pleasence stayed in a separate hotel from the rest of the cast. Once the night shoots started, you learn very quickly that when the sun comes up and you hear the birds start chirping and they call the day, your job is to go home and get a full night's rest, a good meal, and you're passing people going to work. It's really weird. It's not only weird in that way, but it's a gentle reminder to take care of yourself. If you're all wired up and it takes you a while to kind of settle down into your rest, then that's cutting into the whole next night of working. It was an extremely professional, down to the nth degree, professional set, but they expected a lot from us as cast members. That meant cold nights and a lot of physical work. They were just very cognizant of our safety and things like that. But it was up to us as performers to have the discipline to go home and rest when you need to.

I think Danielle Harris and I worked something like thirty-nine out of the total forty days. We worked really, really long hours. You have to have some discipline. So it was such a great lesson to get at an early age, because it's really carried us through. There are some performers that kind of crash and burn early on. For whatever reason, they kind of go off the rails a little bit. We all worked right on through, even down to our drivers, the people that dress us, the people that do our hair and makeup every day—they're all working those long hours. It was also a great lesson in respecting the people that are supporting the work that we do in front of the camera. We are no more important than those folks behind us by any stretch of the imagination. We get treated differently, but without those guys, it doesn't happen. A lot of great first lessons on a first job. I really credit Dwight for taking that leap of faith with so many young people. Even Sasha Jenson [Brady] and Kathleen Kinmont—we were all pretty green at that point. We still had a great time, but we took it seriously.

AG: Your role is very physical, all while working overnight with your natural sleep schedule altered. This is a pre-CGI era, where everything was practical. Let's dive into the physicality of the role for a moment.

Ellie Cornell: A couple months later I read for this movie called *A League of Our Own* that Penny Marshall directed. They were like, "Okay, FYI, you're gonna be actually playing softball for the coaches from USC." They warned you you're gonna be playing softball as part of your audition. But for *Halloween*, there was no "Hey, Ellie, by the way, you're going to be crawling around with Danielle on your back, sliding around, running, leaping over fences." You just do it, though, and adrenaline helps. The part that I didn't do, which is probably no shock to anybody, was actually falling off the roof. That was a stunt double. But a lot of that was Danielle and I, and it's cold out. Dwight was great about prepping us. It wasn't just like, "Okay, you guys, you're gonna run really fast down this foggy, dark alley." No, it was like, "Imagine that he's behind you, and our job as performers is to tell the story." It's not that hard to imagine what it would be like. If that's the case, of course I would run up through the attic and climb out onto the roof. You would do what you had to do. So that's also helpful. It doesn't come from a fake place, and to me it wasn't gratuitous action where it was these ridiculous fight scenes for no reason. I've done those too, and those are fine. That's a different animal. But this to me comes from a really true place. I feel like our audience felt it. Horror movies took a different path after *Halloween 4*. After our film, the genre slowly got darker and darker and gorier and gorier, which is fine. But back in the day, you really had to tell the story in ways that the audience is going to understand and relate to. It's the relatability that I think made it work. I think that's why the character is likable and relatable, because you could relate to being in charge of a child and there's this threat. Of course you're gonna climb out the roof and put them on your back. What else could I do?

AG: It felt very primal. It felt very real. To your point, if you're in that situation, the way that your character behaved and reacted is how most of us would like to think that we would too if we were in that situation.

Ellie Cornell: Right. That's what I mean about horror fans. If I fold it up or did something really stupid, they go, "Oh, come on. Really?" It's like the whole truck sequence. I'm sure you've been told this, but Danielle and I were sitting in the truck on a two-by-four with prop people jumping on the two-by-four to make it look like we were bumbling along. There was a little bit of CGI, when Michael Myers reaches and tears the guy's head off. He wasn't there when we were shooting it, but of course we had to react to it. So again, you rely on that imagination, and it was so fun to see it with all the components put together—the music, the CGI. That's why the movies are so fun, because we were just one component of many that went into it. It was scary.

AG: Something that I really love about this film is that everything makes sense yet still acts as a natural extension of the first film. Jamie Lee Curtis is taking care of these two little kids in a babysitting sequence. Your character is very reminiscent of hers in terms of the girl next door type, and now you actually have a little girl with you the whole time. Kathleen Kinmont's character is a natural extension of P. J. Soles in the first film. And everything makes sense. I think that's why people love this film so much. It doesn't make us question things. It's just a fun, logical film with an awesome cast.

Ellie Cornell: Oh my God. That is so good. You're hitting the nail on the head. Yeah, that's it. That's it. I think what I liked about *Halloween 4* is there was an extra layer to everything. Think about Kathleen Kinmont's role. She was the sheriff's daughter. She was someone's daughter. She wasn't just like a crazy, slutty bimbo. You know what I mean? She wasn't a caricature of that girl. You know, she was just a little bit rebellious. She had a big crush on this kid, but her dad was right there. You're right. It didn't go too far off in any one direction, or it didn't introduce something that was implausible. It was just like a small-town group of people.

AG: It's been said that Dwight was very open to feedback and trying different things on set. How much of the Rachel character was scripted, and what elements perhaps did you bring forth?

Ellie Cornell: Rachel was a good girl, right? Meaning not rebellious, worked hard, studied hard, things like that, but she was also a teenager. I think when her parents said, "We need for you to stay home and take care of Jamie tonight," it was written to where it was like, "Okay, whatever you need for me to do, I'll do." But I think there was an element to Rachel of like, "You gotta be freaking kidding me. Like tonight of all nights, are you kidding me?" I personally don't make a habit of ever going off book. That's the writer's job, and my job is to speak their words. I never fought to change that line necessarily. But I think that there was a certain attitude that I thought needed to be implemented to make her more human and more relatable. What fun is that if all I wanted to do was stay home? It was the same thing with having a crush on Brady. I wanted to be that girl. I wanted to be Kathleen Kinmont. I didn't know how to quite get there, and she did. So she got the guy, but she's still a regular teenage girl that wants to go out, for God's sake. It's Halloween. That's what the eye rolls were all about.

AG: Moving on to *Halloween 5*, who was it that reached out to you about returning for another film?

Ellie Cornell: Well, my agent said the script was coming, and I knew it would because obviously I had lived through *Halloween 4*, which is a huge deal to me. It was rare for both Danielle and I to survive to tell the story. So I knew it was coming. They're not gonna completely switch gears. It's probably very typical actor behavior, but as soon as the script arrives, you flip through looking for your character's name. Rachel was not in a lot of it, so it's like, "How is it gonna end?" I wasn't surprised that Rachel was killed off. I've said this before, but I was surprised by how it was written. It was a different kind of script, even the amount of characters. It was a little chaotic—not in a bad way, just a different energy.

So I fussed, and I said that I don't like this, for Rachel to get scissors shoved down her throat. I didn't think it was dignified enough. He changed it to where she just gets the scissors into her chest. What I've come to realize—and this is for all horror directors and producers out there—always leave the possibility that they can keep going and come back. You just never know. I think there was a little bit of a backlash, like, "That's it for Rachel? You gotta be kidding me." Even Moustapha Akkad said that he didn't know at the time that it would be seen as a negative thing.

AG: How did that make you feel to hear that from Moustapha?

Ellie Cornell: Oh, I thought it was supersweet. It wasn't like I was patting myself on the back or anything. It was a good lesson because at the time, I could have said, "Hey you guys, are you sure you wanna do this?" It's all in retrospect, but I did know the value of bringing characters back even then. They had a really cool opportunity.

AG: Dwight Little doesn't hold back with his feelings on *Halloween 5* in general.

Ellie Cornell: You know what's so weird is that you think it's easy to create a film like that because it's so formulaic, but it's also so elusive. Somehow Dwight got this little lightning in a bottle, this little chemistry between me and Danielle and a good story. He told it well, he told it simply, and you're like, "Well, how hard can that be?" But look at other horror films out there. It's not that easy.

AG: I think the most simple way to compare the two films is that *Halloween 4* is Americana. It's the Midwest on a fall night. It's a lot of things that we are accustomed to. *Halloween 5* has a harsh, European feel to it. The two styles feel very strange next to each other back-to-back. Your character feels drastically different in the two films. In *Halloween 4*, it's sweaters-and-girl-next-door vibes. In *Halloween 5*, you're in a state of undress right before you die. It almost seemed like we're gonna take her from good girl babysitter to slightly bad girlish right before she dies. I don't wanna use the word upsetting, but it's like you look at somebody one way and then we're told to look at them a different way, and as a viewer it's off-kilter.

Ellie Cornell: Yeah. Oh my God, that's so true. Wow. I guess in retrospect I could have put my foot down and said, "You can't get me to do this." But the whole shower scene was all done very respectfully. Like I said, Moustapha ran a very professional set. Everything was done by the book. It's all protected. The union protects its actors in terms of how it's shot, who's in the room, and all that stuff. So that I didn't have a problem with. But what bothered me the most in *Halloween 5*, just in the little bit that I was in, besides the fact that I would run out in the yard in a towel, was the slapstick quality to the policeman. There was a silliness that felt disingenuous. The whole shower thing, it felt gratuitous. Fans were superbummed. The one positive thing that came out of it is that the fans were very generous in that they will always like Rachel.

I'm not panning [Dominique Othenin-Girard's] direction, because that's not my job as a performer, but we even spoke different languages in that way. He wanted something very sexy, and it was like trying to get apple juice from an orange. It's like no, no, no. We didn't clash on set, but creatively, in my bones, I was like, *No, I don't think so.* You just know when it's not genuine, when it's not coming from a real place. That means story; that means character and the way it looks.

Interview: Kathleen Kinmont (Kelly, *Halloween 4: The Return of Michael Myers*)

AG: What was the casting process like?

Kathleen Kinmont: I was nineteen. It was easy, not any kind of a big deal. I'm sure I went in once, maybe twice, and they cast me pretty quickly. I don't remember there being any kind of real long, lengthy process. I think they found their cast swiftly. I probably read for the casting director and Dwight Little. These days, so much stuff is done on tape. You don't really get that real personal meeting and instant notes. You just kind of do it to the best of your ability and throw it in there and see if it sticks. I love going into a room and meeting with the people and feeling the vibe and getting the notes, making the adjustments right there on the spot. I think they can see how pliable you are. That was back then, and those were the good old days.

AG: What are some of your memories of working with Dwight Little? What was he like as a director?

Kathleen Kinmont: He was really very kind, careful, and funny. The scripted line at the beginning that introduces my character was "Get lost, Wade," when he came up to me with the sunglasses on. We filmed that, and then Dwight said, "You know, just for shits and giggles, why don't we try 'Fuck off, Wade?'" So I laughed for a second, and I thought, *Wow, that's pretty damn funny*. I didn't recall the F word being in the original script. It was one of those things where I thought this will probably never make it because it's so R-rated, and this was such a child-driven film, very youth oriented. I thought, *It'll never make it, but it was fun to do*. It was my first foray into kind of going off book from what the script was. I didn't really know that you could do that, change lines like that. That's big, you know. Now it was like, *Think on your feet*. Don't try to make anything other than what you did with the other line and just deliver it the same way. Don't lean on it; just make it happen. It made it into the film, and it's so iconic and such a memory for everyone that loves the film. I sign that primarily on all of the convention photographs I've signed. That was really neat. I thought that Dwight was super collaborative that way. I thought that he was really trusting and was having fun and being in the moment. We were all so young and so brand-new to so much of it. He just made it really relaxed, which was good because you're dealing with kids, and attention spans aren't really that long yet. He knew how to take care of the kids. He knew to make sure we had a hotel with an indoor swimming pool so we could go and blow off some energy at the end of every day. He really made the set supersafe. He had an excellent stunt crew and coordinators, which is important when dealing with contraptions you're putting young kids into. There's always a possibility for people getting hurt on any set, just tripping over any kind of lighting equipment or whatever. I love Dwight Little and would love to work with him again.

AG: Your character is kind of the sultry, bad girl of the film. How much of that was written? Walk me through the character a little bit.

Kathleen Kinmont: The character was completely written, for sure. Who says things like, "Wise up to what men want Rachel or Brady won't be the last man you lose to another woman"? I'm like nineteen years old. That's such a great line. It's really stuck in my head forever. It's so kind of ridiculous. But also it just says a lot about the intelligence of that character, where she's at and her maturity. I think that people who know me know that I'm so far from being anything like that, but I love her so much for just having so much balls to be slaying on somebody else's boyfriend right in front of them. It's such a small town, and there's not a lot to pick from. "Hey, are you done with that one? Because as soon as you're gone, I'm in there." That's what it kind of feels like. So it's not like she's a bad girl. It was a small town. Brady was the one cute guy, and she set her sights on him. Rachel, if you're not gonna freaking go for it, then step aside, small fry.

AG: How long did you film for?

Kathleen Kinmont: I would say about four weeks. It wasn't a tremendously long shoot, but it wasn't really short either. It never felt like we were rushing through anything. It felt like they definitely made ample time for all of it. You can always feel it, how quickly you're getting ushered through the day, how stressed out the first AD is, and we didn't have that. I think it was because Dwight was so conscious of the fact that he had younger performers here. They're gonna need some support, and what's more important than supporting somebody with giving them some time? It never felt like, "Come on, act faster." It always felt like, "We want you to do great." You never feel compromised or unsure. It was just a very comfortable set, superorganized and superconsiderate. You can't get any better than that.

AG: This film rebooted the *Halloween* franchise. John Carpenter and Debra Hill had exited the series. This film was reintroducing Micheal Myers after he had been removed for the third film. Most people assumed this franchise wasn't coming back. Was there any pressure amongst the cast to reboot this franchise, or was the feeling more "Let's go make a cool horror movie"?

Kathleen Kinmont: I don't feel like we felt any pressure. I don't think that any of us were old enough to understand the impact of bringing back a franchise. I feel like we were just all excited to be at work, superexcited to be on location, working with Donald Pleasence and thinking that he's the real actor here. We were all very respectful and in awe of him because he was so relaxed and didn't have any kind of tonality like, "Come on everybody, we gotta do a good job because this ship is sinking." It was just like we were making our own film. It was a stand-alone film regardless of what had ever predated it or what was ever expected after it. I don't think that any of us felt like we were shouldering this franchise from being obscure anymore. Everyone was just really present in what we were doing. Nobody was thinking about anything from before or what was gonna happen afterwards. We were all just saying that this is gonna be cool because we're all cool and we're all doing our thing. Everybody likes each other, and we're getting along great. We're having fun, and all the adults are telling us that we're doing a really good job. That was validation enough. Nobody cared about anything other than that. Nobody was reading *Variety* on set. We just weren't that crew. We weren't that cast.

I grew up in the business. The entertainment industry is so fickle. You don't know what anything is gonna be. You don't even know if it's gonna get finished. You don't even know if it's gonna find a platform when it does get finished. Who's gonna see it? There's so many platforms now. You never know when you're making it, and you really shouldn't be caring. You really should just be in the character of what you're doing.

AG: You brought up Donald Pleasence. One of my questions was asking for stories that perhaps you had from working with him and being around him on set.

Kathleen Kinmont: Well, he was pleasantly toasty all the way through this movie. He definitely had acquired a huge résumé at that point and was very respected. He was comfortable, and the nights were cold. He had a flask, or he had a red cup, and I just remember thinking, God, can you really do this kind of stuff if you've been drinking? But you know what? He could have done anything like that with his eyes closed. I just remember that he was the first person I ever witnessed getting a little toasty on set, but it didn't affect him or make him anything different than what he was when he arrived on set. Maybe that was just him. I have huge respect for the man, and I thought he was so great in the film. He just has a gravitas that gives everything credibility. He lent a lot of credibility to all of our performances. I thought when you have people like that in the same cast list, it kind of resonates with everybody. Even if you're not working with him, you know he's somewhere on the set, and it makes you want to have your shit together. *I want to be good. I wanna know my lines.*

Certain people will always rise to the level of personal best. It gets better when certain people walk in the room. You thought you were doing your personal best, and then here's Tom Hanks. He just came in now. You feel it when you just say the name, and Donald had that. So it was really neat because even if he wasn't around, he was still around because he was part of the call sheet. You'd see his name on the call sheet either with a "W" [for working] next to it or a "hold" next to it or a "work finish" next to it. We weren't just making a little film, which can be great and do really well. But this gave us confidence. *I'm in something that's gonna be seen.* I think it was that and the fact that it was a franchise movie. It was exciting. We knew that there was gonna be some buzz. We didn't know that it was gonna be as great as it was. I really do feel like *Halloween 4* is probably one of the best *Halloween* movies, not just from being biased because I'm in it, but because of everything I've heard from the fans.

AG: Let's talk about your death scene. We were in the pre-CGI era, and everything was practical effects. What was that experience like for you?

Kathleen Kinmont: Well, they drilled a bike seat onto the door so I had something to sit on and my legs would be dangling. To get me upright on that, they had to put me into a harness that was underneath my shirt. They drilled a hole in the back of the shirt where there was a wire that went from the harness through the door so that they could pull my torso up and back in the same swift movement that he's drilling that sawed-off shotgun into the torso. It was a contraption that really lasted only for about fifteen or twenty minutes of filming, but it was intense and uncomfortable. They were very careful with me and gave me a lot of support, but it was definitely a lot of work. It was a big work moment because I wanted it to look real, and I wanted it to feel shocking. I wanted to sell it with my face and the timing of the movement and not slam myself so hard into the door that I'm giving myself a concussion. Fortunately, I'm a pretty physical person and strong, willing, and able. I thought it was great. I saw it on the big screen and was like, *Holy shit.* It was really fucking realistic and scary. A very vulnerable feeling scene. I thought, Here's this girl that was having the time of her life just twenty minutes ago in front of the fire with Brady. Then Dad comes home, and shit hits the fan. It was a good night up until that moment.

AG: It is a very vulnerable moment. There's a lot of theories about Michael Myers and his violence perhaps being of a sexual nature. Your character does kind of lend itself to that theory: dressed only in an oversized T-shirt, exposed legs, and there is a bit of a sexuality to the murder, as well as vulnerability. What was that like for you as a young actress?

Kathleen Kinmont: I was completely down for it. There's always going to be sexuality in every film. Any time you cast a female, she represents sexuality and sensuality. Women have been chased by King

Kong forever. It's the formula. It's what stimulates the hero concept for men, and it's what stimulates the fight-or-flight concept for women. Women can fight back. I think it's important to show all of that, the human condition. Women have been preyed upon forever, so to not show that is unrealistic, and it's basically what the *Halloween* franchise has been all about from the get-go. They stayed true to that.

AG: Any fun on-set stories you care to share?

Kathleen Kinmont: Sasha Jenson, who played Brady, I knew from high school. In fact, I set him up with one of my friends to take her to our prom. He ended up coming to my prom with me and my girlfriend and my friend Frankie Avalon Jr. That was a lot of fun. When I got to the hotel in Utah and there he was in the lobby, I was like, "Oh my God! What are you doing here?" And he's like, "I'm doing a movie." I'm like, "I'm doing a movie. Is it *Halloween*? Are you Brady?" He's like, "Are you Kelly?" It got really awkward, knowing that our characters are going to have this love scene. He says, "This is how we're gonna fix this. We're gonna go up to your room or mine, and we're gonna rehearse that scene so we can get all the giggles and all the weirdness out, just so we can get into it. We gotta be able to trust each other." I said, "You're right." We both were studied actors, but we're still very young. We can't buy alcohol; we're that young. It's not like we can get some booze and get really toasty like Donald Pleasence to be relaxed on the set. That wasn't an option.

So we had to do the work, and it really helped. We were up in my room, and we rehearsed, and it was fun. When it came time to do the scene, I was really relaxed because he was my friend and we had talked about it, and we did our own intimate choreography so that we could get it to that place where they could cut away. But I was comfortable with it so that I wasn't so self-conscious. I thought it went really well and was pretty hot stuff. What's really funny is that when I did go see the movie in the theater, my brother Matt Smith went with me. He and I were sitting behind these two guys, and right at that scene when my bra started to drop, the two guys were like, "Oh my God, that was worth the $7.50 right there!" I'm so glad that I rehearsed with Sasha, because you have to be that in the moment and not feel like I've got to cover myself or feel insecure. I was like, "Let's play." That's a really great memory, because Sasha is just the coolest guy ever and one of my favorite people.

I also remember just playing with Danielle Harris in that hotel swimming pool every day after work. We had the best time. We could be kids, play with the little kid, and do cannonballs. That was really fun. Being at the pool was like our martini at the end of the evening, jumping into this great big chlorinated, heated indoor swimming pool in Utah during the winter. We felt like little movie stars. We'd all sit in the jacuzzi and talk about the day. You've been up since five in the morning or whatever, and you're just too wound up to have some pizza and go to sleep right now. I think all filmmakers should take that to heart. If you're working with kids, make sure you put them in a hotel with an indoor swimming pool, give them a space to go take a dip together and wash the day off. Some healthy exercise and camaraderie. I think that's probably why we still love each other so much. We had such a great time playing Marco Polo and just being stupid, splashing each other and just getting it all out.

Interview: Dominique Othenin-Girard (Director, *Halloween 5: The Revenge of Michael Myers*)

AG: How did you get involved with *Halloween 5: The Revenge of Michael Myers*?

Dominique Othenin-Girard: Debra Hill, the producer and cowriter of the first *Halloween* film, I met her at the Sundance film festival. She saw my film *Piège à flics*, [*Black Sequence*], and she asked if I would consider directing a horror movie. I just finished *Night Angel*, which was a horror movie in the States that I did before *Halloween 5*. She called Moustapha, and the next week I received a script on a Friday, and then on Monday I had an appointment with Moustapha and the team.

AG: Did you have any additional meetings or collaborations with Debra Hill beyond that initial meeting at Sundance?

Dominique Othenin-Girard: Yes, I did. She was brilliant at analyzing stories and then putting the story on track. She was a very clever producer. She knew exactly what the ingredients of *Halloween* were, and Moustapha paid her residual money as well as to John every time he was doing a new sequel, as well as paying her for the rights. He also asked her for her advice. They were not close, because Moustapha was not close to very many people. But let's say they were talking. She was the founding partner to Moustapha, not John, who was uninvolved then. She was not involved in the production of *Halloween 5* at all, but she was a counselor on the script with Michael Jacobs and myself. I sort of didn't know where to go from Dwight Little's *Halloween 4*, where he had the little girl who put on the mask and stabbed her mother. Is it the mask that made her evil? Is it the little girl who became evil? Do we have Michael and Jamie both as villains? I hesitated, and with Michael Jacobs, we were looking at *The Eyes of Laura Mars*. Michael brought that to the table and said, "Look, Dominique, it's like a haunted hypnosis of sorts." We brought that to Debra, and she said to be careful. She put a stop on our going into psychedelic cinema. She said to stay down to earth. Don't go into lyrical dreams and so on.

I also said, "Let's not mix genres between the three franchises that were on the market at the time." *Friday the 13th* was the body-count series, the gore. I didn't want to go into the genre of *Nightmare on Elm Street*, where it was during your dream, during your sleep, that evil could strike. I didn't want to go into that, but I had inherited a strange thing I had to get out of, the little girl stabbing her mother. I sort of chose the direction to go in, and Debra went with me, and Michael Jacobs as well, of Jamie and Michael being connected in a very special way, especially feeling when he's getting aroused, when he's getting into the killing mode. There she has a sense of crisis, and in those moments she can be helpful to the police, to locate him or to sort of try to see if they can hinder his killing. Debra was very helpful. She's so smart. She was the defender of John Carpenter's down-to-earth horror movie style, but she knew it had to evolve. This couldn't be another John Carpenter movie. To tell you the truth, the first *Halloween* was my only reference for making *Halloween 5*. You've probably read this, but I didn't see the second or third films. I saw *Halloween 4*, and I thought it was very good of Dwight Little to come back to the Hitchcockian suspense and not to go elsewhere. I only saw it once. I didn't study it so much. I didn't think the lighting or the acting were too exceptional. I thought it was totally acceptable but not interesting.

AG: I'm very curious about the psychedelic concepts that Debra Hill was warning you against. Did you have any particular ideas for that type of direction that you wanted to take the film in?

Dominique Othenin-Girard: I know Michael Jacobs had put on the table this concept of psychedelic. We wanted to do visions from Jamie of what Michael was seeing. For me, that was something interesting because it was visual. But I think it went further with kinetic powers. Then Debra said, "Careful, guys, you're going outside the realm of *Halloween* movies. You're inventing something different." I do not think she liked the second and third *Halloween* films either. I know they were quite different. They were not taking the original idea of suspense of when a kid makes love for the first time, he feels guilty. That's when death strikes through Michael Myers. First-timers get punished. I thought, *Oh, that's very good.* We can relate to this because there's a sense of guiltiness when we first have excitement, sexual arousal. I thought, *Good, let's keep that as the center of the film, because everyone feels it at some point in their life.*

AG: Did you view Michael's violence as being sexual in nature?

Dominique Othenin-Girard: I didn't see sexual violence in any of the *Halloween* films. Mine is certainly not geared that way. I wanted to punish the innocent. I think that's terrible. What is more unjust than during your first time or first time getting aroused to be slashed at that moment? This is unjust. It can't be; you're a bad guy. You die. That's too simple. You're innocent, and you're a first-timer; now you die. That's unjust. Why do I kill the good girl right at the beginning of the movie, Rachel? Because I want to kill the innocent. If the heroine of *Halloween 4* dies right away, this is unsettling, and I think that's what horror is about. So now you have these teenagers who speak about sex and wish to have sex at the party, and it's a big Halloween night, and I killed the blonde, Tamara Glynn's character [Sammy]. It's the first time that she has a boyfriend. But it is not sexual violence, because I don't show Michael aroused. I don't show if he has pleasure or not. I show the unfairness of life by his strike during the first time of pleasure.

AG: It's so cruel.

Dominique Othenin-Girard: It *is* cruel. I've tried to make Michael human. When I show his face, I feel an emotion. I don't want to make him totally unreachable, supernatural and so on. He survived having been shot twenty times, things like that. It's improbable or a superpower kind of gift that he has. But apart from these tricks of the trade, I tried to make him human to link him with Jamie.

AG: One of the most fascinating parts of your film to me is the character of Loomis. Loomis feels more desperate and crazed here, even mean at times. It feels like he is reaching a breaking point of sorts. Let's discuss your thought process behind writing the character of Loomis here, in his fourth film in the series.

Dominique Othenin-Girard: We were with Moustapha, and he said that Donald Pleasence was doing his last *Halloween* film. He had enough. Oh, good, so I can kill him? It's a privilege to have this knowledge at the beginning of writing the character. His character was so repetitive from one film to another, searching to understand this evil and so on. I have to congratulate Michael Jacobs, who wrote some great lines for Loomis here. "I tried to send him to hell, but hell won't have him" was a great line. To write for Loomis and not to be repetitive was a pain. So I cranked it up a notch. He had to use Jamie in order to trap Michael. From the beginning he shakes her in her hospital bed. He maltreated this poor little girl, and Donald was not happy about doing it, but he went in and did the scene very well. He had some kind of resistance because it's a child, but I said, "You've got to." So I was pretty hard on Donald. Donald was in a bad mood making the movie because of the special effects makeup. We wanted him to look burned from the previous films. We wanted him to have suffered a lot. His hand was full of latex, his face, and so on. He hated to sit in the makeup chair. He collaborated extremely well, no problem. But he said, "My character is not really like that." I said, "Yeah, but it's the last time you're doing it; you can evolve. So let's not be boring; let's not do the same thing again." We effectively trap the little girl in order to create a trap for Michael, to imprison the little girl alone and send the cops away, to be alone in that house because he wants to face Michael. So what does he want? It is the big question towards the climax of the movie.

I did not respect at all the architecture of John Carpenter for the Myers house. That was with the blessing of the production designer. We had a great time with Brent Swift [production designer/art director]. He was fantastic. Moustapha didn't realize we were offending the fans so much by creating a new house. I wanted to have that house become a mythical place, something haunted. I didn't put any lights inside the house. The house is lit from the outside, by the windows. We created a really freaky atmosphere in that house. I visited their locations, and I found this laundry chute. So I wrote the scene about the laundry chute. Where can I trap this little girl in the narrowest corner of the house with a man coming after her with a knife? Moustapha said, "What are you going to do? Are you crazy? You can't do this." And I said, "Yes, I can." Everyone was saying, "You're crazy. How are you gonna shoot this?" I took all my freedom that I could, and it became quite a nice scene.

Unfortunately, they've taken out three shots of that scene of the laundry chute. One of the major shots is her falling down it. She's close to the camera, and she slides when her fingers lose her grip on the door when he opens the door. Then she falls away. That shot of her is so scary because she's right in front of the camera and she leaves the camera and she tries to grip on the side. It was all done horizontally in studios. I had seven pieces of the laundry chute built differently so that Rob Draper, the director of photography, could put lights for the different shots that are storyboarded. For each storyboarded shot, we had a new piece of the laundry chute built. Jamie's belly was against these roller skates, and we were pulling the roller skates in the tube by ropes. She loved it.

AG: You had such an effective use of tight close-ups in this film. We felt dangerously close to these characters at pivotal moments.

Dominique Othenin-Girard: I learned low-budget film directing in Europe. You don't have so much of a budget. I've learned to be extremely well-prepared for the shoot so I can do many shots and I can get close to the people. For me, to be close is to film the interior feeling and emotion of the characters. When Jamie's in that big house and Michael is coming to her and she runs before she goes to the attic, she had never seen Don Shanks in the costume of Michael Myers prior. There's a few shots where they were together, but they were not dangerous shots because the whole team was there and so on. She didn't see the aggression of Don Shanks. She didn't understand the manipulation that I had built to make the movie. She only saw her part, so she was never afraid. So to have her totally scared and go away from the camera, what did I do? I ran with her up and down the stairs before she got out of the laundry chute in the kitchen. We were running in that kitchen. She was out of breath. I said, "Now go to the shoot." I would sort of scream at her like this, and she would go, and she opened her eyes because this madman is screaming at her now. She would do the take because she would be out of breath. She was so available. I saw Danielle as a baby bird in the nest, all the way up on a tree. I was the guy who said, "Go ahead, jump. You see your wings will open; you won't get crushed." Danielle was that little baby bird looking down and saying, "No, I'm not. You're crazy." But then she would jump. She would see that with her preparation and me doing the dialogue with her before, it's like her wings would open up and she'd fly in the scene. She would be inside the character. Several times she got tears out of me because I was seeing this, and I just got emotionally taken away by her performance. She was so true—authentic, not calculating, not preserving herself. She just threw herself out of the nest and hoped that things would work out. After the first time she did it, she needed courage to do it the second time. She was fantastic.

Actors are the most precious thing to me. If you don't have a performance from an actor, the audience is not gonna relate to the film. They're not gonna empathize with the character; they're not gonna identify. I care about this. We were under pressure because to shoot that movie with the number of effects and the night shoots that we had in thirty-five days was a grueling schedule, especially because it was union rules. We had ten hours a day and sometimes a little more but not much more. We had a child on the set most of the time. So I can see many directors not having time for actors. For me, that was my priority. I love my job directing. I love children, but directing children is a tough task—lots of patience, and it needs to be genuine. You can't build patience. It has to be true, because otherwise the kid feels, *God, I'm doing wrong, and he doesn't like me* or *I did wrong one time, and he won't like me anymore.* If you show that to a child, then the child won't do it again. Well, you have to let the child make the mistake and try it out, and then we go back and we build, and then we trust each other. It's a question of trust, and it's a question of true communication. I would have Danielle be fresh and not tired or waiting for hours. She went with Greg Nicotero [special effects supervisor] and the special effects team. She was hanging out with them and the makeup department and the costume department. That was her playground on the set. I would send her away to play, to not have thoughts about the film or the shots. But I would be directing, and suddenly my hand would be picked up and she would bite my little finger, gently. I was concentrating on seeing what the camera was seeing. I didn't really mind my hand being taken, but I didn't realize that she was biting my little finger, a sign of affection, saying to me, "Hey, I exist. Could you pay attention to me?" I want to be in front of the camera. I don't want you to take care of other people. I wanna be the center of attention.

AG: I wanted to get back to the house. It was more gothic than what the franchise had previously been. There's almost this sense of European cinema and culture coming into a franchise that had always been Midwestern Americana, which creates an interesting dichotomy.

Dominique Othenin-Girard: An astute observation. Very good. Without you guys—the watchers and the critics—sometimes we wouldn't evolve so much. I wanted to have a concept of lighting. Rob Draper was fantastic. I said to Rob, "I want to start with daylight." So in the screenplay, we wrote most of the scenes at the beginning of the screenplay during daylight. I wanted to have pastel colors. Nothing too bright or too flashy, just gentle pastel. Then from this daylight, colorful and normal environment, I wanted to end the film with black and gold—nothing else, just black and gold—so that I could narrow the field of pleasure for the eyes. That was a concept way before Rob came in because it was in the screenplay. The gothic house became part of that concept because I wanted to have a feel of the evilness of Michael. How do I give the evilness of Michael feeling? John Carpenter invented the thing. So this little house in Midwest America in a one-

or two-story house could work because of the narrow locations and so on. He was very good at it. But you can't do sequels in such a small space. I wanted to have something where I could be behind Loomis entering into this house and going through the cobweb, see the total space. He sees nothing, but we know there is a tattoo on the wall. We know Michael is somewhere in there. I just felt that is what the bogeyman is about. He's not seen, but he's present, and I wanted to have him present all the time.

AG: Your film added a mythology for this franchise by introducing not only this mysterious character in black who's seen all throughout the film, but also the symbol that we are now seeing for the first time. Where did these ideas come from, and did you have an idea of how they should unfold in subsequent films?

Dominique Othenin-Girard: Michael Jacobs, Debra Hill, and I had what we thought was a satisfying ending. We prepped for about six weeks, and we were about two and a half or three weeks into the shoot when Moustapha said he wanted the end to be changed. He said, "It doesn't satisfy me to have Michael be picked up by the police and go to jail. He needs to be freed, and I need someone to free him." I'm like, "Are you serious? Do you want to have a drink and calm down?" It is such a bomb. We all liked the end of our script. As a director, you go somewhere with your story, you aim at something. Now I've got to aim at something else, and I've got new scenes coming in. Part of my decision was now I have to introduce a character. I've got to give him some kind of mythical power or link to Michael. In every location that I was shooting in, I had a different person wear the dark jeans, wear the boots, wear the coat, wear the hat. If you really notice, sometimes he's tall, sometimes he's short, and so on. Sometimes it's a woman who wears that costume. Then I said, "It's not enough in order to link him to Michael. I'm going to put a tattoo on both of them." I chose my rune. The rune are the Celtic forces, and this is the rune Thor. I added a dot, so it's not Thor only. It is Thor plus two dots. I changed it slightly, and I added it in the house and onto the guys and onto Michael. So I had to shoot another close-up of Michael waking up in order to see the tattoo. We did this onstage somewhere where we could sort of recreate the lighting of his waking up. Keeping him mysterious was essential in order to get the audience to say, "What the fuck? Who is that crushing a cigarette walking to the house?" This kind of was the only attractive element I could find for him, because I didn't have space in the narrative to add something else. I couldn't have Loomis talk about him. I couldn't have the cops talk about him. I couldn't have any verbal explanation for the character. It had to exist visually, and visually I couldn't give away too much. I needed to retain mystery. As far as a plan for the character in the future after *Halloween 5* and who is he, I'm on the phone with Michael Jacobs, who was in Los Angeles, saying, "Hey Michael, you sort it out. I'm busy shooting it. Write something, Michael." I said, "The best way is to do what Dwight Little did." I'm not so sure he knew why Jamie stabbed her stepmother. I don't know if she died or not, but it is up to me to sort it out. I had thoughts about who this person was—maybe the unknown brother of Michael—but I didn't want to say it. I didn't want to sort of load something that would be too narrow for the next film to open up and to be creative. So I said, "No, I'm gonna let the next film create something with this. I'm gonna leave it totally open. I'm not gonna narrow down the possibilities. I'm gonna leave it open-ended."

AG: Thank you, Dominique. Anything in conclusion you'd like to share or add?

Dominique Othenin-Girard: I did ask myself, "What is it about American culture that I enjoyed so much by living in America, especially when I was sixteen or seventeen, when I did a year in Detroit as an exchange student? What did I like about America?" I know it's the value of a dream. I know it's the value of if you wish to do something, people are going to encourage you to go for it and believe in yourself. Yes, you can do it, as opposed to old Europe, where you wanna do a new driveway to the house for the car. "No, it's expensive. We don't know how to do it," and so on. In America it would be "Yeah, why not? Let's try to see how we can do it," and this basic difference, I've tried to sort of make something out of it with *Halloween 5*. I felt I was walking on dry ground, so I could run. In Europe, it feels like I'm walking on mud, and my feet are much heavier. It's so difficult to go fast and to move a crew and so on. This appreciation that I had about America, I tried to generate it inside the characters, these young characters who believe life is theirs, by having Tina being such a dynamic, eccentric, happy-go-lucky type of girl. So maybe she unnerves people, but for me, she was the freshness of America. She was for me symbolizing that all is possible. The characters were not blasé but innocent people going into life. I wanted to give something else, a message on the positivity of America that I liked personally.

Interview: Shem Bitterman (Writer, *Halloween 5: The Revenge of Michael Myers*)

AG: How did this job on *Halloween 5* come to be?

Shem Bitterman: I did a play in LA called *Tulsa*, and there was a guy named Ramsey Thomas who was working with Moustapha Akkad as a producer. Ramsey was interested in optioning this play. He didn't have money for it, so instead he said, "I've got a job for you," and that's how I got involved.

AG: Interesting. Had you seen any of the *Halloween* films prior to that?

Shem Bitterman: Yeah, I was a fan, like you. *Halloween* was one of those seminal, great, terrifying, fun-to-watch movies. You know what I mean? I love the first film. Watched it in grad school and remember being just terrified by it.

I don't know how Ramsey got involved with Moustapha, but he brought me in to work with Moustapha on *Halloween 4*, and I believe that I did the first draft of *Halloween 4*. What happened is I was hired and did the first draft. Then they hired a director, and the director brought in another writer, which is pretty typical. The Writers Guild called me and said, "This is now going to be a guild project, so you could join the Writers Guild if you want." It's what they call a signatory project.

I said no because I made my deal. I wanted to make little movies, and I didn't know anything about the guild. I didn't feel it was fair to Ramsey or Moustapha to sort of change the terms of my deal. Then there was an arbitration, and I didn't get a credit. Now that I've done a lot of these arbitrations, I find it rather strange because the first writer always gets a credit. It can't be reduced from the first writer. I wonder now in retrospect if that's because I didn't join the Writers Guild. I don't know, but in any event I didn't get a credit, and yet they came to me for *Halloween 5* because, I think, they were grateful that I didn't cost them money by joining the guild. So then I wrote the first draft of *Halloween 5*. Then again they brought another director in, and he brought in another writer, and that writer I share credit with. That credit was not subject to arbitration for the guild because it was not a guild project. So I've never got any residuals from it. Well, very, very, very minimal. Basically none.

For people who wonder what the guild does, having just gone through my third strike with the guild, it's for things like this. Residuals are important, and I was not protected at the end of the day. I did not get any residuals.

AG: Well, that's deeply fascinating, and I'm also sorry to hear that. With a project like this, I would just assume that you would have got residuals.

Shem Bitterman: Yeah, it would be great too. Like you said, it's an iconic franchise. I don't have any dollar figures, but I would assume they're significant. So the net result is I wrote two scripts of two *Halloween* movies, *Halloween 4* and *Halloween 5*.

AG: Well, let's start with *Halloween 4*. The third *Halloween* film attempted to remove Michael Myers from the story and just tell scary stories based on Halloween night. What are the conversations like when you're brought in to write the first script for *Halloween 4*?

Shem Bitterman: I don't remember having a ton of creative conversations. Obviously, they wanted to bring Michael back. I don't wanna say my script was generic. It was paced up. My son has read it and liked it.

In my version of *Halloween 5*, I have Jamie be the killer, the little girl be the killer. I know that I didn't read the final version of either script, because in both cases, the writers came on with the director. I think that if you talk to the writer from *Halloween 4*, he probably won't acknowledge that it was based on a previous script. I've heard that from the guild.

AG: I've heard that there were many incarnations of the *Halloween 4* script, but I've never heard your name attached, to be honest. I feel like I'm getting a scoop here.

Shem Bitterman: Here's my arbitration statement. I'll just read it to you. This is dated 6-28-88. [Shem begins to read] "In December 1987, I was hired to write a treatment for the upcoming *Halloween 4* and given the instruction that it was to involve Michael's return ten years later to Haddonfield to murder his niece. I delivered the treatment to Mr. Akkad around January first. Based on that treatment, I was hired to complete a screenplay, which I did. The first draft I submitted to Mr. Akkad in mid-January. The end of January, another writing team delivered their draft. I don't know to what degree it was influenced by my early treatment, first or second drafts. [Alan] McElroy was the third writer involved with the *Halloween* project. He was hired as a rewriter to combine the two previous drafts and to alter a crucial element of the story, namely that the girl Brittan [original name for the Jamie Lloyd character] was to be afraid of her Uncle Michael from the start.

While Mr. McElroy did a significant amount of work altering and combining the two scripts and creating new incidents, I do not believe this work was sufficiently original to allow him complete credit for either the story structure as well as several specific elements that were taken from my earlier drafts and treatment. Specific borrowed elements include:

- leading attendants past the faces of the insane giving the descriptions of their crimes, medical establishments, hostility toward Loom
- Brittan's box of family photos
- Brittan's bad dreams of Uncle Michael
- Loomis fighting with the head of the asylum about Michael's disappearance
- a roadside scene with Loomis, state troopers, and the asylum head from which Loomis departs alone after Michael
- Loomis stopping by at the gas station
- Michael dressing in the clothing of one of his victims
- Loomis having to change cars en route to Haddonfield

- Michael first being seen at Brittan's school
- the argument with the boyfriend
- use of the clown costume on Brittan
- Michael luring Brittan and Rachel away from the group of the children trick or treating
- a scene with several Michaels
- Loomis being the one to find Rachel and Brittan after they had begun being on the run
- hiding Brittan in the police captain's house
- the final confrontation scene in a locked house
- Brittan screaming "come alive!" to the apparently dead Rachel.

In addition, much of the basic overall structure is mine:

- Michael's unexpected escape from the asylum
- crosscutting to Brittan's bad dream in Haddonfield
- Michael stalking Brittan through the town
- the police force isolating Brittan from the final confrontation in a closed house and picking off Brittan's protectors one by one so she must face Michael alone
- several crucial points of characterization: Brittan's problem with her foster home, desire for real family members, sense of uneasiness, bad dreams, her relationship with an older sister who acts as her protector; Loomis's obsession with Michael to the degree that it cripples him in a professional world; Rachel's desire to win Brittan's love.

For those reasons outlined, I believe I should have shared credit for the story with [Larry] Rattner and for the screenplay with Mr. McElroy. I hope this matter can be adjudicated fairly."

AG: A majority of the things that you just read there do appear in the final version of the film.

Shem Bitterman: Well, I'll send you this, and you can include it to write the record.

AG: I very much appreciate that. Interesting to note the name change: Brittan is her name there, but she's Jamie in the finalized version—a little nod to Jamie Lee Curtis, of course—but so much of what you outlined there does make the final film.

RECEIVED 1

JUN 29 1988

CR[illegible]EPT.

Shem Bitterman
854 W. 181 St Apt # 5K
New York, NY 10033
(212) 928-4342

6/28/88

Grace Reiner & Arbitration Committee
Writer's Guild Of America, West, Inc.
8955 Beverly Boulevard
West Hollywood, CA 90048-2456

RE: "HALLOWEEN IV"

Dear Ms. Reiner & Arbitration Committee,

In December, 1987, I was hired to write a treatment for the upcoming Halloween IV, and given the instructions that it was to involve Michael's return ten years later to Haddonfield to murder his niece. I delivered the treatment to Mr. Akkad around January first and based on that treatment I was hired to complete a screenplay, which I did. The first draft I submitted to Mr. Akkad in mid January, the second a week later.

At the end of January the Rattner team delivered their draft. I don't know to what degree it was influenced by my early treatment, first or second drafts.

Mr. McElroy was the third writer involved with the Halloween project.

He was hired as a rewriter to combine the two previous drafts, and to alter a crucial element of the story, namely, that the girl- Brittan- was to be afraid of her uncle, Michael, from the start.

While Mr. McElroy did a significant amount of work altering and combining the two scripts and creating new incidents, I do not believe this work was sufficiently original to allow him complete credit for either the story or the screenplay, particularly since much of the basic structure as well as several specific elements were taken from my earlier drafts and treatment.

Arbitration letter. Provided by Shem Bitterman

Shem Bitterman: Well, you can rearbitrate it for me. I remember my own experience from that time as feeling like the fourth film was much more like mine, and I didn't get a credit, than the fifth film, where I did get a credit.

AG: I'm curious about your ideas for *Halloween 5*. Let's dive in there.

Shem Bitterman: Well, my idea was called *The Killer Inside Me.* I think some of my ideas were influenced by Jim Thompson, the idea that she was a killer. That's the main thing I remember about it, that it was about the interior life of that girl.

AG: So the film would have focused on her as a killer?

Shem Bitterman: Yes, that was my basic premise. It picks up right where *Halloween 4* ends, with a little girl dressed in a clown suit spattered with blood.

After this question, Shem asked to pause the interview so he could revisit his script. We unfortunately never got to conclude our conversation.

Interview: Daniel Farrands (Writer, *Halloween: The Curse of Michael Myers*)

AG: Let's start with a fun question. Memories of working with Paul Rudd?

Daniel Farrands: I met Paul, I think for the first time, when we showed up in Salt Lake City to shoot the movie. So this would have been in the fall of 1994. I remember I'd seen his audition. I thought he was really good—quirky, you know. I thought that he was an interesting choice for the part because he gave off a sort of slightly different vibe than I had imagined in my head for that character. Everything that everybody knows about him today was true back then—very humble, funny, kind of self-deprecating. He was levelheaded and really committed to the project and was really excited to be there. We spent a lot of time together because we were all the same age. We're these young kids getting this first break in our careers. We naturally gravitated toward each other, and we were kind of like the young rookies, and then it was like those older guys that don't know anything. We were kind of the— I won't call it the rebels, but we had a little bit of a renegade streak, I think, in this little posse of ours. He was just part of the group, and it was fun. Spent a lot of evenings just going to each other's hotel rooms and piling on a bed and watching movies on VHS tapes because there was nothing to do. I mean, everything in Salt Lake City shuts down at a certain hour because of the Mormon influence there.

We were young and wanted to have some fun in between the long days, and we just found ways to have fun together. I remember when we came back to Los Angeles, we all went and played pool together. It was fun. He was a cool guy and up for all of it, loved being a part of it. I know that later he probably had not the greatest things to say about the movie, but then again, I was the same. I think he would tell you today that he was always on Team Dan, so to speak. I was the one kind of going "God, this isn't right. This is not *Halloween*," and I think he understood it. I do remember one little anecdote on set that he confessed to me, which was that he didn't know at first that I was like this uber-*Halloween* geek, that literally my entire life I had been obsessed with the *Halloween* movies. He didn't know that, and when he found it out, everything changed for him. It became less of just a gig and more of an "Oh my God, this is really important; I gotta get it right for him." I think in a weird way it just became more meaningful to him once he knew how passionate I was about it and how long I had lobbied for this and how much it literally was life-changing for me. I remember him pulling me aside one day and telling me a story about seeing *Close Encounters of the Third Kind* for the first time, how much it affected him, to the point where his parents had to talk him off a ledge because his brain couldn't handle it at that age. I remember him saying, "If there's anything in my life that I could say that altered me, it would have been that movie, like *Halloween* was for you."

AG: *Halloween*: *The Curse of Michael Myers* serves as both an end and a beginning, but a beginning of something that never came to be. When you were writing it, were these things that you were cognizant of?

Daniel Farrands: I don't know if I thought of it concretely, but I would say yes, I was maybe slightly, subconsciously aware that we needed to wrap up some things and then start a new chapter of this. I knew this was not the end. It never is. I remember even the vibe on the set, some of the local people that were hired to be on the crew, they were like, "*Halloween 6*, you mean there's been five of them?" You know, people are just mystified at the shelf life of this franchise, which is unbelievable to me.

I think that is the challenge with a sequel. You're always trying to kinda tip your hat to the original and elevate the movie to the point where it's become this iconic thing that we all remember from those signature moments from the first film but also to do something slightly different. I think that was the challenge: to not make it just a carbon copy of the earlier ones. So from that standpoint, yes, but I don't know if I had any master plan other than my original treatment that I went off and wrote after I first met Moustapha Akkad, God rest his soul. I just thank the man and credit him with giving me this opportunity. It changed my life forever in the best of ways. I kind of owe it all to Moustapha. He saw something in this weirdly obsessed kid, by far the youngest person who walked through his door. He would often say, and I think his son, Malek, who now obviously holds the reins of the franchise and has been guiding it ever since, they would both often say, "You know more about it than we do." Moustapha would be walking around the set with his little pipe or cigar or whatever. I don't know what he was thinking. He was always one of those people that you wondered what he was actually thinking. *Does he hate me? Does he want to kill me?* He always had a little twinkle in his eye, and he would come to me, and he'd try to stump me on a *Halloween* trivia question. I would answer it like in a second, and he'd just laugh and walk off. He thought it was hilarious that I didn't hesitate. I think for those weird reasons, he saw something in me, because the passion was there. I didn't come in there telling him to talk to my agent. I didn't even have one. I think that my sheer love of it all is what sold him on hiring me and taking a chance on a twenty-four-year-old kid.

AG: It really is one of those special Hollywood stories.

Daniel Farrands: Weirdly enough, I went to my high school reunion a few years after that, and everyone who knew me in high school was like, "Well, of course you did; we knew you were gonna do that." That's who I always was to them. I was that weirdly obsessed kid making horror movies in the halls of the school. Here's the other weird irony of it: the high school that I went to and graduated from is the same high school where Wes Craven was supposed to have filmed the original *Scream*, and they shut him down because of the violent content.

This is my life. Isn't that bizarre? I'll never forget one of the Dimension Films executives found out that I went to that high school there. They called me and asked if I could call the school board and tell them I went to school there and now I make horror movies. They're basically asking me for help—the weird kind of synchronicities of life. Sometimes I'm like, "Maybe there's really no mistakes." I know *Halloween* is always about fate; then maybe, maybe, this was mine? I don't know why, but be careful what you wish for.

AG: Jamie Lloyd in this film, her fate is her demise early on in the film. I was very curious about the decision to kill her so early in the film, especially after *Halloween 5* did something very similar with the Rachel character.

Daniel Farrands: It was a product of its time, the early to midnineties, coming off the eighties, where that was the format. The survivor of the last movie always ends up dead in the first or second reel of the sequel. That was kind of a trope but wasn't the trope that I wanted to follow, to be completely transparent. I did not want to kill this character. Then I was told, "You have to." Then I was told, "You have to do it earlier." I was told originally, "You can't have her in this movie at all because nobody cares." And I'm like, "Yes, they do." You know, that's the fanboy in me. We can't just make a movie and just not talk about her. She was literally on the poster of the last movie. The only person who got what I was saying was Moustapha Akkad. Certainly nobody at Miramax [Dimension's parent company] cared. In fact, it's part of the reason that poor Danielle Harris walked from the project, when Miramax said, "Well, you're not worth anything to us."

AG: That was my next question, about Danielle Harris and her potential involvement in the film.

Daniel Farrands: She was cast. I mean, not only was she cast, she walked into the auditions without an invitation. As I recall, there was an open casting call that was put out for this character. I think they even put in her picture, like, "We need actresses who look like this." She came over one day to the casting office and said, "Well, wait a minute, that's me." Whoever was in that room had said to her, "Well, we didn't know you wanted to do it," and she's like, "Of course I wanna do it." She was only seventeen. I think they used it as an excuse, like, "Well, we need you to work late hours, and we don't wanna put this teacher on the set, and, you know, then you have to have a guardian because you're not eighteen yet," and all this rigmarole. She's like, "Fine, I'll get emancipated." So she dug into her own pocket, spent thousands of dollars to go through the legal process of emancipating herself only to be told, "Well, you're really not worth that much. This part is not that big. So we're gonna pay you basically scale wages." I completely understood why she dropped after that. I mean, of course it was heartbreaking that she was treated this way. I know Mr. Akkad went to bat for her because he had discovered her for *Halloween 4*, and they had remained in each other's lives as far as I know. Even he couldn't convince the studio people to pay her what she was asking for, which wasn't much. It's not like she was asking for a million dollars. I think it was just enough to cover legal fees and a little extra to pay her bills. I don't think she was doing it for the money. I think she wanted to do it because it was her character. You can't put somebody else in this part, which obviously is what they did. It was all very disappointing. The script that she got was the original version, where Jamie actually lived until the very end of the movie—not the middle, not the first act. She made it to the very last five minutes of the film in my script. I can't remember exactly how it was all set up. She had either been taken back to those tunnels or had found her way back there, and when all hell is breaking loose, she's the one that was gonna show everyone how to get out of this maze. In doing so, she turns to protect them and the baby, and she's mortally wounded herself at this point. She's like, "Take my baby; save the baby," kind of like what happened in the beginning of the movie, and she puts up this massive fight with Michael Myers, like it's a fight to the death between the two of them. I mean she does inflict some serious damage on the guy, and then finally he does poor Jamie in, and then the rest of the movie happens, but that was all in the last five minutes.

AG: That feels like such a fitting ending to the character.

Daniel Farrands: That's what I said, but I was just a writer, and what did I know? That was the process of that movie, just eliminating everything that felt like it belonged there, all in service of the almighty, or not so almighty, dollar. They didn't wanna spend the money on her. They didn't wanna give this character more than a couple days on the schedule. Everything that I was trying to do to make it what the fans would have wanted to see was all just being chucked out and thrown into the bin. That was the original conceit for Jamie. It never was the plan to kill her off that way—never, not even in the producers' cut, where she gets shot in the head. That wasn't in the script either.

AG: The alternative ending and footage from *Halloween: The Curse of Michael Myers* was eventually turned into what is now known as the producers' cut. It was finally released in 2014 as a separate version of the film. Personally, I think it's been romanticized a lot over the years.

Daniel Farrands: Oh yeah, I agree. In some ways, it's better. But for me, it was never the movie that I wrote. I've been very vocal about it over the years, although I love the fact that it's kind of become this kind of cult—no pun intended— thing that for years and years fans were trying to track it down and finding terrible bootleg copies online. Thank God for our friends at Shout Factory that actually wanted to do it. For years, I felt like I was the same person I was during the reshoots, screaming at the back of the room and nobody was listening. "Somebody release the producer's cut!" So finally that happened, and I'm grateful for it, because now people don't ask me all the time about it. I think that what you said is true. Because it was this weird, holy grail kind of thing, the thing that can't be found, they did romanticize it a little bit. I think you see the problems with it when watching it now, just like the studio and the test audiences did. I think it just left so many questions because again, they just really never, in any substantial way, really followed the script or at least what I had in my mind that it was supposed to look like or how it was supposed to feel. The homage is the original movie, but also just making it much more dark and kind of gothic and ominous, even down to the casting. I had written the role of Dr. Wynn specifically with Christopher Lee in mind because Loomis was originally offered to him, and he turned it down. Allegedly, according to Debra Hill, Christopher Lee said that was the biggest mistake of his career. So as a nod to that, I said, "Let's make these two titans of terror, Donald Pleasence and Christopher Lee, on-screen together. Oh my God, the fans will go nuts." But the studio said no, and they got the guy from *Lethal Weapon* [Mitch Ryan]. I'm not putting anybody down, but that's not what I wanted it to be. Listen, I wasn't a casting person. I wasn't a producer. I certainly wasn't the director. I think one of the early lessons I learned in this industry was writing is like putting your kid up for adoption. Once you give it up, you have no say in how it's being cared for. That's a really brutal lesson learned. I just thought, Oh, everybody making these movies knows what it's supposed to be like. I never questioned it at the beginning like that, that I was gonna be put in the mix with a bunch of studio bean counters, but the problems didn't end with *Halloween: The Curse of Michael Myers*. It went on and on and on for years with the Akkads versus the crazy, fucking Weinsteins. It wasn't isolated to our movie.

AG: As a writer, what sense of pressure did you feel to pay off the threads that were laid in *Halloween 5*? Sometimes in this genre, people tend to ignore things that were laid out and totally change plans.

Daniel Farrands: I felt like I needed to. I think I owed it to myself. I remember specifically, and I have two people in my life who will attest to this, we saw *Halloween 5* at what used to be a movie theater in Studio City the night that it came out. I walked out of that theater and stood in the lobby with these two friends of mine and said, "I'm writing *Halloween 6*." I just declared it to the universe, and in my mind that was just a given. That's what was gonna happen. Didn't know how. Didn't know anyone. Had no agent. Sometimes you speak to the universe and it provides; sometimes it doesn't. But I just had this like myopic, tunnel-vision, this-is-gonna-happen kind of attitude. I think going into this project, I just felt like, *Okay, I know what this is supposed to be*. Everything you write is for yourself first, but there was an intense amount of pressure to get it done quickly. They hired me in June, and they were shooting by October, so there was no time to really develop the script. It was almost like a rush to production because they had gone through allegedly, from what I've heard over the years, a whole bunch of writers had taken, pardon the pun again, a stab at it, and it all kind of had not worked, at least as far as most of it was concerned. I think the reason they called me was like, "We need somebody who knows how to do this. We can't just be hiring some TV writer to write this. We need an expert." So I think that was kind of also the motivation. But that being said, it was high pressure to get it done fast. So that was scary. It was almost like, *Well, you've been preparing yourself for this for years.* Between *Halloween 5* and *Halloween: The Curse of Michael Myers* was like six years. So when I made that declaration to the universe, it was like a five-year overnight success. It literally took that long. Then you're handed the keys, and they're like, "Go kid!" and then you're like, *Oh fuck, now I gotta really do this.*

I remember the thing that scared me and intimidated me the most was writing all that Loomis dialogue. I was like, *I can't write this.* I had the elevated Donald Pleasence in my mind, and knowing he was gonna be in the movie and knowing he was gonna read these pages, I was like, *I'm not worthy. I can't do this.* I would just sit there in absolute frozen fear, like *I can't do it. I'm gonna give them their money back.* I had got $10,000 at that point, but I was like, *I'll give it back.* It was that kind of icy-cold, frozen-in-your-footsteps terror that I experienced when I would get to the Loomis stuff. So I just thought to myself, *You know who Loomis is. You know every word of every movie and every syllable in the way he said it.* Just imagine if he was in this house in this situation, and go. So that's kinda how I just gave myself permission to write it badly. It was an intense amount of pressure to deliver something.

AG: Where did you want to take the character? Loomis had obviously been through a lot, and in the previous film, he'd teetered a bit on the edge of insanity.

Daniel Farrands: I didn't wanna go that route. I remember thinking, *Well, it's been six years.* Everybody took a breath, and although he didn't give up the ghost, as it were, he just kind of went into seclusion. I imagined him, weirdly enough, like Alec Guinness in the original *Star Wars*, kind of being that person that was gonna come out of retirement because he was forced to. It was a little bit of that. I think there are a lot of parallels to Loomis and Obi-Wan Kenobi. I think they're in many ways the same character. I mean, one is slightly more twisted, but with Loomis, I just wanted to bring him back into a place where he's like, Okay, I'm safe, and maybe he's still out there, maybe he's not, but I've had to kind of reconcile this, and so that's why I came to the idea he's writing this book, his memoir, and it sort of built out of that.

AG: What is it like for you now, knowing that you scripted his final film?

Daniel Farrands: We all knew that he had slowed down. It was so evident the minute he showed up on the set. He didn't move the way he used to; he had really, really slowed down. Some of the stuff that was in the script that was maybe more physical had to be pared back. I remember one of the things was that we don't wanna sit him in that makeup chair for hours to put those burns on. I didn't write it, but somebody came up with the line "Oh, I had plastic surgery." I don't think it made the final movie, but it's in the producer's cut. It's just corny. The reason for that was that Donald was obviously in failing health but glad to be there. Let me tell you, when he called me on the phone, after my endless, all-night cram sessions that were like writing your term paper and turning it in and being terrified of the grade, to hear his voice on the other end of the line and telling me it was like the best thing he'd read since the original movie, how excited he was, what a great new turn this was for the series and the character, "I'm so thrilled to be a part of it; thank you for writing this for me"—that's what I got from him. So for me, it was like *Holy shit, that was the stamp of approval from the God of* Halloween. That was magic for me; it was really a special moment in my life. I'll never ever forget it. To this day, I get the chills thinking about it.

AG: My wife has studied paganism. She's not a huge fan of slashers, but she loved the mythology behind *Halloween*: *The Curse of Michael Myers*. She explained to me that the writer of this film has obviously spent some time studying paganism and how everything was very factual and well researched.

Daniel Farrands: That is maybe one of the nicest compliments I've ever heard, so please tell her from the bottom of my heart thank you, because I can't tell you the number of hours that I spent with my nose in the pages of books, like one called *Rune Magic* by Donald Tyson. Isn't it crazy that to this day I can tell you the title and the author's name? It *is* crazy. What I did was deep dive into this stuff, stuff that I knew would never make it to the screen. A lot of times when you're writing stuff, it's like there's a whole world of things that you've researched, and now it's all kind of sitting there and you can draw on little bits and pieces of that as you go along. You know that you can't have a two-hour origin story of Michael Myers. So much was set up in the earlier films. For me, to this day, I will say if you wanna talk about sequels, my favorite of the sequels is *Halloween II*, the Rick Rosenthal and John Carpenter *Halloween II*. It's a continuation of the original movie. It's the same night. It's building on the story, giving it context and history and mythology, and then they stopped. *Halloween III* kind of had it because it was its own kind of adjunct movie, which was purely about druidism and kind of modernizing it. So I went back and skipped the fourth and fifth films in a way, but I did take this grain of something in from *Halloween 5*. There's a mysterious guy in black with the fedora and the John Wayne boots, and it's like an evil guy coming, this gunslinger coming into town. How do I connect all this stuff? How do I take all these threads of things that have been there and kind of draw them all into one narrative? That was the impetus behind the movie, all of that. I think the thorn itself, the symbol we saw in *Halloween 5*, was tattooed on Michael Myers's wrist. They did a close-up on it a couple of times, and I was like, What the hell is that? We've never seen that on his wrist. What does it mean? I had no clue. So I remember vividly, and this was long before I ever got the job, I had my very first pitch meeting with Moustapha when I was nineteen, not long after *Halloween 5* came out, and that's a whole story unto itself. But I did get a meeting with him. I did go into his office as a nineteen-year-old with my bible of *Halloween*. I had spent weeks and weeks prepping for this meeting that lasted all of five minutes, maybe.

I had spent those weeks at the occult section of every weird, New Age bookstore. The one in particular, and it's not here anymore in Los Angeles, called the Bodi Tree, was on Melrose Avenue. It was very well-known back into the fifties and sixties. It was a hippie kind of place to get all your charms and amulets. I actually had drawn the little symbol, the Thorn, and I brought it to some old hippie that worked at the bookstore. I was like, "Do you know what this is?" and they told me that it looks like a rune. They took me to this section of the store with the ancient myths and legends of the UK. That's where I bought that book, *Rune Magic* by Donald Tyson. That's where the mythology of the thorn came directly from. When applied to a person, it is said that this will ensure a visit from the demon upon them. It all goes back to very ancient stuff. There was even a way that if you placed it one way it meant one thing, but if you inverted, it meant something else.

I did a whole deep dive into the mythology of what this rune was. It was in *Halloween 5*. I had to do something with this. You can't just put that out there and just forget it. I think all the people who came before me and had written a draft of this, nobody bothered to acknowledge it. There wasn't a single version that I was ever told about or aware of where anybody had taken the time to delve into that. I think that was another reason Moustapha was like, "Well, this kid knows what he's fucking talking about." Dominique, who had directed *Halloween 5*, his movie is very European and had some odd ideas about it, even the way the movie was shot, like tilting the camera upside down, stuff that people weren't really doing in American movies. When you look at *Halloween 4* and *Halloween 5* stylistically, they're completely different movies. Dominique apparently was the one who said, "Let's put this weird guy in the movie and let him walk around." Literally nobody knew who it was or who he was supposed to be. I was coming in with this approach of "Let's figure this out this and what it means," and it's this rune that has forced a demon on Michael Myers. How did that happen? I was taken back to the original movie and that very first shot of the movie, when you come out of the main credits and the camera's coming from right across the street from the little six-year-old's point of view and it's Panagliding across the street to see the sister in the window. Where was he coming from? What if he was with the old lady across the way? That's where it all began that night. They marked him as the one, and it all led back to babysitters. The old lady was babysitting him. To add an even more weird cyclical thing that came from *Rosemary's Baby*, one of my favorite movies of all time, her name literally was Mrs. Blankenship. Her name was Minnie Blankenship. It wasn't in the movie, but her name was Minnie. In *Rosemary's Baby*, Ruth Gordon played Minnie. She was the leader of the coven. This is how I went into it. All these weird, disparate ideas of witchcraft and druidism and runic symbols. All of that really informed the direction I was gonna go in. There's an even weirder homage that fans have picked up on it. It took a long time for fans to find this Easter egg, but Mrs. Blankenship, Minnie Blankenship, is actually referred to in *Halloween III*. There's a scene where they go to the toy store where

Ellie's father had worked. They look at his calendar and it says he was supposed to have either lunch or dinner with Minnie Blankenship, but he never showed up.

We were gonna connect our movie to *Halloween III* if we had done another one. It was that this whole coven thing was part of the experience of Conal Cochran. It was all over the world. Halloween is a festival of the dead that is celebrated everywhere. So all of these stories, all these myths, are all connected. I had a master plan, and it wasn't very well worked out, obviously, because we didn't get there. I wanted to really impress them, so I wrote this epic treatment. I think I did it in two days. It was like thirty pages of what the story was, and the whole thing was so big that Moustapha read it, and I remember he called me, and he said, "You know, this is great, but it's too big. But the first part is *Halloween 6*, and the second part is *Halloween 7*." In his mind, I think, he already saw where we were gonna go. The bigger reveal was you're gonna find out the whole town of Haddonfield was part of this coven. They were all in on this thing. It was very much inspired by movies like *The Wicker Man*.

I think it's fun when you can nod back to what came before you and show an appreciation for it. Imitation is the most sincere form of flattery, as the old expression goes. Every sequel is trying to flatter the original and the things that came before you. So that was my nod. I mean, there's even references to *The Fog* in *Halloween: The Curse of Michael Myers*. I wanted this to feel like we were in the world of John Carpenter somehow.

AG: Are there any misconceptions about the film or its production that you've heard over the years that you wanted to speak on?

Daniel Farrands: There is one that comes to mind: that Joe Chappelle, our director, was this tyrant. He was anything but that. He was an incredibly nice person. Do I necessarily think Joe was up for a movie called *Halloween: The Curse of Michael Myers* at that time? Not that he looked down on it in any way, but I feel like he wasn't as mad about it as I was. I felt like if the director had been as mad about it as I was, then maybe he would have fought battles that would have made the movie better. I felt like sometimes Joe wasn't fighting enough for the movie or for what we were trying to do with it. Maybe he wasn't seeing some of those big picture stuff and how it all kinda interconnected. If I have a criticism, it's that. But people just came down on him, awful things that were said about him over the years. It's part of the reason I think that I haven't spoken to him in over twenty years. I think it's probably the reason he doesn't go to the conventions or do the commentaries. I think he was really kind of traumatized by the way he was treated. I just feel like he got really fucking beaten up in a way that just wasn't warranted. They don't know Joe. They don't know that he's a great guy and a father. I think he had two kids at the time and a third one on the way when we made that movie. He was dealing with a lot of stuff in his life. People don't realize that we're human beings. People have real lives, and this is a job, and the dehumanization of people really fucking bothers me. The way that he was unfairly demonized in the genre press and certainly by the fan base all felt unfortunate. He didn't deserve that.

I remember when he first got hired, he picked me up in his rental car. He came from Chicago and had flown in to do the movie, and he picked me up, and I think we went to lunch or something. We drove around to random places, and he was listening to the *Last Temptation of Christ* soundtrack if I'm not mistaken. The soundtrack, it was just eerie shit and had this black magic kind of vibe to it. I think we started off on the right foot. I think Joe got a lot of pressure from a lot of sides. This is a business. He was a young dad with a growing family, and there were the poisonous snakes that are Bob and Harvey Weinstein dangling the proverbial apple in front of him. "Come with us, and we will make you a star." I don't mean this in a negative way, but I don't think there's many people in that position that would have turned that down. He did reshoots on the *Hellraiser* movie they were doing at the time that apparently was a complete mess. Then he did another movie called *Phantoms for Dimension*. I think that opened up a door for him to do other things. He went on to have a supersuccessful career in television as a director and a producer. Good for him, and never in my heart did I ever have any kind of personal vendetta against Joe Chappelle. It just shocked me, the vitriol that was being directed not just at the movie, but at him personally. It was just awful. I got a taste of that myself when I started directing my own movies. You start to see just how at the mercy of the public that you become. And it's a scary proposition for anyone. You don't think about that stuff when you're creating a movie and you're on a set for twelve hours a day or longer.

AG: Since you mentioned Bob and Harvey Weinstein . . .

Daniel Farrands: Listen, the gloves are off. You can print this: I said "Go fuck yourself" here in the pages of your book. One is a fucking rapist, a fucking rapist in prison for the rest of his life. Thank God. So they can go fuck yourself, both of them. Robert Zappia, the writer of *Halloween H20*, and I had lunch together after his film. We didn't know each other, but it was like a survivors' group after dealing with the Weinsteins. He had really funny stories. He had it worse than me. His movie was much more high-profile.

AG: How do you feel about being attached to his name tangentially in a movie?

Daniel Farrands: There's no feeling about it. This is all credit to Moustapha Akkad, but because I was so young and so green, I was really isolated from that group of people, like I had no direct contact with them, not until the movie came out and there were a couple—we'll call them assistants—who had just been promoted, and they would ask, "Can you do this interview?" and whatever, that kind of stuff. Again, one of the reasons I respected Moustapha so much is that he really shielded me from studio people.

I don't have any personal shame or anything. I never stepped foot in their office. I will tell you this: many years later—either 2010 or 2011—I had the rights to continue the legitimate, not the straight-to-video ones, for *Amityville Horror*. I went to Jason Blum with this. Jason Blum was not Jason Blum back then. He made this little movie called *Paranormal Activity*, and people were thinking, *Oh, that's gonna be a hit.* So he was new in the scene, although he'd worked in the studios and had worked for the Weinsteins early in his career and had a real falling out with them. But when I went to him and I said, "Listen, I have the rights to this because I know the family behind that story, and they've kind of entrusted me with this, but the problem is that Dimension kind of also inherited rights." Jason was like, "Oh my God, no." He said, "As a courtesy, let's just go pitch them. Bob is not gonna buy this. He hates me, and he'll just say no, but let's just go there and pitch Dimension, and that way we have done our due diligence and given them an opportunity." So we go, and I'm literally sitting at a table with Bob—first time ever meeting the man, all these years later. And we come in with this whole pitch, and we have like pitch boards. We're trying to impress, and he's literally at the table like, "I love it! How soon can you get started?" I remember Jason and I looking at each other like literally our worst nightmares come to life.

It began this couple of months where me and a guy I was working with at the time were being kind of pulled into that family. I remember saying to one of the younger executives who was not there when we did *Halloween: The Curse of Michael Myers*, "Does he even know that I was the writer of *Halloween: The Curse of Michael Myers*?" He said, "I don't think so, and you don't need to say anything. It'll make him feel stupid that he didn't know that." I literally was tiptoeing around. They gave me an office at Dimension. I was like literally out of my own office there at this point. They were ready to go make this movie, and it all collapsed. That being said, I'll never forget the day that some assistant calls and says Bob wants to see you right away in the conference room. I'm like, Oh fuck, I guess I'm fired already. So I was terrified, but I'm old enough now to hold my own. So Bob tells me that we have those *Halloween* movies, and I'm like, uh-huh. My partner and I, we're both looking at each other. I don't know what's happening here. And Bob says, "Do you have any ideas for the next *Halloween* movie?" and then my partner at the time starts rambling, "Well, you could do Michael in the sanitarium in his early years," and he starts going on with this whole thing for a couple minutes. And Bob's like, "We made a movie about the sanitarium. It had Paul Rudd." He had no idea I was the guy who wrote that film. That's my story. The end.

AG: You're in a unique position as both a lifelong fan of this franchise and as somebody who has made a film in this franchise.

Daniel Farrands: Written a script that became a film that I didn't necessarily recognize. But yes.

AG: Where would you like to see this franchise go?

Daniel Farrands: There was obviously this big splash announcement recently that Malek and his company had teamed up with the new Miramax to create kind of a *Halloween* universe. I think that's kind of interesting. I don't know where else you go. He's been put through a metal shredder, and I don't think there's coming back from that. Listen, he will be back, Michael Myers. Evil is eternal. Thorn will live again. Minnie Blankenship will resurrect him.

I think they were onto something creatively with *Halloween III* because it was really stepping into an anthology Halloween kind of stories. Each one would sort of stand on its own and be centered around the holiday of Halloween but not have any sort of thing to do with those first couple films. There'll be a time when they need to give it a nice pause and reset it. I think you'll see more in terms of the actual direction. I did pitch Malek around the time of *Halloween H20* about doing a television series. The conceit of the series was that it would be the early case files of Dr. Loomis. So it was almost kind of like *Night Stalker* in that it would be centered around Smith's Grove and in the late fifties, early sixties, before Michael became part of his quest to stop all evil. He was also being dragged into these other cases, and some of them would have been true stories, like the Ed Gein story. He would have been the psychologist that interviewed him. It never got beyond very early conversations about the idea, but Malek was really interested. I think the rights were a huge mess back then.

Interview: Marianne Hagan (Kara, *Halloween: The Curse of Michael Myers*)

AG: I've been excited to speak with you ever since my conversation with Daniel Farrands. He spoke so highly of you.

Marianne Hagan: Dan and I became soulmates from the very beginning. We understood what his script was supposed to be and how it was gonna be the best *Halloween* since the first one. Dan is very, very smart, and we just got along like a house on fire. Dan is a really amazing person. I haven't talked to him in years, but I just love him, and if I ran into him out in LA, it would be a scene and a half of jumping up and down and hugging. The situation has never come up, but we'd love to work together again someday.

AG: So let's start at the beginning. What was the casting process like for you?

Marianne Hagan: I was living in Los Angeles at the time, and my manager, Barbara Lawrence, the best manager in the whole world, and my agent, J. Michael Bloom, also the best agent in the world, got me the audition. Pretty much every gal of my age, women in their twenties, wanted to audition for this part. There hadn't been a new *Halloween* movie in six years. Now also the new arm of Miramax known as Dimension, run by Harvey's dear younger brother, Bob Weinstein, was involved. Bob was running Dimension, which was the Miramax arm of sci-fi and horror. So I just went in on the audition, and I got a callback, and then I got another callback, and then I got it. So I guess I got this role the old-fashioned way in that I auditioned for it.

AG: With the previous five movies, they were independent films. Now we have a bigger studio involved. Were you auditioning for the director and producers here or was it a more corporate environment?

Marianne Hagan: I recall Moustapha Akkad being there and his son Malek too. The casting director, whose name I can't remember, said really mean things to me. I went in once; then I got a callback. I went in again, got a callback to do a chemistry read with Paul Rudd, to see if we had chemistry. That's the first time I met Paul Rudd, and I knew, standing off to the side of the room looking at Paul Rudd, that he was gonna be a star. I just knew it.

AG: Like you said, it had been about six years since the previous *Halloween* movie. Can you describe the general feeling at the start of filming? Was there a buzz about bringing the franchise back among the cast and crew?

Marianne Hagan: I can only speak for Paul and I, but we wanted to make this the best horror movie ever. Mariah O'Brien, who played Beth, cared a lot. We were told that fans were chomping at the bit because there hadn't been a new *Halloween* in years, and they were really antsy about it. We just thought, *We're gonna make this the best* *horror movie ever, at least since the first* Halloween. We cared a lot about it.

AG: This movie is infamous in the fact that it's Donald Pleasence's last film and it's also George Wilbur's final time playing Michael Myers. What was George like to work with?

Marianne Hagan: George Wilbur was the loveliest of lovely—a gentleman stuntman of old Hollywood style, and he could not have been more classy. I just adored him. Out in Salt Lake City—that's where we did the primary shoot . . . then we got word eight months later that we had to come back to Los Angeles and do reshoots for a week. Dimension wanted there to be reshoots. Apparently they wanted more gore, which Paul and I were very against. We didn't sign up for that movie. We signed up for Daniel Farrands's script. So we got on set in August of '95, eight months after finishing the whole movie, and we're like, "What are we doing here? This is so weird," and George Wilbur isn't there. We then were told that the powers that be thought George Wilbur was too short and too tubby to play Michael Myers. So they brought in a different actor, a stuntman named A. Michael Lerner, who was like six foot two and very thin, I guess.

The reshoots were just a week, but I had cut my hair shorter. Paul Rudd had grown his hair longer, and I had to get extensions put in my hair. He didn't wanna cut his hair and rightfully so, but he agreed to cut a little bit off and try to make it work for continuity.

AG: The reshoots all centered around increasing the gore?

Marianne Hagan: Dimension did screenings with fourteen-year-old boys, and their feedback was number one, not enough gore, and number two, the ending sucks. I'm fairly positive that those are direct quotes. So based on the knowledge and genius of fourteen-year-old boys, everybody was brought back to Los Angeles, not Salt Lake City, where we had originally shot it. So if a kill was a three, they wanted it a ten. We were just so confused. We would have never signed up for this movie if Paul and I had read the gore and the brains splattering and all this gross stuff. We wouldn't have even auditioned for it. Daniel wrote this extraordinary script that was so intellectual and so smart, and it brought all these themes of Samhain and just really yummy, fun Halloween stuff in it. It wasn't supposed to be *Texas Chainsaw Massacre 10*.

AG: Donald Pleasence died shortly after shooting this film. How was he on set? Any particular memories that stick out to you of working with him?

Marianne Hagan: I adored him. He was a bit frail; I just didn't know just how frail he was. It only became apparent months later, when we got the news that he had passed away. Donald Pleasence was an absolute joy to work with. I know Paul felt the same way because we had numerous discussions about how honored we were to be working with Donald freaking Pleasence. His wife was with him on that shoot. Pretty much all the time when he wasn't shooting, he was in his trailer, and his wife was with him. I didn't think anything of it because he was an older man, and it was freezing. I swear to Christ, I've never been more cold in my life than when I was shooting *Halloween: The Curse of Michael Myers*. I didn't have a lot of body fat on me at the time, so I was so cold.

Okay, here's a story about Donald Pleasence and his wicked sense of humor. I was sitting in one of those director's chairs even though I wasn't a director, but I was just hanging out on the set. I was reading Vanity Fair magazine. Donald comes over, and he sits down next to me, and he asks me what I'm reading. I hold up the magazine, and I show him the cover that says Vanity Fair, and without missing a beat, he says "Thackeray's best." William Makepeace Thackeray's Vanity Fair.

I was like, *Did I just hear what I thought I heard?* Because that's the most brilliant joke I've ever heard in my fucking life. Then I burst out howling laughing. I had to tell Paul later. We were in worship of Donald Pleasence because Donald Pleasence was a brilliant theater actor. He was Harold Pinter's muse, the amazing British playwright. He and Donald were very close friends. You don't make money doing theater, whether it's New York or London or anywhere. What I had heard was that Donald took his last breath at his chateau in the south of France. The only way he could have bought that chateau in the south of France was because of *Halloween* and Loomis.

AG: Obviously the script changes in your film are notorious. Everybody has heard the stories about what Dan's original script was and what the film wound up being. How did that impact you as an actress and your day-to-day work on set?

Marianne Hagan: It was all done on set, very last moment. We had a huge blizzard the very first week of shooting in Salt Lake City. It was October, and even though it's Salt Lake City, it's still very unusual to get a big snowstorm in October. So they had to blow the snow away, and then they had to rake the leaves and try to make it look like Halloween and not like it's time to go snowboarding. So they had to rearrange the shooting schedule. We couldn't shoot outside because there was all the snow. So once you change one thing in a movie, everything else gets changed, and it becomes the ripple effect. They started having to rip pages out of the script, mostly mine, by the way. My character, Kara, was supersmart. She was on the computer. She was looking up stuff. She was finding her own information in the library at the high school. There were all these amazing scenes where she was a proactive, supersmart gal. That's what I loved about the character, and all those scenes were just ripped out of the script because there was no time to shoot them. We had to go, go, go.

Daniel is so smart. Paul and I went to him when we had any question about anything. I don't know what really happened, but Daniel eventually went back to LA, and he was no longer on set. Paul and I were beside ourselves. I was practically crying. Paul and I needed his brilliance. We needed his knowledge of the entire *Halloween* franchise. He knew it inside and out. There's all sorts of theories. The director was insecure about Daniel being on set because Daniel was smarter and more knowledgeable. What's his name again, the director?

AG: Joe Chappelle.

Marianne Hagan: Yeah, there you go. I want you to keep that in that I couldn't remember his name. . . . He went on to have quite a career directing in television—hourlong, episodic, procedural kinda things. Even Paul, who didn't need the work at that point, was like, "Yeah, I'm kind of insulted that he never called me in for an audition." I know Mariah O'Brien felt the same way. She was just like, "We froze ourselves to death on your first movie, helping you get this amazing career to support your seven kids, or however many he had. You never even called any of us for an audition." That just doesn't happen in our world. They don't have any responsibility to give you a part. What most people do is say, "You know what, this actually could be a good role for Marianne Hagen. Let's bring her in on this. She can audition," and that's cool. If I come in and I'm not the best one or I don't look the part, then that's up to the producers or the showrunners. But I would always have really respected Joe Chappelle for doing that, because that's class, and that's what you do. He did not do that for any of us. Didn't even bring us in on an audition for one of these one-hour shows, which is how we actors make our freaking money. That's how we get our health insurance. He must have had a very bad experience on *Halloween: The Curse of Michael Myers*, because you just don't do that. But he didn't have such a bad experience, because he definitely schmoozed up to Bob Weinstein.

[Author's note: Multiple attempts were made to Joe Chappelle to be interviewed for this book. I never received a response.]

AG: What was he like as a director?

Marianne Hagan: He didn't say anything. You would do a scene and then cut is yelled. Paul would say, "Was that okay? Was that good? Did that work?" Joe Chappelle would say, "It was fine; it was fine. Let's do it again." But with no notes, like, "Play it scarier," or any notes whatsoever. Paul and I would talk about it like, "Are we so bad that he doesn't even know what to say to us?" We were both getting really insecure, because when he yells cut, he won't look at you. He won't talk to you. You have to go over to him and say, "So, Joe, any notes or adjustments?" And he would just say, "No, it was fine. We're just gonna go again." I'm actually surprised he got a career in television because actors can be pretty fragile sometimes, and they need support direction, which is what the director is there for. And he gave us nothing.

AG: Did Bob or Harvey Weinstein have a presence on set?

Marianne Hagan: Harvey was never on the set. As far as I knew, Bob never came to the set.

AG: Were there ever any discussions about you coming back for the next film, prior to the Jamie Lee Curtis announcement for what would become *Halloween H20*?

Marianne Hagan: Paul and I had to sign agreements saying that we would do it, but it didn't matter anymore because all of a sudden, Jamie wanted back in. While we were doing *Halloween: The Curse of Michael Myers*, Jamie Lee Curtis was doing interviews saying she never wanted to talk about *Halloween* ever again. Then, suddenly, Jamie Lee was back in. Paul and I called each other like, "Can you believe this shit?" But beyond the agreement we signed, there were no real discussions about returning, no.

AG: We haven't discussed the producers' cut of the film yet.

Marianne Hagan: The producers' cut wasn't Daniel's script either. Daniel can tell you that. That's when the ripping of the pages out of the script started happening, when we were shooting in Salt Lake City and then the reshoots we did eight months later in Los Angeles. The look of the film is so different—it just looks completely different. We didn't know what on earth was happening. Daniel's whole thing about the cult in the town and the sacrifice was shot on set in Salt Lake City back in 1994. And that was just cut out completely.

AG: Any on-set memories or filming stories that stand out to you still?

Marianne Hagan: So we're in Salt Lake City, and we're doing night shoots. It's 2:30 in the morning, and Paul and I had gotten just punch-drunk giddy. We're so freaking tired. It's the scene at Mrs. Blankenship's house where Tommy says, "Kara, whatever you do, don't go back to that house." So that's his line, and I'm supposed to hear it in a very heavy way like, "Yeah, I get it." The camera is on my back, and it's on Paul. We could not keep a straight face for that entire scene. Our best friend and director, Joe Chappelle, would say action, and Paul would say "Kara, whatever you do" and then lose it laughing. Joe is yelling

"You guys get it together," and we're like, "Okay, fuck you, Joe." We were busting a gut for some reason, because it sounds like this very dramatic kind of line in a horror movie. Nothing against Daniel, of course, but we were just exhausted. It was freezing, and it was dark. Finally Joe got pissed, and he's like, "Come on, you guys," and then we got it out. I didn't laugh; he didn't laugh. Okay, great. Let's go home and go to sleep. But that was one of my favorite memories. It was pure joy.

-CHAPTER 4-
THE JLC ERA

The year 1998 was not only the twentieth anniversary of John Carpenter's *Halloween*, it was also the year that the franchise embraced its most radical change yet. The story is well-known by this point: Jamie Lee Curtis had the idea to return for the anniversary of her star-making role. She pitched a story about trauma and closure. The only problem was that in the years since she and John Carpenter had left, the story had moved on without them. In order to capitalize on both Curtis's return and the milestone anniversary, the decision was made to ignore everything after *Halloween II*, the last film Jamie Lee Curtis had appeared in for the franchise. *Halloween H20: 20 Years Later* was thought of by Curtis as the final film of a trilogy, preceded by the first two films of the series. Some of the key players loved the idea of having Laurie Strode return and triumph over her mass-murdering older brother once and for all so that she could heal. Others, namely Moustapha Akkad, refused to get on board with Laurie Strode chopping Michael's head off and killing him for good. A compromise was reached so that Laurie could have her moment of victory and take her power back, but it would not be Michael under the mask. Michael had subdued a paramedic and switched places with him, placing the mask on him and sealing his untimely fate, as would be explained in *Halloween: Resurrection*. Jamie Lee Curtis would return for the follow-up film so that she could be killed off as part of this compromise.

While I don't think anyone was happy with Laurie's death in the opening minutes of *Halloween: Resurrection*, from a narrative perspective there's a lot to unpack here. If *H20* was the story of Laurie fighting through her pain, trauma, and fear only to decapitate the wrong man, imagine what that would do to her psyche? What if Jamie Lee Curtis had had more of a role in *Halloween: Resurrection* so that we really got to see the impact of her actions from the previous film. It's incredibly heavy to think about Laurie's character arc in this light. Even one scene in *Halloween: Resurrection* in which she displays the full range of her pain would have made the eighth film pack so much more of a punch.

Brad & Jamie Lee Curtis. Image courtesy of Brad Loree

While *Halloween H20* has its flaws, it deserves credit for its emphasis on psychology over jump scares. Laurie Strode's trauma would be further explored in Rob Zombie's *Halloween II* and the duration of David Gordon Green's trilogy, but it started here. It's easy to remember *Halloween H20* merely for bouncing multiple earlier films out of franchise continuity, but it was equally impactful for setting the template for the franchise moving forward. Horrible things had happened in Haddonfield at the hands of Michael Myers, and the emotional scars that result are just as frightening. This dedication to exploring the psychology of trauma is another reason *Halloween* stands out from most of its peers.

Halloween H20 makes some interesting creative choices. For example, the first half of the film is shot almost exclusively in daylight, the second half almost exclusively at night. A lot of narrative is packed into a relatively short run time (eighty-six minutes). We spend virtually the whole first half of the film immersing ourselves in Laurie's life twenty years after we last saw her, before the action picks up. The body count is low (seven kills, the second lowest in the franchise), and an argument can be made that each of them has a significant impact on the story. The point of this film is not blood, guts, and jump scares; rather, this is a nuanced story originally intended to place a bow on Laurie Strode's role in the franchise, even if it didn't wind up that way.

There will always be the question of why franchise darling Jamie Lloyd couldn't at least be mentioned, to make the Michael-verse feel slightly more cohesive. Laurie's personal turmoil could have been amplified with a mention of Jamie or even a picture of her shown—the child she gave up in an attempt to escape Michael Myers. We learn here that Laurie is an alcoholic, and we have seen on-screen the source of her pain. Some kind of reference to Jamie Lloyd and Laurie having to give her up (especially since Laurie tells us she faked her own death) would have added another layer of trauma to this already troubled character while also appeasing longtime fans.

Halloween: Resurrection was intended as a series reset after the first scene of the film. With Laurie's death in the opening moments, all of the ongoing stories were complete, and the franchise was free to pivot in new directions. The concept isn't bad on paper; it was an attempt to modernize the franchise and capitalize on the found-footage craze, which was still in its infancy, all while breaking away from the mythology and backstories that had dominated the series for several films. Free of Laurie, free of Jamie, free of cults, the franchise could move in any direction it wanted to. However, instead of leveraging this clean slate to create a new blueprint for the next few entries in the franchise, the filmmakers opted for a self-contained story that didn't set up anything. Stand-alone films work for franchises like *Friday the 13th* but *Halloween* had always favored the ongoing narrative approach (minus *Halloween III*). and the strategy likely caught some viewers off guard, simultaneously leaving producers with an uncertain future.

Halloween: Resurrection is a mixed bag. The new characters are entertaining and three-dimensional, which makes the film enjoyable and adds to its value in rewatches. The ideas are fresh and make the story feel more timely, and keeping the Myers house as the central location is another benefit. However, several creative decisions left a bad taste in the mouths of audiences. Laurie's death feels underwhelming and hokey. We already had an intimate moment between Michael and Laurie in *H20*. To jump right into another and kill our leading lady while she's wearing a bathrobe feels insulting. She doesn't put up the kind of fight we're accustomed to from the character. There's no buildup or climax. It feels forced and unimportant. Then there's Busta Rhymes karate kicking Michael Myers. We've seen Michael get beat up a lot in previous films, so this was nothing new, but it was much more intentionally comedic than other is customary for the series. Watching a legendary rapper do his best Bruce Lee impression and wipe the floor with this horror icon, all while making us laugh, is off-putting to say the least. Whether or not it diminished the Michael Myers character and his mystique is debatable, but the franchise couldn't figure out how to move forward after this film and wound up rebooting. That's not entirely because of the Busta beatdown, but it sure didn't help. Many audience members walked out of theaters shaking their heads. Tonally, it just felt out of character for the *Halloween* franchise.

We can look at *H20* as the third and final part of the Laurie Strode trilogy and *Resurrection*'s opening scene as an epilogue of sorts, before the film moves in its own direction. These two films occupy an interesting space in the franchise in that they were the last films before the series entered its remake era with Rob Zombie. After that, a reimaging era with Blumhouse, where we're asked to ignore all but the first film. *Resurrection* ended a timeline in the series, with Laurie finally losing her fight and dying at the hands of her older brother, who then goes home. In that timeline, Michael is still alive, as seen in the closing shot of *Resurrection*, and we have to use our imagination as to what comes next. But the bogeyman lived, more people died, and there's still horror in Haddonfield. There's part of me that thinks about how the story could have progressed coming out of the eighth film. Laurie's son John Tate is still alive. He could have picked up his mother's fight and attempted to avenge her death. But it was not meant to be, and this franchise would move in a new direction.

Interview: Patrick Lussier (Editor, *Halloween H20: 20 Years Later*)

AG: So let's start at the beginning. How did this job come to be?

Patrick Lussier: I had edited *Scream*, *Mimic*, and *Scream 2* for Dimension. At the end of *Scream 2*, they were talking to me about possibly directing one of their direct-to-video movies, of which they were beginning to ramp up. They had *Children of the Corn* and obviously *The Prophecy*, which ended up being the one I did. They also asked me to consider editing for Steve Miner this *Halloween* movie they were doing. I think it was just called *Halloween 7* at the time. *H20* didn't become the official title until halfway through photography.

I met with Steve Miner, who was an assistant editor and did a bunch of things on the original *Last House on the Left* for Wes Craven, who I had worked with a lot. Wes put in a good word for me and vice versa, and I hit it off with Steve immediately. Steve's a very laid-back guy in some circumstances. He certainly is really specific about how he likes stuff. But at the same time, he's very collaborative and knew exactly how to make the movie. He's somebody who completely understood the assignment. I think they originally had gone after John Carpenter to direct it, who had passed. I think it was Jamie herself who had suggested Steve, because they had worked together previously. Steve had done a lot of genre stuff already. He'd done a couple of *Friday the 13th* films. He'd also done *Warlock* and *House*. He'd also worked in TV on *The Wonder Years* and then had done the pilot for *Dawson's Creek*. Kevin Williamson, who's a huge *Halloween* fan, also highly recommended Steve. Because of my affiliation with the *Scream* movies, I was suggested as a good collaborative partner for Steve.

AG: There's definitely a crossover in style between the early *Scream* films and *Halloween H20*. Was this deliberate? If so, what were those conversations like?

Patrick Lussier: I will tell you that that was completely intentional. That's not a subtle thing. I think a lot of it came out of Kevin originally. When he was writing *Scream*, back when it was called *Scary*

Movie, he was a huge fan of *Halloween* and all those slasher movies of the early eighties, which *Halloween* spawned. *Halloween* came out in 1978, but it spawned so many other movies that followed: *Prom Night*, *Happy Birthday to Me*, *My Bloody Valentine*, *Terror Train*, which were all basically murder mysteries, right? *Scream* was a really good murder mystery, even though *Halloween* was not. In *Halloween*, you knew exactly who the killer was from the beginning, which was pretty brilliant in its own right. It's a great introduction, how you meet Michael Myers in the original film. Then of course the original *Halloween II*, they retcon in the brother-sister relationship, especially for the TV version, where a lot of those new scenes showed up to establish that because they had to cut out some stuff for TV. *Scream* was sort of a love letter to those movies, yet it was very self-aware and had a very sort of youthful vibe, like *Halloween*. *Halloween* has the whole babysitter dynamic. You have the Loomis story and the babysitter story. Now, with Jamie being the age she was when *H20* was made, she sort of takes on the Loomis role. So in order to have the kids' story, it's now her son and his friends. So it's the same dynamics, but because of the success of *Scream* and *Scream 2* under the Dimension label, they understood the importance of anchoring it with a real strong youth presence.

They cast Michelle Williams from *Dawson's Creek* at the time, which was pretty huge. Then, introducing Josh Hartnett, those two together, that was a real coup for the marketing of the film. You can really look at it as the babysitter taking over the psychiatrist mantle. In order to do that, you had to bring in the younger characters, who are directly linked to her, as opposed to in the original film, where Loomis and Laurie don't even meet till the end of the movie. They're total strangers. Because of the family dynamic that's already built in, with Josh Hartnett's character, Jamie's character, and Michael himself there, this is all a family drama with knives. I think that was a natural sort of dynamic. Kevin's influence on the script was very strong. The final shooting script Kevin rewrote. The version before that, Beau Billingslea's character, who's one of the cops in the beginning scene, was originally going to be played by Charles Dutton. He was cast and got paid for the movie and had a whole sequence during the part where Michelle Williams's character looks out the school window and sees Michael Myers outside the gate—the echo of Laurie Strode looking out at the laundry on the clothesline. There was a whole scene in the script up to probably ten days before photography where Charles Dutton comes up to and is looking at Michael, and Michael Myers kills him. That was a whole sequence that was cut before photography in order to bring the film's budget down.

When you watch the movie, it doesn't just feel short, it is short. It's seventy-nine minutes long or eighty minutes long minus credits, and of course it has a very lengthy main title to bring that up. What it's missing is that kill scene, which is interesting because in *Scream*, we added a kill scene, and that's Henry Winkler's death. That wasn't in the original draft that Kevin wrote. They added that in because they felt they needed something at that point of film. It was added before photography.

AG: My next question was actually about the short run time despite the jam-packed narrative. There's a lot of story that's told in a very short amount of time.

Patrick Lussier: Yeah, and it's told really economically. A lot of that is a credit to Steve and how he tells a story. We would get maybe between ten and twenty minutes of dailies a day, which is very light. Usually you get double or triple that amount timewise. Steve shot a minimal movie. Normally you have eight to ten weeks for a director's cut. This director's cut was done in a day and a half. Then you have like two or three weeks for a studio cut. This studio cut was done in half a day. The entire time from the editor's cut that I presented to what became the final picture lock was two days. We cut out two little scenes, neither of which served the story and slowed the pace down a little bit. Then that was the movie.

The movie never changed. We had moved our cutting rooms very close to where Steve Miner lived thinking we were gonna be working with him for weeks, which was the way we would often do it with Wes. Steve was in on Monday and then Tuesday at noon, he was like, "Well, that's me. I'm done. Show it to the studio and let me know what they think." Then he left, and we went to the studio, and they had no more than like a half day's notes. I think after the preview we did like less than half a day of changes. The movie scored an eighty-eight out of a hundred. The preview went incredibly well for such a lean movie.

A lot of that is because the ending is so strong. The last forty minutes of that movie are nonstop. When we used the John Carpenter music at the very end, we pulled it off the CD, because any version we tried to make was not as good. Watching it with an audience, the moment that Michael's and Jamie's hands touch, people start to boo. Then, when she winds up and cuts his head off, it's like your team won the Super Bowl. Just a massive liftoff. And that's how you go out. You go out on such a high that people are incredibly generous to what is a very lean cinematic experience.

AG: The movie has two equal halves, with the first half of the movie in daylight. Then you move to nighttime, and there's this clear contrast of exposition during the daytime and madness at nighttime.

Patrick Lussier: That was basically how the shooting script showed up after Kevin rewrote Robert Zappia's script. I think Zappia did the first version, then Matt Greenberg did a version, and then Kevin did the final shooting version and just ripped it of any excess. There would have been that daytime kill scene with Charles Dutton had it not been cut. Those scenes were written, and it was, I think, between ten days and two weeks before production that it was removed. Charles Dutton was ready to report to work and die at Michael Myers's hands until that got removed, and they paid him anyway, although you don't get any residuals if you're not in the movie.

I think that evolved without intent. You have a little bit of night in the opening with Jimmy and the nurse. Originally it was a different character than the nurse in the opening. I think it was Steve who had the idea of Dr. Loomis's nurse. Donald Pleasence had obviously passed away beforehand, so that wasn't on the table, to have him. They have the voice-over of him, which they did a soundalike with an actor named Tom Kane, mostly because of there wasn't a clean version of it to use in the movie. That's why that was done. But we worked very hard to make it sound as close to Donald Pleasence as we could, which made sense, to have that character tie in. If you watch the first two *Halloween* films and then *H20*, they go together pretty well. Dr. Loomis of course seems to die at the end of Rick Rosenthal's *Halloween II*, but by *Halloween 4* you know he's less dead. You would have had more day mayhem if the script hadn't been truncated. That wasn't like a mastermind or intent or ever even discussed with me. Maybe it was discussed by others, but it just worked out that way, like so many things in movies that evolve through a series of changes, notes, or budget compromises. Suddenly you have a movie that either works great or doesn't with things that nobody thought of. And people read into it afterwards.

AG: The film is very low on gore and has the second-lowest kill count in the franchise. Was there a conscious effort to replicate the Hitchcockian suspense of the first film?

Patrick Lussier: Maybe. That's really a Steve Miner question. It was certainly in the day and a half we had the cutting room never discussed in those terms. I think it may have been in part a reaction to the original *Scream*. We had so many problems with the [Motion Picture Association of America]. On *Scream 2*, we expected to have a lot of problems with the MPAA but didn't. I think it was a preemptive take on it to make it effective and make all the suspense work without going overkill and getting into glorious *Friday the 13th* territory. And part of that, I think, has to do with Steve having done that before. He had done *Friday the 13th Part 2* and *Friday 13th [Part 3] 3D*. He was very aware of how to do that and had done it already, so that was not his intention here. He didn't need to do it again.

Some filmmakers are doing something in a genre that isn't a place they play a lot, so they winna basically use all the toys available, whether that be blood, body parts and limbs, or whatever, and he didn't need to do that. That wasn't his intent. I think he very much wanted to make something that was classier. Didn't have to put a head in the fish tank here.

AG: These death scenes do resonate more, which makes for a more memorable film.

Patrick Lussier: Yeah, I think so too. I think it's a very effective end to the *Halloween* mythology. For *Halloween: Resurrection*, they forced Steve to shoot the shot of Michael Myers walking through the gate in the ambulance driver's outfit. We're supposed to think that maybe it was the ambulance driver killed. To Steve, that was bullshit, and

I don't think he'd mind me saying that. That wasn't the real version of the movie. The version of the movie he shot was Michael Myers dying at the end and getting his head cut off. That was the end of it. Moustapha Akkad and Paul Freeman didn't want to kill the cash cow that Michael Myers had become, so of course they wanted a parachute. Then the subsequent sort of retcon of the three Blumhouse movies I find just odd in that it takes a bit of a shit on everything that came before it. There's probably a much better way to do that. Each one of those three movies to me gets a little further astray, especially the third one, even Jamie's character. In *H20*, you can tell that both Steve and Kevin are huge fans of hers and wanted to give her this amazing cinematic payoff—for the character that she created, what it spawned, and the audience's love of her and her interaction with Michael. It felt like in the three Blumhouse movies, she was there out of obligation, as opposed to out of reverence.

AG: *H20* created the blueprint for everything that came after. It was the first film to heavily deal with Laurie's trauma and to look at the emotional state of the Laurie character. Rob Zombie's two films are really all about trauma. They just look drastically different from what you guys did in *H20*. And the three Blumhouse films are also about trauma but again look completely different from what you guys did. But everything that came after *H20* followed its thematic lead.

Patrick Lussier: There are some great moments in the Blumhouse films. I think Judy Greer's character is probably the most interesting, so that when she's not in it, it's a real problem. I think it's a shame they couldn't get Paul Rudd to come back to play Tommy Doyle, mostly because Anthony Michael Hall is so physically big. He's a big guy, and it feels like he's beating up an old man when he's fighting with Michael Myers. It just felt sort of ugly in every way. They did themselves a disservice with casting, because you cast somebody who is bigger than Michael Myers. To Rob Zombie's credit, nobody was bigger than Tyler Mane. Tyler's a monster. Sweetheart of a guy, though. I feel Zombie's movies are completely outside. They're unrelated in my mind.

I had heard that there was one note that Kevin had about it, so I'm quoting hearsay. He said that Zombie's *Halloween* demystified Michael Myers. When you get to the creation of Michael Myers, you completely understand why that guy's a serial killer. His life is utter shit. I think to Carpenter's credit, that beginning, when you get no explanation other than it's a seven-year-old kid standing there with a knife, that's the reveal, and it's scarier that he's come from a middle-class family which shows no bad signs and also that created Laurie. How did that happen? There's a leanness to Carpenter's version and a lack of explanation. That is why I think the series perpetuated. I think if Zombie's movies had been the first two movies, that the series never would have had its legs, because there was never any mystery the audience could overlay onto the character. You couldn't apply your own sense of what that enigma was. There was no mystery in the Zombie version. It's like, *Oh, I'm just watching a white-trash train wreck. Oh, okay. So Michael Myers wears a red hat and votes for Trump? Got it.*

AG: You came close to making the sequel to Rob Zombie's *Halloween II*, correct?

Patrick Lussier: We got very close. We got five weeks away from shooting. We had a script that I think would have gotten better. We were forced to write it very fast, Todd Farmer and I. The thing we wanted to do was remythologize the character from what Rob had done. I think his second film is more interesting than his first film. I think the trailer for the second film, the one that had "Nights in White Satin," is actually the best encapsulation of that movie—the trailer they were never supposed to release, and of course "it got released by accident." I have it on good authority that it did not get released by accident, but that's neither here nor there. In our opening, we stripped everything down to its brass tacks. At the end of the opening sequence, we killed Brad Dourif's character. Michael Myers is caught in an ambulance that goes over the side of a dam on fire. The Laurie Strode character is locked up, and we introduce a new final girl. There was also some concern from Dimension. They weren't crazy about the Laurie Strode that they had. How could you compare to Jamie, though? Poor Scout [Taylor-Compton, Laurie Strode in Rob Zombie's *Halloween* and *Halloween II*] had that comparison, which would have been an unwelcome thing to try and live up to. Those are massive shoes to try and fill. In the writing of her version of that character, she wasn't the hero. Michael was the hero in Zombie's movies. So we worked with that when he shows up later in our movie. We had some characterization stuff that I think we could have done better and would have done better if we had a chance to evolve the script more. But some of the kills were great that we had. Michael killing somebody with an iron was wonderfully horrific, then pummeling somebody with a side-view mirror, which was a 3D gag that was going to be amazing. Tom Atkins was gonna come back and play a doctor in a psychiatric hospital. He was all for it, and we even got permission to use the Silver Shamrock song in it. When Michael comes back, there's a point where he finds the original Shatner mask and he puts it on, so you don't see his face. But in the end, the mask is ripped off, and you see that the original Zombie mask is melted into his skin. So Michael no longer exists. He is only the Shape. Michael has been utterly eradicated, and the Shape has completely consumed him. So that was the big reveal.

AG: You have me sold.

Patrick Lussier: We were five weeks out. We had locations. We had the crew. Suddenly, Dimension went dark. They didn't answer their phones over the weekend. Then I got a call from Bob Weinstein on Monday, and he said we don't have the money; we can't make it. I think it's 2009. So it was after they had to sell all their interest in *Inglourious Bastards*, which made a bunch of money. But it didn't make it for them, because in order to get the movie released, they had to sell so much of their stake. They had lost their Disney backing. We had wanted to make it, I think, for $12.5 million in full 3D. I look back now, and it's like, God, we could have made that movie for half that now if somebody gave us the opportunity, but it was a different time.

AG: Scout shared with me that they went dark on her as well.

Patrick Lussier: We had a great resolution for her. There was a point where she and Michael are handcuffed together through the whole last third of the movie. They are handcuffed together, and it's pretty crazy. We had a sort of new Loomis-type character named Goodman.

We had another final girl character who hadn't been cast at that time. Tom Atkins was gonna come back, and Tyler we had talked to, and he was all on board.

But there's a point where Tyler and Scout would have been handcuffed together for a large period of time and going on this murder spree through the town. It would have been a fun, unique sort of way to do it. I think we had Laurie cut her own hand off at the end. At first they were like, "Oh, we don't know if we need Laurie in it." We told them that we think we have a really cool thing for Scout in this that'll be different and to make her really go the opposite way of Jamie's Laurie Strode, lean into the idea of is Laurie going to be the prodigy or not? She's so damaged. Rob sets that up at the end of his second film. Is she gonna go fully to the dark side or not? She does indeed have a conclusion in our script. She doesn't go all the way upriver.

It was great fun to write. Todd and I wrote it incredibly quickly because of the pressure of knowing how quickly they wanted to do it. We were gonna go off and do *Drive Angry*, and they wanted us to shoot it beforehand. We had a whole plan to do it. We had everything laid out. We were gonna shoot it in the same town and had scouted locations. We were ready. Then they were like, "We don't actually have the money." So a script is still out there. They paid for it. They own it; they can do whatever they want with it.

Tyler Mane as Michael, walking the hospital hallways. Image courtesy of Phil Parmet

AG: The direction you're talking about moves the series back into traditional *Halloween* kind of lore, it sounds like, while still acknowledging Rob's films and the stories they laid out.

Patrick Lussier: Exactly. We wanted to make it. Because Laurie was in a psychiatric hospital where Tom Atkins was a doctor, we did kill Tom Atkins by cutting his head off in a fish tank but with the fish in 3D. Would have been really cool. Laurie had an affair with one of the orderlies, and Michael kills the orderly, and that's the one he kills with the iron, and it's horrifically awesome. I think there's a line where somebody says, "You should never bang a serial killer's kid sister," or something like that. It wasn't Shakespeare.

AG: Any final stories or memories you'd like to share from your experience with the *Halloween* franchise?

Patrick Lussier: Other than the challenges with the music score on *Halloween H20*, which was problematic, it was a really fun experience. It was fun to step into that world. Every time I would go to set, there was a real excitement and enthusiasm for the project. I think Steve's sparse and lean approach to it matched, or at least echoed, a lot of the cinematic stylings of the original film and the limitations that it had. I think he did that very deliberately.

The sequences with LL Cool J and Adam Arkin, there's all these great sort of misdirections, and then we have sort of a fantastic escalation. As you talked about before, it hits night in the second half of the movie, and it just doesn't stop. It's a forty-minute tour de force, and then it's over. It didn't waste any time. There were a lot of issues with the mask. There was the original, sort of featureless mask because they were told they weren't allowed to use the Shatner mask because everybody was afraid that Shatner would sue them. And of course if we couldn't get Tom Atkins to be the psychiatrist for *Halloween 3D*, we would have gone for William Shatner, just because seeing Michael kill William Shatner and Shatner reach up and touch his face—his own face—would have been amazing. That is a meta version that needed to happen.

I think the mask issues created a lot of drama behind the scenes that was challenging for Steve. He found that to be really problematic. We went through the same mask drama on *Scream*. There were a whole bunch of mask issues with the Ghostface mask. You can watch the opening of *Scream* and you can see the different masks that appear. So that to me was all very familiar. There was a mask at one point they demanded Steve shoot with. I think the mask is from either *Halloween 4* or *5*? Steve hated that. I think he shot one shot with it and hated it. Steve was doing *Lake Placid* at the same time, prepping the film, working with Stan Winston, who was designing the crocodile that they were gonna use. So he asked Stan as a favor to design a mask. So the main mask in the movie that has the real hair, Stan designed. Matt Winston, Stan's son, is also in the movie at the beginning.

I remember the conversations with the studio when that mask showed up, saying, "For everybody to save face, you guys really need to like that mask because Steve will die on this hill." To everyone's credit, they all got on board. There was one we shot they couldn't redo. They redid a bunch of other stuff. I think they ran out of time, because the original ending, in the kitchen area where Michael is flipping the tables, that was shot with all the lights on with the other featureless mask, and it wasn't as creepy. So when Steve got to reshoot that with the lights off, it became so much more engaging. But because they were reshooting a bunch of stuff with the new mask and still within the original shooting schedule, they ran out of time to redo the shot of Charlie's death, which you don't see on camera. But Charlie sticking his hand in the garbage disposal and then turns around, and Michael's standing there with that terrible digital mask, which was from a company out of Vancouver and in Los Angeles. They had said, "It will be 100 percent. We guarantee it. It's gonna work. You're not even gonna be able to tell the difference." The problem is you're going on faith until the movie is finished. Then we pulled up the release date of the movie. The movie was set for September, and suddenly it releases in the beginning of August, and that's the shot we got. And it was like, "Oh well, that shot was shitty." Basically, it's a very bad digital cartoon over the old mask. It's too big because they're trying to cover up the thing that was underneath. That was an example of "Oh look, the visual effects guys fucked us." And there was nothing we could do about it. There was no time to deal with it because they pulled up the release date so far.

Other than that, I was always just amazed at how inventive Steve was with so little. He could shoot so few minutes of material and get so much out of it. His economical approach to directing was really, really inspiring. There's that scene when he plays the bursar. The interesting thing about that scene is it makes that campus look huge. So you think there are buildings on either side and they're in the middle when in fact the shots this way are at the front of the building, and the shots the other way are on the back of the same building. So he just moved people. It's really ingenious. It's just little clever camera stuff that he did. I love the scene with the little girl and her mom. It's just really effective. Nobody dies in it. You could have killed them both, but he didn't need to. It's the glimpses of Michael through the bathroom stall. It's creepy, and you're vulnerable.

I remember there being a big studio note because the actress playing the mother mimed pulling her underwear down to use the bathroom. One of the studio guys was like, "I don't want to think about her ass on the toilet seat. I can't think about that. You have to cut that out." So we did. But it was the weirdest note. That was one of their notes from their half day of notes.

I think we were very lucky to have Marco Beltrami come in and write a few new cues and reformat a bunch of his music from both *Mimic* and *Scream 2* into the movie. The John Ottman music was interesting, and there's still a fair amount of it in the movie, but it wasn't scary. It was so complexly orchestrated; it took away from the simplicity of the character. The Shape's simplicity needed to be reflected in the music, the way Carpenter had done that. Marco had rewritten Carpenter's music for the end of the film, trying to make it sound like the original Carpenter score, but he was the one who finally said, "Can't we just use it from the CD?" We cut that in, and it's a spectacular moment when you're using the original Carpenter synth. It takes it all back right to the beginning. Nobody planned that. It was a choice of necessity. There's a lot of things in that movie that happened because of desperation and time, and every one of the things that work that way work to the film's benefit.

Interview: Chris Durand (Michael Myers, *Halloween H20: 20 Years Later*)

AG: I wanted to start with your characterization of Michael. It was unique in the fact that a lot of your physical movements were different from your predecessors'. More jungle predator like.

Chris Durand: You hit the nail on the head exactly with that one. To back up a little, I got called in for an interview. What I understood is they had looked at something like a hundred actors and said, "Why are we doing this? It's originally someone who came from the stunt world, and this is a physical acting role. Let's do that." The woman they had hired to double Jamie Lee Curtis and also to run the show as a coordinator is named Donna Keegan. Donna said, "I'm not gonna do some big cattle call. I'm gonna give you five guys. They're all qualified. Pick one." I went in, sat down, and talked to the director, Steve Miner, and the first AD. The other guys up for the role were there as well. We just kind of cycled through. They knew a little bit about my background with physical work. I was a gymnast at six foot two and a martial artist. So two things happen. The first was that I didn't realize I was Donna's first choice. So that was lovely to find out later. And the second was that part of their decision-making was—and this happens all the time—"Who do you wanna hang out with for the next three months?" I'm a pretty friendly guy, so I won that one, not that the other guys weren't great. I know them. One of them had a little bit of a spark, if you know what I mean. You'd look at him like, "That's a great performer," but you're like, "Do you really wanna deal with that?"

Now, during the interview, they were talking for a moment among themselves. They were saying, "We are not going to reference what came between. Or what came before." That's what I heard, "what came before." I think it was within a couple of weeks they told me that I landed the role. I said to myself, *We're not doing what came before. Why look at anything?* So I didn't watch any of the other movies. Then you get to the set, and you're a guy in a mask. Granted, the mask is scary in its own right. The lighting makes it more so; the music makes it more so, but it's not enough. So here's a guy with no facial expressions. No dialogue. Maybe you see my eyes, maybe. Now be scary. So it's like, "What do you do," right? Obviously there's a fair amount built in, but the thing that pushes it over the top is that you have to have an intent behind your movements, an intent behind your performance. So I kind of thought about this guy for a little while and said, "What is he?" You nailed it on the head earlier. What I landed on was how a tiger or a lion locked on prey. They crouch and lock. You can't break that gaze. That's what I decided this guy was. He was coming for you. You're not gonna break that gaze; you're not gonna break that connection. There's nothing you can do really to stop him. I'm also not in a hurry. So it wasn't "I'm gonna chase you down like a cheetah." It was more like, "When I'm ready, I'm pouncing. I'm very much methodically stalking." I guess it would be more "I'm toying with you and I can get you anytime I want, but I'm coming, and there's nothing you can do about it." That's how I landed on playing him. I actually would tilt my head slightly down, with my eyes raised up, locked on whoever I was coming for, and gutterly, under my breath, I would do a little growl. The sound guy actually picked up on that because they have very sensitive microphones. I think he kept it in there as a deep kind of a layer to everything. It's nothing you're gonna really notice, but he kind of worked it into the overall soundtrack.

AG: Were your motivations or preparations different at all for the final forty-five minutes of the film, when it's just pure, unadulterated terror and you're coming for these characters, versus the first half of the film, when you're almost more of an apparition, a visual representation of Laurie's trauma? Did you play those scenes any differently?

Chris Durand: No, you can't. They have to be the same because of that trauma. Whether she's hallucinating that I'm there or whether I'm there, it has to have that same feeling of coming after her. So there's moments when I'm coming down the driveway and she's trying to blink me away. If you don't have that same kind of energy behind it, it'll separate it for the audience, and you'll know that it's not me, and it'll separate it for her. Her trauma is deep enough that everything she sees with me is real.

She's not happy-go-lucky. She's reliving this. It's been twenty years. She's drinking, she's popping pills, she can't sleep, she's hallucinating, and a lot of it has to do with the fact that her son is the age that she was when all this started. He's roughly that same age. So now, as a mom, the stakes are much, much higher. You're worried about your own safety, but if you've got your kid with you, it's a different game. She's really freaked out because she's got an extra layer in there she didn't have the first time. Part of her turning around and going back to finish it with me is that I'm after the kids, and she's like, "Hell, no. It's not happening."

AG: When she sees that her son has been stabbed in the leg, it is a turning point for her.

Chris Durand: Correct, and as an audience, you know I'm there the whole time. You know there's moments where she's hallucinating me, having flashbacks and feeling her trauma, but you also know that I'm real, that I'm there and I'm chasing the kids. She doesn't until we come face-to-face at the door. She doesn't know that I'm actually back. So that's a powerful moment of realization, where it's like, *Oh shit, he's actually here. I'm not just hallucinating; he's here*, and then you add in the layer of "Yes, I've been trying to kill her kid and the other kids," and it just ramps it up really, really fast.

AG: You mentioned the face-to-face moment in the mirror. That and the moment where you come down from the ceiling are two of the most iconic moments in the franchise. I wanted to ask about filming those scenes and dive into both.

Chris Durand: The little bit of action right before coming face-to-face at the window is when Josh [Hartnett] and Michelle [Williams] get trapped behind the gate and I'm reaching through and then fiddling with the keys to get them. For a good hour and a half before that scene, I avoided them completely. Wherever they went, I went somewhere else. I kept my distance. When they were lining up the shot, there was kind of a small courtyard between where I got ready and where they were already in scene in front of the camera. I made sure I was stacked up behind the camera so they couldn't see me getting ready. When they were ready for me, they said, "We're ready to go forward." I said, "Go ahead and roll." They rolled the cameras and started the scene without me there. The first bit of that is them banging on the door before I arrive. When they started rolling, I was already moving, but I stacked myself up behind the camera so they couldn't see me. So by the time they said action, I arrived at that gate with force, first time they've seen me in a couple hours in character, and you get a much better reaction. That was something I very purposely did. I thought that out. This is something I've done for years just performing anyway. You want to help somebody who's on camera by giving them eyeline dialogue reactions so they're not acting to nothing. But also it helps to not be just standing around, goofing around, and then try to get into character in the last two seconds. It helps to come in and show up in character on any scene you do. You don't want to have egg on your face. You don't want those dead moments that don't fit. So I learned long ago you start acting before they yell action, as soon as the rolling cameras are already going. But that moment where we come face-to-face, that's the first time she really realizes I'm back. The brilliance of the whole thing is when she fumbles for the gun and comes back up, I'm gone.

I'll give you the analogy. If you're swimming in a small bay somewhere and you see a shark fin go by, that's bad, right? You know what's worse? When you've seen it and then you don't see it anymore. That's what that scene is. She sees me; she knows I'm there. She fumbles, looks back up, and I'm gone. She has no idea where I am, which leads me to the next scene, with the lowering down from the ceiling. That was actually an on-the-spot decision. She's in the house and goes up the small staircase just before she gets into the room with all the tables. Steve Miner was questioning if I should come from behind or rise up behind her. There were fairly tall ceilings in this place, and he looked up and there was a pipe that ran across, just about a foot below the ceiling. He's like, "Can you fit up there?" I was like, "I don't know. Get a ladder. Let's see." Half an hour later, that scene was on film.

What's really cool about that scene is the pacing. I didn't drop down like a ninja, right? It's very controlled coming down, and then you add to that the whole creepiness of it being Michael coming from some unexpected place, and she doesn't know I'm there. It's almost like a spider if you saw a spider repelling down your friend's shirt and they don't know it. Your visceral reaction is to jump at that. It was a little bit of that. But as Michael Myers, it's like that on steroids.

AG: You brought up Michelle Williams and Josh Hartnett, who both would go on to become pretty big stars in their own right. What were they like to work with so early in their careers?

Chris Durand: It was Josh's first film. Michelle was coming off *Dawson's Creek*. They were both great. Everyone was very respectful of everything. They were both really excited to meet me when they first got there. I guess because it's an iconic character. They were very deferential at first. Of course, they both have gone on to become very big stars. They were absolutely wonderful to work with. It was kind of fun because we were isolated up at that mansion, so we could wander around during the in-between time and explore and hang out with each other. There wasn't a lot of exterior noise. We weren't somewhere where there were cars going by or people walking around talking to us. We were isolated. That was fun.

AG: Steve Miner was a brilliant choice for the director here. His name carried a lot of gravitas within the genre, which was exciting for fans. What was the experience of working with him like?

Chris Durand: Steve was funny because he let me do what I thought was right. In this business, no news is good news. If you do something that's not working, you'll hear about it and we'll fix it. But if they love it, you usually don't get any feedback. There were a couple of times, though, when I think I made him really happy because you could hear him giggling in the next room at video village. We knew we nailed the shot. So that was always fun. Steve was great. He was a straight-up, no-nonsense kind of director. He played the principal—he gave himself a little cameo, as he should have. There was one funny scene when we're in the kitchen. Donna and I are working out a little piece where they've stabbed the drawer, and then I knock her back through a whole dish rack of stuff that flips over and she scrambles out of the room. We're trying to figure it out, and we're setting it up, and it's kind of a quarter-speed rehearsal. We're very much just marking things. "We'll go here and then we'll come by this and then chip over here," and of course that's when Steve walks by and says, "That sucks." So we're like, "Well, what would you like us to change?" He says, "Make it not suck." Of course it's ribbing each other. He knows full well what we're doing, and as soon as you roll cameras, you ramp up. We slam through everything and everything flies, and it's what you knew it would be. He would give you a hard time like that in a fun way. I think he kept the truck, by the way. He had a small ranch somewhere, and he bought the truck off production.

AG: It's common knowledge at this point that there were three masks used for this film. I wanted to hear about that from your perspective, though, as the person wearing the mask. What was that like for you to go through these changes?

Chris Durand: It's frustrating, because we did mask tests two weeks before principal photography. They landed on the mask made by KNB [Greg Nicotero's special effects company]. Whatever versions they molded together to get to the KNB mask, they wanted that. Then of course you watch dailies every day, basically. It's a delay of a day or two before the film is developed, and you sit down and watch what you've shot. So for them to watch daily for five weeks and then go, "We don't like the mask," it was fairly disheartening.

The opening sequence, we shot the exterior fairly early on. It was right at the mask change that we were shooting the interior where I killed the nurse. There was a huge kerfuffle on set. Steve was horribly upset because he's done all this work. With each shot, sometimes you get what's called a happy accident, where things work out in a way that you're like, "Wow, we can't even replicate that." A little piece of business slipped through, and it's great. We had a lot of that already built up. I believe it was the *Halloween 6* mask that we shot that scene with and also the KNB mask. When I pulled the knife from the little knife holder and flipped it around and went around the corner and then we tracked down the hall, we shot that very dark on purpose. That was the Friday that everything went down, and we shot it with both masks. So by Monday we had the Winston mask and had to go back and reshoot a bunch of stuff. Some big scenes too, and that gets very disheartening for the crew. Now, I came from the world of stunts. That was my original position in the film industry. I always like to do things once, but there's times when you have to do things twice because the camera missed it or something happens and there's some big thumper you do, like you get thrown through something or they slip and fall and they don't catch it. The tendency on the second take is you're wary of what's coming, and you don't sell the same way. So you have to override that instinct and go even harder the second time around. So I was used to doing that. It's like, "Whatever, let's go reshoot it." But it was a little disheartening for the crew because there were some big setups, but I think it helps with my attitude of "Let's go; let's nail it again." You lose some of those happy accidents along the way, and hopefully you gain others. It was a big issue, though, and we had to go through and reshoot some big scenes. Like flipping the tables, we reshot that. But we kind of knew what we were up against, and the setup is five times faster the second time around because you've been through it.

AG: I wanted to ask if you had any Moustapha Akkad stories you could share?

Chris Durand: He wasn't around a lot on set. He was busy in the office, I'm sure, dealing with finances and everything else. Early on, I remember discussions, though, around early scripts. I believe it was when I killed Adam Arkin's character. I think he has a gun at that point, because he shoots down the stairs at LL Cool J's character. Then I come out of nowhere and I stab him, and of course he twitches and we do that whole thing. Somebody suggested, "Why doesn't Michael pick up the gun?" Of course that's ethically wrong on every level for the character, and it was just one of those suggestions that somebody threw out at the spur of the moment. Moustapha was like, "No gun, no gun!"—just a way over-the-top reaction. Of course everyone agreed, but they thought it was funny. So then we get to the flipping-the-table scene. Before we flip the tables, I'm walking down the top of the tables, and Jamie's underneath, scrambling along. There's a shot where she stops and looks back and forth. It pans up, and you see me right above her on the table. So it was that shot—and this exists somewhere still—but everyone decided to play a joke on Moustapha because he was on set. Of course, this means I'm playing a joke on Moustapha. So I'm like, "Man, I hope this goes well because I don't really wanna get fired from this job." We roll the camera; we do the whole thing with her scrambling. Rise up to see me there, and there's this pause. I dropped the knife, and I pulled a gun out of my back pocket. It's just dead silent for like three or four seconds. There's nothing. I'm like, "Oh, man." Then he goes, "Ah, you got me, you got me." He thought it was really funny. Then we then backed up and shot the scene for real. Somewhere that exists on film.

AG: The fight sequence that ensues between Will's death and Laurie sending the teenagers away is a standout moment for the film as well as the franchise. Walk me through what that is like as a stuntman and as an actor for you. It's obviously very physical work. You're working with Jamie Lee Curtis, who is back in this franchise, and now she's tapping into something that she hasn't done in twenty years. The stakes are high; the emotions are high.

Chris Durand: Well, the first thing I would say is Adam Arkin's kill is probably my favorite kill in the movie and for reasons that you wouldn't probably guess. It's got nothing to do with killing Adam. He's completely incidental to it. I stab him and raise him up, and I'm staring her down.

It's all about "Look what I just did to your boy, and I'm coming for you." This is the psychological aspect of it again that I tried to add. I'm focused again on her. That's my end goal. He's incidental; he's in the way. But it's also something that's important to her, and I'm taking it away from her. So very slowly, I'm stripping things away, which will also go to the tables after. It's a stalking sequence, and she's desperately scrambling, and once again I'm coming—this is where I'm actually coming for her at this point. I'm really focused on coming and getting her, but I'm still not in a huge hurry because I'm gonna get her. The physicality part is all stuff I've done a bunch of times—little serendipitous moments again, the happy accidents, like when I stabbed the drawer, then shake it off. It was actually stuck. I was starting to go and it wasn't gonna go, so I ramped it up and just angrily flicked it off of there, which really worked, because then he's really after her. So the tables, I would say that part of it was superfun to do. But think of that as almost a reverse tidal wave. Usually you get chased by something and you run away. What I'm doing is I'm ripping away her hiding spots. So once again, I'm exposing her. Will's dead. Her ally is gone. Tables are gone. Where are you gonna hide now? So the psychology of it was "I'm gonna get you, but I'm just gonna rip you down first."

When she steals the van and we do that whole sequence, we did that practically. We built a platform even with the dashboard of the van, but there's a very short windshield height. I was on the platform and had a couple of little blocks to push off of. I can brace myself, and we drove in at like forty-five miles an hour and hit the brakes on the mark. I duck to my head and got spit out, and I'm totally blind going out the window. Recover in the air, roll up, and the whole thing of rolling up, sitting up, standing up is all still in the same shot.

This is another thing like the reaction I got with the kids at the gate. When she hit me and we went down the hill, the impact of her hitting me was onstage. We had a van up on a riser, kind of a big platform, and they got me ready. Again, I was about twenty-five to thirty feet away. They thought I was gonna stand on the platform and pop up into the windshield. They rolled cameras, and I took off running and leaped. I slammed into her windshield right at her face, and she jumped back, and that's what you need. I didn't tell her; I just did it. You get a much better, honest reaction out of her. It all works better, and it's also much more of an impact that she slammed me. Just to pop up and kind of smack into the windshield is not gonna look very powerful. You gotta come at it with a little force.

Getting pinned by the van we were trying to figure out. There was a crane that was holding the van up, and they're trying to figure out how I am gonna roll into this spot and guarantee that this van lands where it's supposed to and doesn't smack me. So what I did, again because of experience, I said shoot it backwards, this will flip the film. So I acted backwards from when I got pinned. I do a reaction arch, and then I bend forward. They yank the van, and I roll out. Flip the film. I figured out what my action was, what it would be to get to that spot smoothly, and we could shoot all the lead-ups to that spot smoothly. What do I need for this shot? It's like this last little bit hit here, how would I act? I'd land this way, draped. The thing hits me; I arch up like it broke my back. That's the shot. So do all those motions in reverse and yank the van away, and you know the placement is gonna be perfect every time because we placed it where we needed it. Then you just flip the film.

AG: That's incredibly impressive.

Chris Durand: Coming from a physical background, I wanna have things smooth, as safe as possible, as easy as possible, as predictable as possible. There's a shot where she sees me in the store window, camera flips around, and it's Adam Arkin. They were trying to figure out how to get the effect shot here. I say, "Stand Adam next to me just off my shoulder." You see me in the reflection as soon as the camera flipped. I ducked. They whip around and they land on Adam, who wasn't in the reflection because he's off set from me. It's what you would call a cowboy switch. If you think about the old westerns, you'd see someone come flying out the second-story window of the saloon, roll off the roof, and fall behind the horse trough, and then pop up. The stunt guy would do all the beginning, disappear behind the horse trough, and the actor would pop up, and you believe that he did it, right? So it's the same thing. It was just a switch, but that's just years of experience from knowing how to do this the simple way, because they were starting to get in their heads about how we're gonna pull this effect off, and it's like it isn't an effect.

AG: You're at the van; you're pinned. The moment where you stick your hand out for her to take your hand was one that caught many viewers by surprise, the emotional connection between the two of them. Was that scripted?

Chris Durand: This is where Steve let me do a little bit of what I wanted, but it was scripted in terms of reaching out. In terms of how I did it, he kind of let me do what I thought was right. Let me back up on you a little bit. In the original script, there's the description of his eyes—the darkest eyes, the blackest eyes, the Devil's eyes, something like that. Then, in this one, you can see my eyes on the close-ups. I'm a California kid with blue eyes, which doesn't exactly match that description. But there's a couple of reasons that that choice was made. The first is when we come face-to-face in the window, that doesn't work if you don't have an emotional connection between me and Jamie. That scene doesn't work if I had blacked-out eyes. It's freaky in a different way but here is much more meaningful because it's like, "Oh, hey, sis, what's going on?" If you give it that human touch, that's much more impactful, in my mind.

One of the discussions early on, backing up even further, was "Do you tuck the mask in or leave it untucked?" I always feel that if it's untucked, I want to grab it, lift it up, and see who's under there. But if it's tucked in, you're walking the razor-thin line between Michael as an entity and Michael as a person. You're somewhere in between.

So seeing the eyes for the face-to-face is very important. Same at the end. That scene doesn't work on a couple of levels if we don't have that connection. I had to play that on three levels, and it actually worked on all three, so it's probably my proudest moment actingwise in that film. We knew before we started *H2O* that they were going to carry the franchise forward, and they knew they needed a device to say it wasn't Michael, which was "We're gonna do the switch with the paramedic." You can't have blacked-out eyes if I somehow switch with the paramedic. How would he have blacked-out eyes? Logistically, it doesn't work. I'm supposed to be at that moment a paramedic who's got his mouth taped shut. He's just gone through this trauma saying, "What the hell's going on? Help me." I'm supposed to be Michael, who just got sense knocked into him, saying, "Oh my gosh, what have I done all these years?" Forgive me," reaching out and then, "Just touch me and I'll finish it." It had to include all of this as an undertone. So seeing the eyes and having that connection with her had to happen, because if you look at her reaction to everything, she's torn between "This is my brother" and "Hell, no." I go through this little arc right there, and she goes through a little arc right there because she doesn't want to kill her brother. She wants to believe that he can be reformed in that regard at that moment. Obviously we know what she did.

AG: So it was known by all that the franchise would carry on when you were filming?

Chris Durand: The deal as I understood it was that Jamie wanted to finish Michael and finish a trilogy. If you watch *H2O* as the third in a trilogy, that's what was intended, taking me back to my original story about how I got this role and they said, "We're not gonna reference what came before," but they meant "what came between." They meant *Halloween 4*, *5* and *6*. I thought they meant everything, so I never watched anything. But this was always intended as the third in a trilogy and to finish it. Moustapha and company were not going to kill the franchise, so they came up with a device to carry the franchise forward and still allow her to have what she wanted for this one. It was the only way she was gonna do the film and the only way that they were gonna let that happen at the end of the film, because again, it's business. They weren't gonna give up the franchise.

Interview: Robert Zappia (Writer, *Halloween H20: 20 Years Later*)

This conversation was conducted through email.
AG: How did you come to be involved with the seventh *Halloween* film?

Robert Zappia: At the time, my career was focused on television, where I contributed to sitcoms, notably *Home Improvement* and a brief stint on a show featuring David Chapelle, *Buddies*. In between these projects, I pursued my passion for film writing, creating a speculative sci-fi script titled *Population Zero*. My aspiration was always to break into the feature film industry, so I consistently used these breaks to craft new scripts, hoping for a breakthrough. Although *Population Zero* never found a buyer, it succeeded in drawing the attention of Richard Potter, an executive at Dimension Films. Subsequently, my agent set up a meeting with Richard at the Miramax/Dimension office. I recall a lengthy wait in the lobby, nearly an hour, which almost led me to abandon the meeting. These general meetings had often ended in mere compliments about my writing, but something told me to stay. When Richard finally appeared, he was apologetic about the delay. We instantly connected as we discussed my script. Richard came across as a genuine, down-to-earth executive, a rarity in the industry. He mentioned they were looking for someone to write *Halloween 7*, intended for direct-to-home video release. Being an ardent fan of the original *Halloween* series, the prospect of contributing to such a renowned franchise, irrespective of its release format, was an opportunity I couldn't pass up. I was told by Richard Potter that I would have to meet with Moustapha Akkad along with a few other writers who would pitch their idea to Moustapha and producer Paul Freeman. They would then decide who to hire based on the initial pitches. So I set about coming up with a pitch in June of 1996. Having seen Moustapha's name on screen for so many years, it was a thrill (and quite surreal) to be sitting across from him pitching an idea for *Halloween 7*. Moustapha looked like he stepped out of a time machine. He was impeccably dressed (a sport coat with patched elbows), with a pipe in hand, sitting in a high-back leather chair, salt-and-pepper hair neatly combed. And he had this great smile—a very subtle, wry smile. It sounds cliché, but he had a twinkle in his eye when he smiled. I pitched to Moustapha, Paul Freeman, and Moustapha's son, Malek (who was a student at USC Cinema School at the time). I was incredibly nervous, but I had prepared a brief document to help me through the nerves! I think it was within a week that I heard I got the writing assignment.

AG: The film prior to yours, *Halloween*: *The Curse of Michael Myers*, has a reputation for last-minute rewrites, an increased amount of studio involvement, and nobody being truly happy with the final product. What directions or notes did you receive pertaining to the sixth film before you started writing your initial script?

Robert Zappia: When I began working on *Halloween H20*, there wasn't much discussion about the specifics of *Halloween*: *The Curse of Michael Myers*. The focus was more on streamlining the story and returning to the roots of the original films. The intention from the start was to drop the complex plotlines like the druid cult and curse of Thorn story, which were considered too far removed from the original concept of Michael Myers. I haven't had the chance to watch the producers' cut of *Halloween: The Curse of Michael Myers*, which many claim far surpasses the version released in theaters. Personally, I wasn't particularly fond of the theatrical release. To me, it ventured too far into camp territory, with a plot teetering on the ridiculous (involving elements like the Man in Black and genetic experiments), not to mention Michael Myers's less-than-intimidating physical appearance. With *Two Faces of Evil*, I saw an opportunity to help right the ship.

AG: Your first script had nothing to do with Laurie Strode returning. Where did you as a writer want to take the series prior to the announcement of Laurie's return?

Robert Zappia: My original pitch for *Halloween 7* was to set the movie in an all-girl boarding school. The movie starts when Michael is found dead in a maximum-security penitentiary. He's transported to the local morgue. As you can imagine, things didn't go well for the mortician. And soon Michael is out and about wreaking havoc on the students at the boarding school. I believe it was producer Paul

Freeman who had the idea of adding a copycat killer to the fray who was captured and served the same purpose as Hannibal Lecter in *Silence of the Lambs*. The draft *Two Faces of Evil*—the two faces being Michael Myers and the copycat killer—evolved from there. Before it became *H20* with Jamie Lee Curtis reprising her role, I really wanted to make a film that I would enjoy as a fan of the original. I wanted to try and recapture as best I could what John Carpenter had in the first Halloween. It had the lowest budget of any of them, and yet, in my mind, it was the scariest of them all. Carpenter couldn't rely on big-budget effects; he didn't have unlimited setups and unlimited shoot days. He had to boil down the story and characters to their most primal level. Ultimately, the boarding school afforded me a "micro-Haddonfield" where I could let Michael Myers loose and focus on the inventiveness rather than the goriness of the murders. And the copycat element added a distinct story device that added a layer of complexity to the script. It also afforded me the opportunity to bring in a character to fill the shoes of Dr. Loomis (as impossibly large shoes to fill as they were!).

AG: How did the story evolve once Kevin Williamson was brought in? What was your working relationship like with him?

Robert Zappia: Rewinding to the early stages, before Jamie Lee Curtis's involvement, I had finalized either the first or perhaps the second version of *Two Faces of Evil*. It wasn't long after that when I received a call from my agent conveying Bob Weinstein's excitement about the script and his desire to meet. During our meeting, Bob revealed that he had personally discussed the project with Jamie Lee Curtis, who had agreed to join for the film's twentieth anniversary. He expressed enthusiasm about the boarding school setting and sought my input on integrating Jamie Lee's character into this context. I proposed making her character a teacher or headmistress, which led to the initial draft, titled *Halloween: Blood Ties*, followed by versions named *Halloween: The Revenge of Laurie Strode*. The latter title was a nod to my fondness for *Star Wars*, recalling when *Return of the Jedi* was initially titled *Revenge of the Jedi*. Surprisingly, I was unaware of Kevin Williamson's involvement and his treatment until months after I submitted my revised drafts. The details of what Dimension communicated to Kevin about my work or the existence of my drafts were unclear to me; they might have even suggested the boarding school concept to him. A dispute arose over the script's credit. Dimension Films was keen on accrediting Kevin with the story. This led to arbitration by the Writers Guild of America, where an independent panel anonymously reviewed all submissions—outlines, drafts, etc.—to determine the final credits. This process is crucial to ensure unbiased decisions in a field where everyone has a stake and opinion on credit allocation. From the get-go, the original pitch and its evolution were crafted by myself, shaped with insights from Moustapha Akkad, Paul Freeman, and Malek Akkad. Kevin Williamson's involvement came at a pivotal time. By then, Jamie Lee Curtis was already attached, and the script had undergone significant changes. Kevin, known for his success with *Scream*, was more involved as a producer. Our interactions were limited but productive—primarily a single, significant notes call. His influence steered the script toward a contemporary horror sensibility while maintaining the classic *Halloween* ethos and brought a fresh perspective, especially given his success with redefining the horror genre with *Scream*.

AG: Would you like to have had Jamie Lloyd mentioned or acknowledged or do you think the story works better ignoring the films involving that character?

Robert Zappia: In the early drafts, acknowledging Jamie Lloyd was part of the story. There was even a draft where Laurie Strode's alcoholism was attributed to her grief over Jamie's death. However, when it was decided to focus more directly on Laurie's story with Michael Myers and omit references to *Halloween 4* through six, that aspect was dropped. Although part of me wishes we could have included it, the final script benefited from a more streamlined narrative that honed in on Laurie's personal battle.

AG: Are there ideas that you had at any point of scripting that you still wish would have made it to screen in this film or a subsequent sequel?

Robert Zappia: There were several creative ideas in the early drafts that didn't make the final cut but still resonate with me. These ideas, I believe, could have added unique layers to the narrative and potentially could have been explored in future sequels, Expanding on the concepts that didn't make it to the screen:

1. The gymnasium with a hidden pool: This particular concept was inspired by a scene from the classic film *It's A Wonderful Life*. The idea was to stage a climactic confrontation between Laurie and Michael in a gymnasium, which would then dramatically reveal a pool underneath. The tension would have peaked as Michael crashes the dance, and Laurie, in a desperate struggle, impales him with a javelin. He would fall into the pool, and the floor would close above him. I envisioned this scene as a mix of suspense and a grandiose set piece, a nod to the theatricality that can exist within the horror genre.
2. The high-stakes bus chase: Another concept involved Laurie driving a bus full of students, trying to escape from Michael Myers. The bus crashes and ends up teetering on the edge of a cliff, creating a nail-biting scenario. Laurie's character would have been pushed to new limits, showcasing her resilience and bravery as she ensures the safety of all students before the bus eventually falls off the cliff with Michael hanging from the bumper. This scene was designed to be an adrenaline-pumping sequence, blending horror with high-octane action.
3. Helicopter decapitation: In a draft, we toyed with an ending involving a helicopter decapitating Michael Myers in a spectacular fashion. This idea was born from a desire to give Michael an over-the-top, seemingly definitive end. It was our *Mission: Impossible*-style ending, albeit too extravagant for the production budget at the time.
4. Exploration of Laurie Strode's psychology: In earlier drafts, there was a deeper exploration of Laurie Strode's psychological trauma and how she coped with the horrors of her past. This included more detailed exposition of her alcoholism and its roots in her experiences (giving up Jamie for adoption, for example). I believe that delving deeper into Laurie's psyche would have added more depth to her character and provided a more nuanced portrayal of her struggles and resilience.

Each of these ideas, while not making the final cut, represented avenues to explore different facets of fear and suspense. They could have introduced new elements to the *Halloween* series, maintaining its horror roots while expanding its narrative scope and stylistic boundaries.

AG: Coming out of *H20*, what direction would you like to have seen the series go in?

Robert Zappia: I generally hesitate to critique the work of others, understanding the immense challenge of harmonizing various creative perspectives in filmmaking. However, I must admit feeling a sense of letdown with how *Resurrection* seemingly squandered the narrative momentum we had carefully built up in *H20*. Under my agreement, I was granted the initial opportunity to propose a concept for *Halloween 8*. Aiming to keep the storyline authentic and concise, my pitch involved the capture and incarceration of Michael Myers. This approach was designed not only to maintain continuity but also to reunite actors from the franchise's history. Unfortunately, this direction was set aside in favor of what ultimately became *Resurrection*.

AG: In writing the ending, did you know that it wasn't really Michael Myers who got his head chopped off?

Robert Zappia: Short answer: yes. Long answer: besides typical minor creative differences, the biggest issue between the two camps was to kill or not to kill Michael Myers. Myers was not only Akkad's bread and butter, but I think he truly had a fondness for the character, whereas the other camp (Jamie/Dimension) wanted to put a proper end to the "trilogy." Personally, I preferred the idea of Laurie Strode killing Myers. In terms of story, it was the ideal conclusion to the franchise. And I knew, as a fan, that's what I would love to see. What convinced Moustapha to go along with the decapitation scene was the explanation that Michael had done the ol' switcheroo with a security guard and, maybe more importantly, that Jamie Lee agreed to do a cameo in the sequel to *H20*. It was also important to me to show that fear must be faced and dealt with—you can avoid it for some time, but ultimately you have to confront it or it will consume you. In *H20*, Laurie confronts her fear and ultimately triumphs over it. It sounds cliché, but in the end good wins over evil. Laurie slays her Goliath. On a side note, when I saw the film on opening night with a sold-out crowd, that moment where Laurie Strode takes an axe to Myers got an enormous cheer that gave me chills. In my mind, that was and forever will have been Michael Myers.

AG: What are some highlights from your *H20* experience?

Robert Zappia: I have great memories of visiting the set. It was quite surreal. I remember at one point standing on the set between takes and having Chris Durand dressed in full Michael Myers attire, including having the mask on, approach me. He leaned in and said something to the effect that he was a writer too and asked if I'd read a script he'd written. I was being pitched a movie by Michael Myers. It doesn't get any more surreal than that! And who would say no? Jamie Lee was also so gracious. She asked if I'd seen any of the dailies. When I said I hadn't, she invited me to watch some of them in her bungalow. Another surreal and very memorable moment!

I first saw the complete film at the premiere in Westwood. My wife and I sat behind Jamie Lee Curtis and her parents, Tony Curtis and Janet Leigh! Watching the film was (and still is) one of the highlights

Robert & Jamie Lee Curtis. Image courtesy of Robert Zappia

of my career. I was extremely proud of the end result. And all that everyone in that theater contributed to the final product!

AG: What was your biggest goal in working on the twentieth anniversary installment of the series?

Robert Zappia: First and foremost, my biggest goal was not to be an embarrassment to the franchise. I wanted to honor the purity of the characters Carpenter and Hill created in the original—*Halloween* was unencumbered by twisted plot devices, exploding heads, gruesome kills, etc. . . . It was horror in its most base and raw form. I figured if I could capture some of the same elements that made Carpenter's *Halloween* so frightening, then it would connect with horror fans old and new. Fear is timeless. As long as humans have roamed the Earth, we've been afraid of the dark, of the predator, of being the hunted . . . Michael Myers (the Shape) embodies all those fears. I think that's why Michael Myers has remained relevant for thirty-five years. And as long as future writers and filmmakers understand what makes him truly terrifying, he will remain relevant for another thirty-five years. For example, there's an important distinction that has been missed in some of the films; it's not the brutality of the killings that make the Shape so frightening, it's the inevitability that you will be killed if you are his target. He is certain that he will succeed. He is deliberate. He is patient—after all, how many serial killers can wait 364 days between killing sprees? That is what makes him so terrifying. Like Laurie Strode crouched in the bedroom closet—there is no escape.

AG: Do you recall what role, if any, the producers behind the original film, specifically John Carpenter, Debra Hill, and Moustapha Akkad, played in terms of the overall story and concept?

Robert Zappia: Unfortunately, neither Debra Hill or John Carpenter were involved in the film. The original pitch and subsequent versions were crafted by myself (along with input from Moustapha, Paul Freeman, and Malek Akkad). Later, Kevin Williamson was brought aboard as a producer. I had one notes call with him on a first or second draft of the film. Moustapha was heavily involved with the concept. He really had an affinity for the franchise and Michael. He was incredibly protective, in the best possible way, of the characters and the franchise as a whole. A funny story regarding John Carpenter: I went to a live concert of his in 2018 where there was a backstage meet and greet. I put my *H20* DVD cover down for him to sign. This was the dialogue exchange we had. John Carpenter: "I had absolutely nothing to do with this one." Me: "I know. Because I wrote it." He turns for the first time and looks at me, surprised. Not sure he heard right. John Carpenter: "You wrote it?" Me: "Yes, I'm Robert Zappia. And my biggest regret is that you had absolutely nothing to do with it." He smiled (also for the first time) and signed the DVD. Here's a picture (taken before our exchange).

Robert & John Carpenter. Image courtesy of Robert Zappia

Interview: Brad Loree (Michael Myers, *Halloween: Resurrection*)

AG: How did this job come to be?

Brad Loree: I was working on a low-budget television show for Fox called *Los Luchadores*. The protagonists were Mexican wrestlers by day and crime fighters by night. For the first eight episodes, I was the stunt double for the lead guy. Then my coordinator went off to do a feature, and he convinced production to let me also be the stunt coordinator. So for the five last episodes, I was the stunt coordinator and the stunt double. It was very lucrative. Every Friday, I went up to the accountant's office to get paid, and the checks were between eight and ten grand a week. We finished the first season, thirteen episodes total, and we knew we were certainly coming back for a second season. But you never count on anything, because in the film industry, you haven't got the job until the sixth check is in the bank.

When you have a break between seasons, you go out and pursue other work because something better might come along or you can keep a couple of things in the chamber, things to work on. A guy named Brian Knight that I was working with went to interview with the *Halloween* people, knowing full well that he wasn't going to take the job. As a professional courtesy, because it's all about networking, he goes and sits down with them, and I guess during his interview, they mentioned they weren't sure yet who they were gonna use for Michael Myers. They didn't have a Canadian stunt coordinator yet either. Back in the day they used to always match a Canadian stunt coordinator with the American coordinator because Americans come up and they don't really know who's who in Vancouver. So they need somebody. The Canadian stunt coordinator is rarely more than a booking agent and a coffee fetcher. Brian said to them, "You should talk to Brad Loree," and he mentioned that I was coordinating now.

I'm driving in my car one day, and the phone rang. It was Tracy Long, the production manager of *Halloween: Resurrection.* She says something about Michael Myers and asks me how tall I am. I'm six foot two and a half. She says, "Perfect, can you come in tomorrow to meet the executives?" Because I'm driving, I only half paid attention to her. I thought they were looking for a stunt double for Mike Myers, the guy from Toronto, Mr. Austin Powers. I thought his career must be taking a turn into the fucking tank. I went in the next day, and everybody was already there, already hired. It was kind of like hiring the Michael Myers performer was an afterthought. I did the walk for the director Rick Rosenthal a few times. He gave me some direction, and I did it three or four times, and he turned to Paul Freeman, the producer, and said, "Yeah, he should be fine." Paul tells me that I'm the first guy they've looked at, and they have to at least consider other people. But if I get the role, they're gonna have to fly me down to LA to cast my head so they can build the mask around the shape of my head. I said, "Wait a minute, I gotta go all the way to LA just to double some actor? "That's when Paul says, "You're not going to double some guy; you're gonna be the guy."

The two horror films that I've always loved are the first two *Halloween* films. The first *Halloween* is an absolute fucking classic. It wasn't overly bloody, gory, or violent, like other films at the time. When I was twenty years old, I dated this girl, and all she wanted to watch was horror films. She was cute. So of course, it's all we watched. When I broke up with her, I thought at least I'd never have to watch a horror film again. And then everybody and their dog a week later was talking about this *Halloween* film. I was like, "I don't care. I don't wanna hear about it." My cousin Diana said she enjoyed it, and I respected her opinion. So anyway, when they told me I was gonna be Michael Myers as opposed to being the stunt double, that's when I went, "Oh, that's different." So I passed on *Los Luchadores* season two, which actually got canceled in the third episode of the second season. I took the Michael Myers job, go down to LA, and Malek Akkad picked me up at the airport and took me to the Cinema Secrets Shop, and they mold my head, which cracked me up because we do all that in Vancouver now. Americans just weren't aware of it at the time, I guess. We did a week of camera testings and wardrobe fittings. It was pretty much the only movie I've been on from the very beginning to the very end.

We shot for five weeks and then a week of reshoots. It was just a dream come true. As a kid, I always wanted to be an actor. It's just that when I fell in love with Bruce Lee at thirteen, I joined the local karate school, and the instructor, Tony Morelli, went on to become a world champion kickboxer, and he dragged me into the stunt world.

So that's where my connections were. I'm very camera shy. I got a lot of compliments and kudos when I was in acting class, though. It's definitely one of the jewels in my crown because it was six weeks of fun. I just loved all the actors. I got along with everybody, and I spent a significant amount of moments with everybody.

AG: You mentioned Rick Rosenthal. What was he like as a director?

Brad Loree: I love Rick. I call him Coach because being Canadian, I really admire the fact that Rick likes hockey. I think he has even played hockey, and I think I started calling him Coach more after we did the film, though. I really liked Rick. We only twice had any kind of misunderstanding, but I really got along with him. I understand that Busta was a little tardy to set, but I wasn't around, wasn't in a lot of scenes with Busta. When they didn't need Michael Myers, and they never needed me as a stunt coordinator because they had Donna Keegan, I was in my trailer. That is what stunt people do when you're not needed. You stay out of the way. To get back to your question, I love Rick, and I always look forward to seeing him at the conventions. He's been to a couple now. I don't know if his memories of me are as fond as my memories are of him. I don't know if you've ever seen the behind-the-scenes on the *Halloween: Resurrection* DVD, but he's talking about me, and I don't know why, but he made some comment like, "Brad was obviously somebody you don't mess with," in reference to my size. Maybe he knew that I got into the business because of my martial arts, I don't know.

AG: In the beginning of the movie, there's that classic scene with Jamie Lee Curtis where you're busting through that door and then you move up to the roof. Walk me through that sequence and working with Jamie Lee.

Brad Loree: Whenever the props guy or the set decorator scores something to make it weak, you never really know how weak it's gonna be. You don't want to go through the door and have it look like a papier-mâché, but you also don't want to go there and have to fight it. There's no real science to how exact the strength is gonna be. I think I went through the door twice. They always have more than one prop setting for you. Going through the door, I went through it assuming it was gonna be a little bit stronger than I was anticipating, but it was perfect. I think we did it the second time, though. The first one sometimes turns out to be a rehearsal, right? Then you get a feel for it, and then you nail it on the second one. That's quite common, really.

Then, when I was in the room coming at Jamie Lee with the knife and she hits me with the lamp, I had what we call an armadillo, which is a Motocross pad, and she was afraid to hurt me of course. So she hit me with the thing, and it felt fine. I told Donna that Jamie Lee could hit me much harder than that if she wants to. We shot it twice, but I'm not sure which take we used. Chasing her in the stairwell, we had time between setups. People don't realize unless you work on a film how much time it is. The lighting has to be right. The framing has to be right. The camera has to be right. Then the performers are supposed to get it right on the first take, right? I spent a lot of time just sitting and chatting with Jamie Lee. I was really kind of starstruck, because it's Jamie Lee Curtis. I was just glad to have the mask on, because it made me less shy. She was in town for four days. Malek Akkad was down in LA and getting my mask finished. He told me, and I don't know how they fucking calculate this shit, but he said that Jamie owed them thirty seconds with no dialogue. She didn't owe them more dialogue, but she owed them thirty seconds of screen time. She said to them, "Whatever you can shoot in a weekend, I'll do." She came up on Thursday, shot for half of the day, shot all day Friday, all day Saturday, and half of the Sunday. She bought everybody a little crew gift. She was really sweet and kind to myself and my girlfriend. She had us hang out in her trailer with her.

I'll tell you about getting up on the roof. If you watch the movie closely, you'll notice that my hair looks like I'm in a fucking hair band. Then, when I stepped through the door onto the roof, my hair was combed back and perfect. Wearing the mask, I could only see my hair on the shadow on the wall. I remember thinking my hair was too puffy. But I did not want to speak up. I didn't want to be that guy. I'm not in charge of hair. They are. Next time you watch the movie, you'll see how fluffy my hair looks. Then, as I get on the roof, it's all combed back the way it was supposed to be. Then we did the thing on the roof. Donna, I have to give her big, big credit. She was very adamant about them not leaving me hung upside down for too long. I don't think I was ever upside down for even a minute because she said if you hang too long, you end up bursting blood vessels in your eyes, which is nothing major, but they don't want a Michael Myers that looks like he's drunk, right? So we shot that scene with Jamie, like I said, in two half days and two full days. She was terrific to work with, very professional. I remember Rick was trying to get her to do one scene or do some kind of dialogue, and she refused to do it. I think they wanted to use this snippet for advertising or something. I don't know what the controversy was, but this went on for like five minutes. He's trying to convince her, and she said, "I'm not doing that. Let's move on." She stood her ground. I don't really understand what the problem is, but I always admired her for standing her ground. That's sort of behind-the-scenes, hush-hush. Not that it was any big deal. But it was the one time I saw them kind of butt heads. It wasn't a major thing or like a big blowout, but for whatever reason, she couldn't say that dialogue or shoot that scene.

AG: You mentioned Malek Akkad. Was Moustapha Akkad a presence on set? This was the last *Halloween* film shot before he passed away.

Brad Loree: Moustapha was there at the beginning. The first two or three shots that we did, they had black mesh in the eyes. I heard somebody suggested that they had done that previously, so of course they thought they would do it again. Moustapha was there, and he said, "No, no, no, I want to be able to see his eyes. I want them to be able to see that there's a human being behind those eyes." So what they did is they took the mesh out, and they just blacked my eyes so that there was kind of a contrast through the mask. I felt like I had to go up and say something to Moustapha. I went up and said, "Mr. Akkad, I just wanna tell you that although I'm not a huge horror fan, I am a gigantic fan of the very first *Halloween*." He put his hand on my face very gently and said, "It would have been that much better if you had been in it," and it almost makes me cry to think about today. He made me feel like the star when I talked to him.

AG: Let's get into the Busta Rhymes fight scene.

Brad Loree: The first dozen people that came up to me at my first-ever convention tore a strip off me because I got beat up by Busta. I said, "Guys, I'm a stuntman in a mask. I do what the script tells me." Being a martial artist, I don't care how superstrong you are. If somebody hits you with a good front kick, you're gonna fly backwards like I did. Shooting the scene where I go through the window, that fucking window was only about a quarter inch wide on either side of my shoulders, and they want me to take like three strong strides and throw myself through the window. I had to run backward, and in the rehearsal, I kept clipping the left side and hitting the right side and stopping dead. But we kind of dialed in, because I think we only shot that once. I think it's a really neat scene, because they had the camera wrapped around me because he's been strangled with the cable. So they even used part of the camera angle as I was going through the window, which I thought was really cool. Once he ends up out on the roof and he comes off the roof and falls and ends up hanging at the end of the cable, and it looks like he's hanging himself. My dad was there that day, and he wasn't prepared for how real it was gonna look. They had me in the harness on the table, and I had to roll off from about ten feet. When I got down there, I think I did some twitching just to make it look good. That was a neat scene. I really liked the way Rick shot it.

I didn't have a lot of time to chat with Busta. I do remember that every morning in the trailer, he would give me the most genuine giant bear hug. The scene where he's following me as Michael Myers thinking that I'm the other guy, when we were rehearsing, I laughed so hard I ended up doubling over. I couldn't help it. He was so funny. I just thought it was the most hilarious thing. He was awesome. I got very close to his acting coach, Tracy. She was a very sweet lady and gave me a copy of her book. I remember when 9/11 happened, I was really scared for Busta and Tracy because I knew they lived in downtown New York. They were the only friends I had that lived in downtown New York. We were anticipating seeing them again for reshoots. I remember when I saw Tracy, telling her how scared I was for them. She thought that was so sweet.

AG: Any other favorite memories you have from the set that you care to share?

Brad holds a knife to Daisy McCrackin's throat. Image courtesy of Brad Loree

Brad Loree: The first day at work, when we were doing camera tests, which I had never experienced before, Bianca [Kajlich] was there, and we hadn't met yet. Even though I was not even in costume yet, she screamed and ran away from me, genuinely afraid of me. I don't know if it was part of her process or what. She was training herself to be afraid of me but literally to the point where she ended up saying, "Okay, I have to hold your hand and walk with you so I can get over this fear." We got along great. That was a really fun memory.

Another bittersweet memory I have now when I watch the film is the first person I kill after I killed Jamie Lee, the kid that's setting up the cameras in the house, Charley. His name was Brad Sihvon. He was a local actor that I knew from around the neighborhood, and we played hockey against each other. A couple of years after we shot the movie, Brad and I ended up being roommates with another guy for a year. In 2004, the film industry slowed down in Vancouver. We all went from working all the time to hardly working at all. He got massively depressed, and he ended up going east out to the next province over to get a plumbing ticket with his brother just to have something to fall back on. But he was so depressed and got hooked on painkillers and vodka. He ended up dying. I watched that scene today. I get a little emotional because he was such a great guy, and I really miss him.

Cutting off Katee Sackhoff's head was such a realistic-looking scene. I have a very special love for Katee. She made us all gifts. She took a bunch of pictures of us all and cut the heads out and put them in this coffee travel mug. She made that for all the actors. I think she's a great actor and just a great person. I remember sitting in the trailer smoking cigars at three in the morning with the kids, the two young guys that were in the room texting Bianca's character. I spent so much time on that set, and when you're between shots, with all the time between shots, you're just hanging out with those guys, bonding. Then, the last day of shooting, at lunchtime we turned the lights off, and Rick had pretty much the first ten or fifteen minutes edited, all the stuff Jamie did. We're all sitting there watching it, and I'm holding hands with my girlfriend. There's the scene where he's walking down the tunnel, and she's squeezing my hand because it's Michael Myers. I remember starting to feel a little bit of that old-school fear of Michael Myers. Then I went "Wait a minute. That's me."

Interview: David Geddes (Director of Photography, *Halloween Resurrection*)

AG: How did this job come to be?

David Geddes: One of the first things people want to know is "How did you get attached to the project?" My agent knew Rick Rosenthal from previous productions, and she felt that the two of us would work well together. I was one of several directors of photography that Rick interviewed for *Halloween Resurrection*, and I guess we did get along, since he hired me to DP the project.

AG: What kind of creative discussions did you have with Rick prior to filming? Any discussions about style or influences?

David Geddes: Rick and I had many creative discussions during prep. Some influences came from previous *Halloween* films, but during these discussions we decided to start the story with a more saturated color palette, specifically in the blue and amber range. As the story unfolds through Act 1 and into Act 2, we started pulling back on the color saturation, working with more neutral tones, and Michael

Myers rained down horror on our heroes.

AG: *Halloween Resurrection* came at a time when the found-footage subgenre was in its infancy, as was internet streaming. Reality TV also wasn't the juggernaut that it would go on to be. In many ways, this was significantly more modern than other films in the franchise. How did being at the forefront of trends to come impact your work here?

David Geddes: The reality TV aspect of *Resurrection*'s script was a fun experience. It introduced audiences both to the concept of the internet, especially as a group activity, and also to the concept of reality shows, particularly the ones that cheated.

Being on the forefront of internet streaming technology for the time required research and testing to find the most efficient small, wearable cameras and recording systems for our heroes. The capture hardware and software needed to produce images that would pass quality-control requirements for feature film projection—not an easy task at the time. That "leading edge technology" we used more than twenty years ago is of course completely antiquated now, as are the cameras. Today you can buy a camera not much bigger than a quarter that generates film quality images.

AG: What was Rick Rosenthal like to work with as a director? Did his experience working on *Halloween II* come into play at all?

David Geddes: Rick Rosenthal and I developed a great working relationship and friendship while shooting *Resurrection*. And let's face it: horror is a lot of fun to plan and shoot. You get to reimagine and recreate your most chilling childhood memories, of shadows under the bed and evil lurking in hallway closets. Shooting this film was a great experience. I don't remember that Rick's work with *Halloween II* specifically came into play with *Resurrection*, but certainly his approach would have been affected by that experience.

AG: When you think back on this film, which shots have stuck with you the most over the years? What are you most proud of from your work here?

David Geddes: A few scenes have really stuck in my mind over the years. About fifteen minutes in, we have just witnessed Michael Myers "supposedly" killing Jamie Lee Curtis. We cut to Michael walking into the clown's room and handing the clown the bloody knife. The clown then starts to dictate Michael Myers's history. That continues over the back of Michael as he walks in an underground hallway. The clown continues his dictation, letting the world know that Michael is definitely back.

AG: Any on-set memories you care to share?

David Geddes: One memory I have involves a night scene that never made it into the movie. We watch through Michael Myers's POV as he is walking in a campsite. He comes across a tent, and on the tent wall you see the shadows of a couple having sex. While we were shooting this scene, one of the producers said, "I don't know that this is ever going to make it into the movie. It's too pornographic." I remember thinking, "Here we are shooting a slasher movie, and filming the shadows of a couple having sex is wrong?" Michael lets the couple live, but he steals their red Camaro. The Camaro appears in a couple of later scenes, but the audience can't appreciate the significance, since the campsite scene was cut, and we didn't see Michael steal it.

AG: The film had a cliffhanger ending, revealing that Michael was in fact still alive. Were there any discussions about doing another film or ideas being discussed for the future of the franchise?

David Geddes: We reshot some of the ending of the film specifically to set up the Michael Myers body bag that ends up in the morgue. As the doctor unzips the body bag, revealing Michael's face, you just knew that he was going to be alive. The franchise needed to survive.

AG: How do you think the film holds up?

David Geddes: *Resurrection* has held up very well over the years, but with the antiquated internet footage, it really has become a period piece as well. It was cutting-edge at the time, introducing something that audiences were not familiar with and that hadn't become part of everyday life. Not anymore!

AG: Any additional stories you'd like to share?

David Geddes: There is also a great logistical story about scheduling the shoot. We were filming *Resurrection* in Vancouver, British Columbia. Unless you live here or have visited here in the early summer months, you wouldn't realize that at that time of the year, there are only about six hours of true night. That meant that we would only have six hours to shoot multiple exterior scenes each night. During prep, when I was doing my night-and-day breakdown, I realized that in order to accomplish all the night shooting in June, we would have to add weeks to the shooting schedule.

That wasn't going to happen, so the decision was made to build the exterior of the house onstage—and on a big stage—because we needed to build both Michael's house and the neighbor's houses on each side, plus the road in front of the house. Then we needed to add blue screen behind it to give the whole area some depth. So we had Michael Myers's house onstage to accommodate the night shoots, but naturally we also needed to shoot day exterior scenes in front of the house.

Normally that would not be a big deal, but the set was so enormous that in order to light it for day, we had to produce enough electrical power that we could have sent the DeLorean back to the future.

-CHAPTER 5- THE ZOMBIE ERA

Much like David Gordon Green's trilogy of *Halloween* films that followed, Rob Zombie's two *Halloween* films are divisive. Franchise continuity became a thing of the past in 1998 when *Halloween H20* brought Jamie Lee Curtis back to the role that had made her a star and all, but the first two films were seemingly forgotten by the powers that be. *Halloween Resurrection* (2002), the eighth film in the franchise, is widely regarded as the creative low point for the franchise. Fans were still invested in Michael Myers, but the series lacked an obvious future direction. Horror remakes were in high demand after 2003's *Texas Chainsaw Massacre* remake, and Dimension opted to follow the trend by remaking its genre classic, but with a highly creative director guaranteed to move the series in bold new directions.

Rob Zombie's two *Halloween* films, again like those of the David Gordon Green trilogy, have to be studied together. Zombie's first film is thirty minutes of his own vision, followed by an almost shot-by-shot remake of John Carpenter's classic. His second film is purely a product of his style and vision. Critics of Zombie's films argue that they indulge in excess and don't reflect the established *Halloween* style and tone. Fans of the films say that's the point. When you step back and take a mile-high view of the thirteen films in this franchise, the various timelines splinter in such a way that setting two films completely in their own bubble makes a strange kind of sense. Rob Zombie's two entries brought a grindhouse aesthetic to the franchise and augured a genre trend referred to as "elevated horror" [a subgenre that emphasizes complex, often psychological themes over gore and jump scares]—a phrase that wouldn't be coined until several years after Rob Zombie had left Haddonfield. Not only are the stories self-contained in Rob's two films, but the themes, motivations, and visual storytelling are also exclusive to Zombie's contribution to the franchise.

Clearly, Zombie was extremely familiar with the eight films that came before. That's not to say that he enjoyed them all, but he was obviously well-versed in them. One take on his two *Halloween* films is that Zombie was attempting to craft a more cohesive narrative and mythology in a franchise prone to changing its story on the fly. It's difficult to do that in the ninth and tenth film in a series, but it could be argued that he was successful. For example, the *Halloween* films had long wavered on what was supernatural and what was rooted in the natural world. *Halloween 6: The Curse of Michael Myers* attempts to create series continuity by mapping a well-thought-out supernatural approach, but it was ultimately neutered by the powers that be. Rob Zombie wasn't handcuffed by the studio, and he made it clear that his films and the character of Michael Myers were rooted in real-world trauma.

Getting ready to roll with Michael. Image courtesy of Phil Parmet

By backing away from the more paranormal explanations, Zombie limned a Michael Myers more like the serial killers of the seventies and eighties who had captured the attention of the nation. The thread of mental illness that runs through Zombie's *Halloween* films feel more relatable and therefore more frightening than most of the other films in the franchise. We weren't required to suspend belief nearly as often. Here Michael Myers is a child from a poor, violent household with a hypersexualized mother and sister. He took out his childhood trauma on everyone in sight. That's a story we see even today on the evening news. That particular brand of evil can lurk anywhere; it evokes the Shape in the original film, lurking in the shadows.

Halloween had long wavered on whether Michael's violence was sexual in nature or not. Certainly, compelling arguments could be made that Michael's motivation was somewhat sexual, although some filmmakers seemed to shy away from that idea. In the films before Zombie's, Michael Myers's mother is a nonfactor. She plays no role in the mythology. She's barely mentioned and has no apparent relevance to Michael's motivation. In Zombie's *Halloween*, we see that Michael has only his mother's love to help him cope with the trauma of growing up in a hugely dysfunctional family with a stepfather who's an abusive drunk. Despite the fact that his mother is a stripper, Michael sees her (and his baby sister) as innocent and pure, as visually represented by his mother appearing in white in his hallucinations in the second film. Yet her line of work can't help but complicate his vision of her. His older sister, Judith, is an overly sexualized teen who likely triggers lust in her younger brother. This is evident from the way Michael strokes her leg before killing her. Michael acts out on these feelings with his sister as well as Lynda and Annie, both undressed when he attacks them. Michael likely would kill even without this sexual repression, but it does trigger his unrelenting rage in Rob Zombie's films.

Most of the previous *Halloween* films embraced a less-is-more sentiment when it comes to gore. Visually however, the films are all over the place. Whereas *Halloween 4* attempted to recreate the Midwestern autumn-night aesthetic of the original, none of the other sequels chose to follow that template. *Halloween II* was set in a dark, dingy hospital, which informed the film's visual style. *Halloween II* was always intended to be distinct in every aspect from the previous two films. *Halloween 5* feels more European gothic. *Halloween: The*

Curse of Michael Myers is the most bipolar of all the films visually, ranging from Midwestern fall nights to nineties industrial music video. *Resurrection* reflected the found-footage craze. Rob Zombie brought a much grittier style to the franchise, evocative of his 2005 film, The Devil's Rejects, and the aesthetic of seventies and eighties grindhouse flicks; it was unsettling for longtime fans of the franchise, although perhaps it shouldn't have been. The series was constantly changing, so why was this visual departure any different? The increase in gore certainly was a change. Zombie didn't shy away from violence, which was par for the course in the genre as a whole at the time. It was just something different for this particular franchise.

The characterization of Laurie undergoes a substantial change. Particularly in Zombie's second film, Scout Taylor-Compton's Laurie is a far cry from Jamie Lee Curtis's portrayal of the character. Laurie in Rob's films is a young woman who can't deal with the trauma she's endured. Her life has been ruined by it, almost as it was just starting. She's going to therapy, has a job, and is surrounded by people who care about her, but she can't move past what's happened to her. It feels authentic. Her life was turned upside down by the discovery of the identity of her real family. Her blood brother goes on a violent rampage, resulting in the deaths of her adoptive parents and her friends, forcing her to fight for her own life. Nobody, especially a teenager, is going to move through that trauma quickly. Zombie's *Halloween II* is a film about trauma long before "trauma" became a buzzword in every movie ever, particularly in the horror genre.

That's not to say *Halloween* both before and after Zombie's films doesn't deal with trauma. *H20* famously does, and the David Gordon Green trilogy that followed does as well. The biggest difference is the execution. In Zombie's *Halloween II*, Scout Taylor-Compton's Laurie Strode explores how messy trauma can look. There are no illusions of control. Scout plays the trauma as primal. It's hard to look at. It's upsetting, but genuine. In a contrast I find deeply fascinating, trauma manifests externally for Scout's Laurie, whereas Danielle Harris's Annie Brackett internalizes her trauma.

In a sense, that's a great metaphor for the contrast between Rob's films and the rest of the franchise. Rob's *Halloween* films are bold, stylish, outside the box. Haddonfield looks different with Rob in town. For some, that's a good thing. For others, maybe not. These two films are beginning to get a second look, with critics and scholars becoming more vocal about their power, especially the second film. It's well documented that Rob Zombie had a tumultuous relationship with Harvey and Bob Weinstein and that his second *Halloween* film especially was a turbulent production. (The director's cut of Rob Zombie's *Halloween II*—the version he prefers—is now the more accessible version to purchase on home video) While the likelihood of Rob ever making his *Halloween III* is small, I can't help but wonder where he would've taken us. The haunting image of Scout Taylor-Compton in an all-white padded room after the mesmerizing scene in the cabin might be where we leave this thread of the *Halloween* narrative forever, which would be unfortunate, but it certainly leaves us room to dream.

Interview: Scout Taylor-Compton (Laurie Strode, Rob Zombie's *Halloween* and *Halloween II*)

AG: Let's discuss the casting process. This was a bigger budget, more high-profile film than most before it in the franchise. What was the casting process like for you?

Scout Taylor-Compton: It was very rough and a long, long process. It's funny, because people ask this question, and they're like, "It must have been something that you've never done before." I'm like, "No, every big movie that I had to audition for or got close to, you would go through this process of six to seven meetings going in to read for this movie." This was no different. It was the original call and then the callback. Then it was a test and then another test, and then it was a triple test. It was just a constant question of *Do I have it? Do I not have it? Is it me? Is it not me?* It was really challenging.

When it really became a reality of how big this project was is when I met Rob for the first time. Rob doesn't like to be in the audition room. He likes to look at tapes. I remember sitting there on this couch in this office, and I remember I was looking at my sides. I was really nervous, and I had these Ugg boots on, and I was just looking at my Uggs. Then, all of a sudden—it was literally like out of a movie—I heard this stomping. Then I saw these boots with spikes. Then I saw these flared seventies pants, this belt, all this hair and this metal band shirt. And I'm just like, *Who is that?* He says, "Hi! I'm Rob Zombie; you're coming in to read for me." You get put into this small, little room that's cubicle size, and you're having to audition for your life. And then they bring in Danielle Harris, who I've watched in these movies and I've watched in other movies, like *Free Willy* or *Wish Upon a Star*. You have this professional and cool actress, and you're working with her. There's like a connection, and it's pretty wild. Then you go home and think *Fuck, I really hope I get that job because that was such a cool experience.* Then to not hear for a long time and when you do get called back, you hear, "Well, they really like you, but the studio is not sure. So you've got to come in one more time and do it all over again." So then you go back. And you try not to piss yourself while you're going into the studio. You're like, *I just really want this job.* And then you're put into costume and someone does your hair. Someone does your makeup, but you haven't actually gotten the part. They're just gonna test you. They're going to bring back Danielle Harris. Now there's this other girl, Kristina Klebe. She's your other friend. "You guys are just gonna go in the backlot and do this scene. We're gonna get our DP, and Rob's gonna direct it. We're just gonna film it like we're filming the movie."

It's just a wild process, and it's really exhausting. To think that other girls were going through that process and they didn't get it, it hurts my heart because I know that feeling, but on the other end, when you do get it, it's very exciting. I remember Rob told me that I was the first person whose tape he saw and that I was his Laurie from the very beginning. But it was a battle with the Weinsteins because of multiple things. But to have someone fight for you that hard is really cool. I do remember something that was really epic from my last testing. I remember sitting on that same couch. It was now the production office, because they were getting ready to roll really soon. I remember looking up, and they had all the headshots of all the actors on the wall. They hadn't cast Laurie Strode yet, but there in the middle was my photo. I hadn't been cast yet, but to see that was so wild. *Did I get it? Am I gonna get it? Are they gonna tell me I got it?* It's a brutal process, and it's very hard to explain to anyone if they hadn't done it before. I've been doing this since I was eight, and I've done that process a lot of times. A lot of times it didn't go my way.

AG: You're seventeen years old for this arduous process. Let's jump forward to your first day of work. You've endured this lengthy and challenging process and won the role. Now you're on set with various genre icons and a maverick director, plus all the fan buzz. What do you remember about your first day of work?

Scout Taylor-Compton: Well, let's take it back before my first day. Everybody knew *Halloween* was coming back and it was Rob Zombie directing. What everybody didn't know was who's Laurie Strode? That's all that anybody wanted to know: who's Laurie Strode? Back then, the internet was pretty big already, with people commenting and being able to voice what they thought about things. Once my name got dropped, it was a lot of people going, "Wait! What? No! Who's that? That's not Jamie Lee!" There were a lot of people being very negative towards me. I was a kid. I was seventeen years old reading stuff online. To see all those comments, I was really hurt. I was really hurt, really scared, and very nervous. So walking on set for my first day of work, that's exactly how I felt. I felt that even more because like you said, I was seeing Danielle Harris. I was seeing Dee Wallace. Rob came up to me, and he took me aside. I don't know if he knew that I had seen those comments or what, but he was like, "I cast you for a reason. I cast you to play your Laurie Strode, not to play Jamie Lee Curtis's Laurie Strode. Let's do this together. No matter what they

Scout, Danielle, and Kristina. Image courtesy of Phil Parmet

say, I got your back." So that's what my first day was like, which was so cool to have someone be there for me without even knowing that person. It really solidified our bond and how much admiration I had for him. He really did settle me down, and we would go on to have a lot of fun, because he did that on the first day.

AG: That's a pretty good springboard into the character too. Having all those feelings and then having somebody like Rob there for you, you can translate that into the work.

Scout Taylor-Compton: I think that was super important. From what I've heard, the Weinsteins wanted somebody older. I don't know if that's for whatever purposes, but they were fighting for older actresses. I've had a couple of conversations with Rob about it, and he said, "You were a kid. You felt like Laurie Strode, babysitter at seventeen, trying to figure out life, doing her best. You felt authentic. That's why I fought for you." It wasn't my first horror movie, but it was my first big one. It was my first huge movie like this. I was going through a lot of my firsts on that set. So it was all real. Me and Laurie Strode were very, very similar at that time.

AG: A quote that I've been told was that the Weinsteins wanted a "WB girl."

Scout Taylor-Compton: It would have been a different movie. It really would have. Like with *Texas Chainsaw Massacre*'s remake, it works because those women are sexy. That's just *Texas Chainsaw*. They're very sexy women. I don't really ever look at *Halloween* and go, "Oh, this is a sexpot." That's why I love this franchise so much, because it does seem very authentic and very real. That's the stuff that I like to watch.

AG: I've got to ask about Dee Wallace, who played your mother. She speaks glowingly about you and particularly your work together. Your work together stands out in that movie. It is silly, and it's also kind of heartwarming. It's a needed counterbalance to the horror and violence in the film.

Scout Taylor-Compton: Yeah, it was. The relationship with Dee and I was very much like mother and daughter, very, very much. She's like my second mom. I absolutely adore her and absolutely love her. I see myself in Dee a lot. We're very similar. And she's said the same stuff about me. She is very bubbly and will say what she feels. Our connection is like no other, and a lot of those scenes that we had, we kind of just improvised with one another. We were having so much fun being in each other's company and creating this really cool art. Our chemistry was just so there that it was very easy. I knew where she was going. She knew where I was going. There was no fear. We would just jump on it. Even with the bagel scene, she didn't know what was happening, but she went with it. She has a daughter that I'm very close with now that's the same age as me. She's one of the coolest scene partners I've ever worked with. She's so talented, and everything just comes very natural for her. She's so badass as well and so hot. She's a sexy woman. She just is who she is, and she just has a natural talent for it. She just takes no bullshit, and I strive to be an ounce of what Dee Wallace is.

AG: The third act of *Halloween* is heavily focused on your character. It's very physically intense and action oriented. What was that like for you?

Scout Taylor-Compton: I grew up an athlete, and I'm ADD [attention deficit disorder]. I was a swimmer growing up. I was either going to go to the Olympics for swimming or I was going to stay an actor. It kind of is the same thing for me. I love physicality, I love movement. I love working my body into the characters. It really helps me. So the third act was so much fun for me. I was having to fight with Rob, telling him I want to do that stunt and that stunt and that stunt. I want to be in an *Alien* franchise or the *Resident Evil* franchise. I just love physical stuff when it comes to my craft. So that was one of my favorite parts of filming, all the tumbling, the screaming, the kicking, and the fighting. I just loved it. It's like dancing for me. I was like, "Let's do more. Let's shoot it again. Can we do it again?" I just love it. Plus it helps you get into the character. It's just fun for me.

AG: What was the dynamic with Tyler Mane [Michael Myers in both

Rob Zombie *Halloween* films] like then? Did you already have a good relationship by the time you started filming the third act, or was it still developing as you shot these physically intense scenes?

Scout Taylor-Compton: I have a weird thing, especially when I was that age. Everybody would have to love me. I would be like, "You have to love me; I already love you. I know I love you. You have to love me back." I had a really big problem with that. So Tyler was one of them. I was like his annoying little sister, but he is like my dad, like my second dad. I'm his annoying little sister, though. Maybe it's because I've known these people since I was seventeen that I have picked personalities and traits from them and kind of incorporated them into who I am now. My goofy side is my Tyler side. We're very goofy people. We'll be cracking jokes and doing funny hand movements and then Rob will say action and then we'll get into it, and then when we cut, we'll be back to dancing. That's just like how we roll, and plus our trailers were connected. We had a wall that connected them, so I would constantly bug him through the wall. I think there's some YouTube videos of me knocking every time I heard the bathroom door open. I was yelling, "What are you doing? What's happening? What's going on?" And he's like, "Leave me alone." It's a big playground; it really is. Tyler wasn't scary to me. He was someone that I looked forward to seeing every day because I just knew we were gonna have a good time. We're gonna laugh. We're gonna joke around. It's gonna be a really good time.

AG: When you look back at filming *Halloween* today, what are the memories that most stick out to you?

Scout Taylor-Compton: I turned eighteen on the set. We were all so sick, and I think it was one of the last scenes, if not the pool scene, and it was an overnight shoot. I'd never really remembered getting birthday cakes, or maybe I'm just not on sets long enough to. I remember we broke for lunch, and then, all of a sudden, this big cake comes out and there's all these candles and everybody's singing "Happy Birthday." I'm just smiling, and I start blowing the candles out, and they're not going out. So I'm blowing harder, and they're not going out. I am so gullible that I'm the last to know anything. Someone might have to even explain it to me, and everybody's just laughing at me. I'm like, "Why are you laughing at me?" They got trick candles. My first instinct was to grab the cake—literally a huge amount—and I just went towards Tyler. Tyler tells me not to do it. So then I turn to Rob. All Rob does is just start sprinting. So I just started running. I am chasing him down the block to base camp to where our makeup trailers are, and we're just in this chase. He gets to the makeup trailer, and I just smush it in his face. I covered him with all this cake, and it was just one of the best moments. I'll always remember that. That is so special to me. I became an adult on that movie and had the best birthday ever, with the best people ever. It's one of those pinch-me moments where you're like, *Wow! This is my life.*

AG: I'm reminded of the tagline for the second movie: "Family is forever."

Scout Taylor-Compton: It's forever, man. It really is when it comes to Rob Zombie's *Halloween.* We really became a family. That's when you know it's special, when you get those connections. I think it's also just the genre itself. Maybe it's because of the brutalness of the job that makes you really close with one another. There's just so much family that I've created in this genre, and I really, really appreciate it.

AG: So *Halloween* comes out. Walk me through what that's like for you from the premiere on. What was that impact like on you at eighteen years old?

Scout Taylor-Compton: I was on cloud nine. All my friends knew about it and people were talking about it nonstop in the media. We just came off of that high, and we really became a family unit. Anything that Rob would send us to see, we were all just jazzed. Then getting ready for the premiere and doing the premiere was the first time I got a taste of the genre fan base. It was wild. The fan base is so cool, so loving, and so supportive, which is kind of how I am as a person anyway. It just really felt comfortable, like a big warm hug. Then to see the movie and see it executed, it was so badass. Then it was like the number one movie. It was just a whirlwind. It was like a tornado, and it was just fun. You're on a high at that point of your life, and of course my thing is like what's next? I can't wait; let's go. But it was a really cool experience.

AG: Earlier you mentioned internet culture. The buzz at that time was that Rob's not gonna do another one. He wasn't coming back for a sequel, and we were all very surprised when that turned out not to be true. I don't know how much of that's just like internet rumors or innuendo, but walk me through you finding out that you were coming back for a second film.

Scout Taylor-Compton: Yeah, I don't know either. I don't know if he was contracted to do a sequel. At some point he was contracted to do three films; then the second film was so brutal that things changed. "I'll finish the second film if you let me out of the third" kind of deal is my understanding. That's the Weinsteins for you. But we all got the call that we're coming back for a sequel, and we were all stoked. Slowly it was like Tyler's attached, Scout's attached, Danielle's attached. People are starting to be attached, and it was just like a camp that you get so excited that you're going to every summer. I was really excited when I got the script. I was really stoked with where Rob took it. I had watched the second *Halloween*, and I loved that it was different. We were all on board with Rob as our captain. We were ready to rock 'n' roll and make another good movie.

AG: How would you describe the differences between filming the two movies beyond just the differences in your character?

Scout Taylor-Compton: It was very different. You could feel the tension behind the scenes. It was not as nice just because Rob was battling the Weinsteins constantly. I don't know what they were doing to him, but it wasn't good and it wasn't nice. You could feel the heaviness, and things were constantly changing. It just seemed very chaotic. Whenever something is getting tense, I'm the first person that's like, "What can I do? How can I help?" In those situations, you can't do anything. You're an actor, and that's all production. You can't really get into that. I was younger, so I wasn't really involved in a lot of those conversations like other actors were, like Tyler or Danielle. They were older, and they got it a little bit more. It was a lot different, and it was hard. We were still a family, but you could tell that one of our family members was not being treated right. It was so hard to be there every day and know that was the case.

To also jump into the character, that was really hard. She was going through her own PTSD, with ups and downs, ups and downs, ups and downs, ups and downs. I also was not in a very good relationship at the time, so I was going through my own personal ups and downs, ups and downs, ups and downs. So it seemed like we were all on this insane roller coaster, and we couldn't get off. We all just wanted to get off. I've said this in so many interviews, that I didn't realize at that time that acting is a massive therapy for me. I am releasing and getting rid of all this trauma and all this stuff within that is just so deep that I just need to get out. That's what I was going through during that movie. There was so much that I was releasing. I'm very emotional, and I was very external with my trauma at that time in my life. I love that dynamic of that's what Laurie was feeling. Danielle and I are two very different people, but we are also very similar. She's more reserved and can hold her trauma deeper within and control it a little bit more, which is what you were seeing with her character. It was a cool dynamic to have, but it was definitely really brutal. It was still fun to come back and have new memories with everybody, though.

I was testing for *The Runaways* during that shoot. That was another project that I went in one, two, three, four, five, six times. I even wrote a letter. I was like, I need to be in this movie. I don't know what it is, but I need to be in this movie, and they put me through the ringer. I remember Rob was so excited when I told him I was up for *The Runaways*. He's like, "I fucking love *The Runaways*. What do you need?" I went out for the drummer because I can kind of play drums, but they think I don't look like her, they think maybe the bass player. He's like, "Oh, I'll get you someone to teach you bass"". Then he would play "Cherry Bomb" on set. It was just that kind of stuff. We were there for each other through the good times and through the bad times. We were there for each other.

AG: "Elevated horror" is somewhat of a buzz phrase at the moment. The argument can absolutely be made that *Halloween II* started that trend. The masses might not see that yet, but writers and journalists seem to be making that connection now.

Scout Taylor-Compton: As much negativity as I got on the first film with my name being announced, or even with the second one, because people were confused and didn't understand it, Rob has gotten so much worse. I don't understand it. When I watch his stuff, there is so much rawness and realness to it. Maybe that's what it is. Maybe it's because it's too real. It's too close to home for people that they just don't want to see it. I think there's gonna be a time and a place, whether that's 5 years from now or 2 years from now, or whatever that people are going to be able to go back and look at *Halloween* or *Halloween II* and look at other Rob's work and go fuck. This guy actually executed this. This guy created a lane for this sort of work. It's interesting that you say that because I do think of that from time to time, especially when people come up to my table when I'm at cons and they say "I didn't like *Halloween II*. But can you sign this?" I really want to ask why you didn't like *Halloween II*? Is it because it stepped too much on trauma and life things? Because it was too deep? I'm always curious. What are you afraid of? What's holding you back from appreciating somebody's art?

I never closed the door, but I would love to, and I would love for Rob to get another opportunity to do a third *Halloween* film. I really think that he was going somewhere really epic with his vision for this franchise.

AG: *Halloween* has become a *Choose Your Own Adventure* book in a sense, with the five different and distinct timelines. It doesn't seem out of the question to have a third film from Rob's plotline happen now. What would that look like now, though? You already kicked in the door on elevated horror. What new trends would you set?

Scout Taylor-Compton: God, I don't know. Time heals all wounds, right? I don't think Rob's issue was ever with Malek. I think it was with the Weinsteins. I don't know what his feelings are towards it, if he would ever be like, "Yeah, I'll come back," or if he's like, "Fuck that." Only he would know, but I really think that he could. I would be so stoked to see what he would come up with for a third film. One thing with Rob is that I think he would listen to what fans want to see, I really do. He really does care about that sort of stuff.

AG: I wanted to ask about the director's cut versus the theatrical cut. There's a stark difference in her trauma journey from one cut to the other.

Scout Taylor-Compton: Rob was going through so much at that time with the Weinsteins and with people being so negative with him about the movies. I can't imagine being the captain of the ship and having all of that darkness come at you. I feel like Rob's version (the director's cut) is kind of Rob saying, "FUCK YOU! Fuck it all!" I was so happy that I could do that for him. I feel like it was both Rob and I playing Laurie Strode at the same time. Honestly, I don't know which one I like more. I liked both of them because both were inside of me. Both of those versions were me internally anyway. It's more interesting to go Rob's way. I think it would have made for an epic third movie if we went with Rob's way. I think it would have opened up something else that I don't think anybody had seen before.

AG: The ending to *Halloween II* was ambiguous in the sense that it's somewhat open to interpretation. Did you and Rob have any discussions about what would happen next for the character?

Scout Taylor-Compton: There was so much trust with Rob. Those are big stages in your life. I'm becoming who I want to be in life at seventeen and eighteen when we filmed these movies, and I'm learning from all these people. I was very embarrassed and shy back then to tell people how much they meant to me. I probably should tell Rob how much he has meant to me in my life. There was so much love and so much trust and appreciation. I admired him so much that there was no pushback. Whatever he was wanting to create and wanting to do, I just kind of went for the ride. I felt like, "I want to learn from you. I wanna soak it all in. Is this where we're going? Cool. I'll hold your hand and jump from the bridge." I think he was trying to do something so much bigger and trying to make Michael Myers and *Halloween* so much bigger. He was just trying to push it to that next level. And I was just so ready to go. I was like, "I trust you, and I believe in you, and I love you so much. This is going to be great, and I'm excited to take the leap."

AG: One of the most striking scenes in the entire franchise is in the cabin at the end of *Halloween II*. Visually, it's stunning. Tell me about filming that scene.

Scout Taylor-Compton: When we wrapped the movie, I had never put the mask on ever during the entire shooting process. Tyler is fucking sweaty. I remember we were having so much fun, and when we wrapped, I yelled to Tyler, "Give me your mask!" and I put it on. Rob looked at me, and I slowly looked at him, and something clicked. We reshot it. We did an alternate take. So we went back to the cabin, and I put the mask on, and I came out. It wasn't reshot because the reviews were not good. It was one of those cool moments, and I loved it. I loved losing myself. I felt like Laurie Strode was losing herself anyway throughout the entire journey, so it made sense being there in that moment, seeing things that aren't there or losing yourself within the truth, within what you know and what you've been through. *Is it real? Is it not? I'm losing myself.* I think I was just so invested in who she was that I was like, *This is what it's like. This is what I'm feeling.* Imagine going through what that woman had gone through! I get a lot of people that come to me that are from the military and have been in wars and have seen the craziest things that no one should ever see. They've come to me and have said that is what my PTSD is like in real time. That is what I feel. And I'm like, of course. To go through that trauma and try to move on with your life, of course that's what it feels like. It's so traumatizing. And there's no magic pill or magic person or magic day where everything will be okay. Unfortunately, it consumes you. Sometimes it consumes someone whole, which I think is what Rob was trying to go for. That's so scary. That's scarier than the fucking bogeyman.

AG: So you at one point you were connected to a potential third film, without Rob. New writer and director both.

Scout Taylor-Compton: The call that Tyler and I both got was "There's going to be a third film. We don't have a script. We don't have a director. We're shooting in a month. Rob's not a part of it. Okay, bye." That was it. Then it was us calling each other and going, "Did you just get a crazy call? What do you mean Rob's not a part of it? What's happening? What's going on?" Then we had to sit back and wait. We were just reading the media shit about it being in 3D or that it was the guy from *My Bloody Valentine* directing [Patrick Lussier]. We were literally like fans in the chat going, "What's happening? Is it happening? Is it not happening? What's going on?" It was wild. Then it just went dark.

AG: It makes no sense.

Scout Taylor-Compton: But it does make sense. It's the Weinsteins. I guarantee you there was a conversation happening of "Hey, Mr. Weinstein, so you got this thing about to come up for you. You might want to buckle down." So that's a bummer it didn't happen, but fuck! Would it have been a great movie and a good movie to do without Rob? Twenty-year- old me was like, "Oh, I want to do the fucking movie." But now I'm glad it didn't happen, and I'm glad it didn't happen without Rob.

AG: So that leads me to my last question. You're now a director yourself. What impact has Rob had on your work now that you're on the other side of the camera?

Scout Taylor-Compton: Everything. I don't think he knows that. I really don't think he knows that I've learned everything from that man, from work ethic to how he treats people and how invested he is. I've learned everything from him, and I really appreciate all the lessons that he's taught me and all the kindness that he's given me. I know that we're gonna work together on a project in the future. I don't know if that's me producing something with him or bringing something to him that I wrote. But we're gonna work together again because now that I'm older, I can sort of look back at all the memories and the lessons that I learned during those movies. I think that he and I could create something really cool and really epic together. He's taught me a lot as a director. I'm very fortunate to have worked with him, because I don't think I ever would have wanted to be a director if I hadn't worked with Rob, to be honest.

I'm not as afraid of things as I used to. That's one thing with Rob. He's never afraid to be his authentic self and do what he believes in and be his truth. I think that's awesome.

AG: And one day you and Rob will do *Halloween II*. I'm throwing it out in the universe.

Scout Taylor-Compton: Or I'm gonna bring him this other franchise idea that I have. "Rob, here we go, babe. Let's do it."

Interview: Dee Wallace (Cynthia Strode, Rob Zombie's *Halloween*)

AG: Were you offered the role or did you audition for Rob Zombie?

Dee Wallace: How can I say this without blowing my own horn? Rob likes to work with icons from the past and the present, right? I got a call asking if I would be interested in meeting with Rob about this film. I was interested more in who Rob Zombie was and is and what he was going to do here. *Halloween* was more of a run-of-the-mill kind of horror film than he usually does. I wanted to see how far he was gonna go, how gruesome it was gonna be compared to the other projects that he done. When I met him, I loved him. He is truly one of the most genuine people that I've ever worked with. I consider him a friend, even though I haven't talked to him in months now. I just sent him a birthday celebration thing.

When I meet a director, usually I click. Sometimes I don't. With Rob, it was an exciting journey learning who Rob was, how to work with him, and how to bring me into his world. It was effortless. I remember at the very beginning we were out by video village [place on set where monitors are set up for the production team to review footage], and we were waiting for him to set up. And I said to Rob, "What's your favorite film this year?" He says, "*Little Miss Sunshine*." I looked at him and I went, "Oh my God, don't tell anybody. Your cover will be totally blown." And he started laughing.

He and Sheri [Moon Zombie] are just the sweetest, most devoted couple. She brings him his health food drink and his vitamins every morning on the set. I just fell in love with both of them and loved working with him. I was finished with *Halloween*, and the producers called and said, "We need you back." I said, "But I've already died."

They said, "Yeah, but Rob wants to kill you better." And he does do that, at least with me. He's done it two or three times now where he's seen something on-screen and he wants to further it or enlarge it or explain it more. So he calls me back. I was shooting *NCIS*, and he called and said, "Dee, I wanna do this pickup shot this afternoon." I said, "I just finished shooting on *NCIS*, so you have to give me time to get out of makeup and fly over there." Fortunately we were shooting in Woodland Hills, so I made it. We did it, and it's just a wonderful scene. It happens out of the creativity of Rob's mind. He trusts himself, and he trusts his actors. One of the best things we got on *Halloween*, the big scene between my husband and my daughter that's in the kitchen, we were working with three cameras. He said, "All right, let's do it as it's written." So we did. And then he said, "Okay, everybody bring in your best shit. Just let's just come on in and play and improv, and let's just see what happens." And that's how all the stuff with the bagels, with Scout and I screwing the bagel, all that stuff just kind of happened because we were given the room to play. It's so important for actors to feel like they've got that room to let stuff happen.

AG: That's really cool to hear. He was pretty early on in his directorial career at this point too. So for him to have that kind of confidence as a relatively new director, that's even more impressive.

Dee Wallace: I think it's a combination of "Hey, I know my shit. I know what I'm doing" and "I don't really care if you like it or not." A director can give me a direction and the character either goes "Oh my God, that's great. I know what to do" or it goes "What the hell are you talking about that?" You as an actor have to feel like you have room to sit down and talk about it with your director. There was one scene in *3 from Hell* where he was giving me all these directions and then said, "Let's go." Okay, hold on. I've gotta drop into her. I told him, "I don't know what she wants to do with it yet, Rob." And he kind of looked at me and said, "Okay, we'll wait." So I'm sitting there on the set. Everybody's staring at me; they're ready to go. And I just asked the character, *Where are we going?* It came to me, and I told Rob, and he yelled to roll action. It's just a fun, interesting creative experience working with Rob Zombie for me. He's one of my favorites.

AG: You guys have worked together on a few films now. Has it always been like that working with him?

Dee Wallace: Yeah. I mean, every set has its tensions because time is money basically on a film set. But that was never thrown at us. For me, it was always fun on Rob's sets. He always gets really good actors who bring all their heart to the situation. Somebody said to me in interview, "When *Halloween* first came out, what did you think about Rob's remake?" I said, "This is not a remake. This is a "Rob-make." It came out that way. But it was so true. I feel like his *Halloween* stands very much on its own, independent of the others.

AG: It does. There are some really jarring parts, but there's also some really sweet parts. The scene with you on the porch with your family is a really sweet kind of moment. It's very reminiscent of the first film. But just a minute later, Michael enters the house, and all hell breaks loose.

Dee Wallace: I have never had more blood on me in my life, and that's saying something with all the horror films I've done. They literally brought a bug sprayer in and sprayed me down. I'm dripping wet walking off the set. And I said, "All right, guys, I can't get into a car. I'm gonna get blood and slime all over." The props department put out a big plastic sheet over the seats in the car so I could get back and take a shower in my dressing room. I mean, seriously, bug sprayer of blood all over me. It was awful.

AG: It's a fascinating scene because part of it is left to the imagination. You're crawling on the floor. We hadn't seen all of what he had done to you, and then he comes back, and he's right behind you. At that point it's just in-your-face violence.

Dee Wallace: I think that's one of the reasons people hire me for these parts. I do have that innocent vulnerability just built into who Dee Wallace is. It was so funny when it premiered: I must have gotten forty or fifty texts and calls, people saying, "We've never seen you die on film. You don't kill Dee Wallace on-screen!" In *The Howling*, you don't see me die on-screen. Everything is inferred in most of my other movies. Maybe I could have been paid a lot more if I'd done this more!

AG: It made for a hell of a death scene.

Dee Wallace: Well, thank you. That's the scene where they called me because Rob wanted to kill me better.

AG: Any other on-set memories you care to share?

Dee Wallace: The scene where the kids were coming up to the house, Scout and I were both running like 103 degree fevers. We were sicker than dogs, both of us, but we just had the time of our lives even with as sick as we were. I think it was two in the morning, and Rob said, "Okay, girls, we're gonna shoot this. Can you still sit up?" "Yeah, we're gonna do it for you, Rob. We're here for you, babe!" It turned out to be a really great scene. We had so much fun doing that scene in the kitchen with the bagels and ad-libbing all that, the three of us. Oh my God, we had three cameras running all the time, which is heaven for an actor. You don't have to match stuff. You just fly. One time, Scout said something so out there and funny and I went, "Oh no, you did not!" I started laughing, totally out of character. I lost it, and I could hear Rob behind the camera losing it when one of the camera operators lost it. There were no light moments in *Cujo*. I couldn't let myself get out of where I was because it was too hard to get back in. On this shoot, we had that freedom every once in a while.

If Rob ever calls, I'm there. I think his stuff is really out there, but the stuff he has me do is out there just far enough that I can go there without being embarrassed about what I did. I said right up front when I went in to meet him, "You know, I'm the mom from *E.T.* I don't do nudity, Rob," and he started laughing. I said, "I can do sex, but I'm not gonna do it nude," and from that moment on, we've had this great working relationship.

Interview: Phil Parmet (Director of Photography, *Rob Zombie's Halloween*)

AG: How did this job come to be?

Phil Parmet: I met Rob through his line producer on *The Devil's Rejects*, Brett Morris, who I had worked with on a film called *American Gun*. Rob had said he was interested in a more realistic rendering than he had done on his first film, *House of 1000 Corpses*—a more handheld, documentary feel. I had shot documentaries for a lot of years when I was just starting out in the business, including work on two Academy Award-winning documentary films, *Harlan County USA* and *American Dream*, both by the great American documentarian Barbara Kopple.

I love the freedom of putting a camera on your shoulder and running and gunning, shooting handheld. It gives an audience the feeling of being in the middle of things as the action unfolds. It also imparts the unsettling feeling of potential danger and of unanticipated shocks to the nervous system. Brett told me this was the sort of work Rob was looking for, and he had already seen a few of my documentary films, including *Harlan County*, and loved them. Brett also thought Rob and I would get along and work well together, so he arranged a meeting. We had an instant rapport; we loved the same films, and stylistically we were on the same page. We had a good meeting. The next day, Rob called me personally and asked me to shoot his film *The Devil's Rejects*. We had a total blast shooting that film. It was one of the best experiences I'd ever had shooting a film. We developed a real bond, and we were both really happy that the film had turned out almost exactly how we had planned.

After *Rejects*, I shot a couple of music videos for Rob, and after that, I went on a musical tour around the USA with him and his band and filmed a music documentary for what was supposed to be his last tour. In the middle of the tour, Rob got word that Miramax was going to finance a new *Halloween* with him directing, and he asked me to shoot it. We were able to spend some downtime on the road between venues talking about how we wanted to do it.

AG: What kind of creative discussions did you have with Rob prior to filming? Any discussions about style or influences?

Phil Parmet: Most people know of Rob as a musician and through his band, White Zombie, but first and foremost, Rob is a visual artist. He went to art school in NYC, and he has a reverence for films of all genres and an encyclopedic knowledge of the history and traditions of cinema as well as an ability to draw and create characters and make them real with precise renditions of his ideas. On *Rejects*, we had talked about how we wanted the film to look: a distressed, homemade western punk, a funky spaghetti western horror film that could have been directed by Sergio Leone, like *A Fistful of Dollars* or *For a Few Dollars More*—a Sergio Leone spaghetti western with the Manson Family as the heroes, a cross between Dario Argento and Sam Peckinpah. We both loved Clint Eastwood and referenced a lot of his work. His film *The Gauntlet*, for example, was the inspiration for the shootout at the Firefly Ranch. We loved *High Plains Drifter*, *The Outlaw Josey Wales*, and *Hang 'Em High*. We watched Frederick Wiseman's *Titicut Follies*, a cinema verité documentary about a New England mental hospital that is perhaps one of the scariest films ever made.

The reason I am talking so much about *The Devil's Rejects* here and now is that when Rob and I first talked about a style for his *Halloween*, the first film he referenced was his own. "I love the way *The Devil's Rejects* looks and feels," Rob told me. "I want to translate that to a larger format and make it look more polished and intentional."

We had shot *The Devil's Rejects* in Super 16 mm with Aaton cameras and Kodak film, scanned it, and blew it up via a digital intermediate to 35 mm for the release prints. We used Zeiss prime lenses primarily and mostly in wide-angle focal lengths because wide-angle lenses again put you in the action as if you are involved, as opposed to telephoto lenses that make you more of an observer from a distance. For *Halloween*, we started out with 35 mm film and Moviecam lightweight cameras configured for handheld. Almost everything would be handheld, and we would shoot with Cooke prime lenses and use the same crew we had used on *Rejects*. One exception was my B camera operator, BJ McDonnell, who was also our Steadicam operator. BJ had worked as a grip for me for years, and this was a big jump for him. He performed brilliantly and went on to a great career operating Steadicam on huge Hollywood movies. My second operator was Dave Daniels, a DP in his own right, who was suggested by the line producer Mike Elliott on *Rejects*. He turned out to be an amazing handheld operator and became a great friend.

With *Halloween*, as with *Rejects*, we wanted to get the unsettled feeling that you get from handheld cinematography, but also we wanted to have a precision that would keep the story moving and the audience on the edge of their seats every moment of the film until its inevitable bloody conclusion.

AG: Your *Halloween* film both creates its own identity as well as faithfully recreating large parts of the original film. Was that a difficult balance to find? How much did you revisit the previous films when trying to find a look and visual style for your film?

Phil Parmet: Of course we looked at the *Halloween* films, but our only actual reference was to the spirit of the films, not really to a particular cinematic style. In addition, we looked at many of Rob's favorite films, looking for what worked in terms of building tension and the actual mechanics of scares. On that list were films like *Last House on the Left, Them, Scanners, The Exorcist, Suspiria, Don't Look Now, Alien, Psycho, Rosemary's Baby, The Ring, The Host, Jacob's Ladder*, and *Repulsion*, to name only a few.

AG: What's it like to work with Rob Zombie as a director?

Rob Zombie on set. Image courtesy of Phil Parmet

Phil Parmet: Rob is great. I knew from working with him on *Rejects* he was an amazing artist. Most people know Rob through White Zombie, but that is only part of his story. He went to art school and studied fine arts, made comic books, and has an encyclopedic knowledge of film, similar to Quentin Tarantino, who I had done the cinematography on *Four Rooms* for and who I met again for *Grindhouse*.

AG: When you think back on this film, which shots have stuck with you most over the years? What are you most proud of from your body of work here?

Phil Parmet: I think there is a real sense of intimacy created by the handheld documentary style, and that's what makes Rob's *Halloween* really different from all the other versions. For me, seeing a couple of scenes up on the big screen for the first time after I had conceptualized them with Rob and then executed the ideas on 35 mm film was gratifying. Most of my lighting choices and camera movements were validated. Back in the day when we shot the film, there were a lot of economic forces that wanted it to be shot digitally. Rob and I both are firm believers in the mystical and magical chemistry of film versus electronic recording of images. I was so happy we were finally able to persuade the producers to shoot on Fuji's film stocks. Personally, I love the grain structure and the warm color palette of the Fuji more than the more modern, fine-grain Kodak films.

The biggest challenge in any scary film for me is what you can and cannot see, to make the lighting seem realistic from natural sources and at the same time dramatically light the night so you can see into the closets, backyards, and dark cellars just enough to see what we want you to see and no more. The irony is in filming we need to create the impression of darkness in a medium that is all about light. I love all the exterior night shots of the house, the scene in the bathroom where the moonlight filters through lace curtains, and the spooky feeling in the cellar with rays of light coming through the high windows.

AG: Any on-set memories you care to share?

Phil Parmet: This is my own speculation. It was a difficult shoot mostly because the Weinstein brothers couldn't keep their hands off the film and were on Rob's case constantly. I think it took a real toll on Rob, who had been promised autonomy after the artistic success of *Rejects*. There was a stream of constant criticism and negative notes Rob was getting from Harvey and Bob, and I think it put Rob on the defensive. It was not a great creative space for an artist to work his magic, and much credit goes to Rob for enduring. There was a lot of tension on the set, and it was not what I would consider a job anybody had fun working on, but we did it. We accomplished what we set out to do, and I think we did justice to the *Halloween* franchise and made a really entertaining film.

AG: The film is controversial within the fandom. Some love it, and for others, it's too different from the original film. How have you felt about criticism of the film over the years?

Phil Parmet: Anytime you do a remake, you're fair game for criticism from the hardcore lovers of the original. I think, however, it is a legitimate exercise for an artist and fan of the original work to try to do a version that is their own. Think how much we enjoy a contemporary musical artist doing their rendition of a classic song. Clearly, it can lend depth and additional meaning to the original work.

AG: If you care to share, why did you not return to work on Rob's second *Halloween* film?

Phil Parmet: I have a lot of respect for Rob's artistry, and I think we made some really interesting work together, but as Rob once said to me, "All things do not end well." I will leave it at that.

AG: How do you think the film holds up almost fifteen years later?

Phil Parmet: I think it holds up pretty well. So much of what is made these days is in a digital format, and although some of it looks good and a small proportion of what gets made looks really great, I still think film is the real stuff of dreams and nightmares and has a magical quality created by the random distribution of silver in an emulsion, among other specific qualities and exigencies of production that cannot be duplicated in a digital format or with the digital style of shooting. For those reasons alone, I think our *Halloween* will survive the test of time and be regarded as one of the most faithful in spirit to the energy of the John Carpenter original.

AG: Any additional stories you'd like to share?

Phil Parmet: The day we had a real horror show. So we were shooting on the grounds of an old VA hospital outside Los Angeles, using the exteriors of disused buildings for the insane asylum sequences. While we were setting up an exterior day establishing shot of the buildings, we began to hear strange animalistic screams from behind a high wooden fence that ran behind our set. My key grip set up a ladder so he could see over the fence and immediately reported back that there was a yard beyond the fence filled with hundreds of monkeys. Word quickly got back to the VA authorities that we had breached their security fence, and word came down we would have to stop shooting and get off the property immediately. Nobody had ever mentioned the monkeys, and of course this would have been a gigantic problem. Apparently, PETA had already made a big stink.

After heated negotiation, it was decided by the authorities that everyone who looked over the fence would have to leave the property. That included me and most of the camera crew. The producers got together some of the union day players, grips, and electrics and asked them if they gave them an additional day's pay, would they leave and pretend they were the camera crew. I don't know the exact details, but as far as I know, the plan worked, and a number of people got an extra day's pay to go home, and we were able to get back to work.

Interview: Daniel Roebuck (Big Lou, Rob Zombie's *Halloween and Halloween II*)

AG: What was it like for you to go from something that you had seen in your younger years on the big screen to being a part of that decades later?

Daniel Roebuck: What a blessing that is. I'll tell you this: it's happened to me a few times. I'm in *Phantasm*, so I got attacked by the ball. I'm in *Star Wars*, in the Skywalker storyline, same storyline that I saw as a kid, and I'm Grandpa Munster, right? So my life has been filled with that full-circle blessing time and again, and that's just the genre stuff I'm talking about. I can give you that in every other aspect of what I've done. But for me, I would say the scariest was the time in *Halloween II* specifically because in *Halloween*, I'm there but I'm holding on by just a little thread. I'm seen so briefly in the movie because Rob cut out all the other stuff. We had done the kill for the slam into the couch, slamming, slamming, slamming, slamming, slamming, slamming. I think if Rob hadn't said cut, he'd still be slamming me into the couch. After about four minutes, I think I said, "Someone for the love of God say cut," because I was losing consciousness. I think Rob only said cut because my screams were bothering people at craft service. I'm either very entertaining or he doesn't like me—I can't tell which. But we did the slamming into the couch. Then we're in the hallway, and it's a question of how do I know when to turn? Because I ran out first, and it was a shot where I turn and I'm facing the camera; then I turn and see him, and then I turn and face the camera. I can't remember if it's in the movie, but we shot it. Tyler just said "Dan" when he came out of the room so I know when to turn because you can't tell, because he has a mask on. So he says "Dan," and I turn. Tyler's seven foot

Big Lou. Image courtesy of Phil Parmet

three—he took four steps, and he was on me. In those four steps, I was screaming. It was horrible, but it was magical and great—one of the many things I'm grateful to Rob Zombie for putting in my path, kind of knowing that these were the kind of things that would make me happy, and he gave me the opportunity to play them, which was very nice.

AG: You have a unique relationship with Rob Zombie. He's done this with others too, but you have been in almost every single one of his films.

Daniel Roebuck: I've shot every one but the first one, because we met right after it was filmed, but I'm making up for it by creating a product from it. He cuts me out. *Lords of Salem*, he cut me out. He really trimmed everything in *Halloween*. In a book I've been writing, I said that he's made a deal for an undisclosed sum of money to have my father cut me out of our home movies too. I love him. I love his creativity. We were shooting *31*, and I had been in makeup with Wayne Toth for about four hours. They put all these cuts and bruises on my face. I had all that rotten, sticky blood on me. They really tie me to the chair, and I'm watching out of the corner of my eye Richard Brake getting ready to do his brilliant monologue. They're like, "Okay, let's start the water." I look up and say, "What water?" "Oh, we're gonna be dripping water on you." Oh, Christ. My hands are tied. The water starts dripping. The first thing it does is take that crappy blood and put it right in my eyes. My eyes start stinging immediately.

I said, "Before we shoot, can I just say one thing?" Rob says yes. I said, "For other people, I star in their movies. I'm the star of the movie. For you, Rob, you kill me in the first five minutes, so you never have to see me again? Okay, I got that off my chest. Let's go." They start rolling the cameras, and we're in the same frame for a lot of what Richard's doing. They were shooting him, and they were shooting us from the same angle. I started thinking, *If that were a gun that he was holding, they would have brought me that gun and showed me that there were no bullets in it, but no one brought me that ax.* I'm just thinking, *Does it look like a foam rubber ax?* Richard's a great actor. He's really getting into this. He's really getting into it. I don't know if that's a real ax. Oh, Jesus.

Getting back to *Halloween*, I took a slam into a wall. We may have done it just for Rob's pleasure twenty times. Every time I hit the wall, I hit the floor. I had foam rubber all over my arms, foam rubber on my face. Every time all that stuff hit the floor, all that sticky blood, I'd have to pull myself off that linoleum floor, and I would leave some of the makeup behind or some of my flesh because it would just stick to the floor, and I'd have to pull myself up. With no exaggeration, that was about hour twenty-two on the set. We shot from the time I went to makeup to have them dye my hair that morning, and until then it was about twenty-two hours. Then, until I got back to the hotel, it was twenty-eight hours.

AG: Your working relationship with Rob started with *The Devil's Rejects*. How did that dynamic grow or change leading to *Halloween*?

Daniel Roebuck: I loved *House of 1000 Corpses*. I thought it was made by a guy who'd seen every movie that I have ever seen and then ingeniously incorporated all of it into one crazy cacophony of horror. I remember being so impressed with his audacity in that shot when Walter Goggins is gonna get killed. He pulls the camera up, and he holds it up there. I don't know how he had the knowledge of how long to hold it there. I could see that this was really a master filmmaker, and then I was intrigued to learn how he got there—not from rock star to there, but from art department on Pee-wee [Pee-wee's Playhouse] to rock star to there. That impressed me a lot. I bumped into him at a screening [horror hostess] Elvira had invited me to. I went with the producer Kevin Burns, and Rob and Sheri [Moon Zombie, Rob Zombie's wife] were there. I had met Rob briefly before at a shop where we were buying monster models. In that moment, my friend John Gilbert said, "Oh hello, Mr, Zombie." John was a rock 'n' roller, and I was like, "What did you call this guy?" That's when I started learning about Mr. Zombie. So I went up to him at this screening and introduced myself and said that I think we've got a lot in common. He said, "Sheri was just saying I should go say hi to you." We both collect Universal monsters and the Munsters. I knew that he had a collection, and he knew I had a collection. He was very great and accessible.

I wrote a movie with Duane Whitaker and Sam Borowski about Al Adamson and Sam Sherman, the guys who made *Dracula vs.*

Frankenstein. I had Rob's ear, and he was definitely into it. So he came over, and we watched some Al Adamson stuff at my house. He asked me if I wanted to be in the next movie. He was looking for a person to play the other guy. He knew Duane from his writing, and he also knew Duane from movies. He said, "What do you think about Duane being the other guy?" So Duane and I did that, and we created that character of Morris Green. Rob is the real deal. He put Morris Green in the cartoon. So I got to be animated, and then he brought it back for part three of the *Firefly* saga in *3 from Hell*—a good opportunity to play the same guy in three movies, albeit briefly. I don't really care. I like being part of stuff. I think we developed a relationship where he knew he could trust me.

Then when I did *Halloween*. I had the character that he cut. I can't put words in his mouth, but I believe that I proved myself. He did say once he cast me as Grandpa Munster that I'm never allowed to complain about how little my part is, which I only ever did once, but he certainly remembered it. For *The Munsters*, we ended up living together, he, Jeff [Daniel Phillips], and Sheri and I. The other actors would come in. They kept us in a bubble in this weird tiny hotel that was, you know, in a 350-year-old building. So to get to our rooms required walking up and around what was like Dracula's staircase twice. We would have to get up every other morning at seven to get our noses swiped for COVID. Then we rehearsed. We lived together, and it was great. We ate together. That was a hard time for him because Universal did not make making that movie easy. What he pulled off with the extraordinarily limited budget is a miracle, simply.

AG: There are a lot of stories floating around about the studio not making *Halloween* easy on Rob. Was that something you were aware of?

Daniel Roebuck: No, not at all. Perhaps we didn't have that relationship where he would have mentioned that to me at that time. What I loved about his first *Halloween* movie was what I love about him. He's a storyteller, and the story isn't a guy stabbing people. The story is why did he stab people? I was surprised that there were a lot of fans who didn't take to it at first. The lesson I learned about Rob is that there is a contingency of the world that I think doesn't like how good things go for Rob Zombie. I don't know how else to say it. He's got a beautiful wife who's a beautiful person too. He's a rock star, and I've been to the concerts. He has ten thousand people come to see him play. That's a lot of people. He should be the representative of every guy who loves this stuff. People should look at him and go, "One of us is making it." But I think he's up against the opposite, which is to some extent people resent that he's good at a lot of things.

In *Halloween II*, he wrote that character who is wearing Frankenstein makeup. He calls and says this was going to be someone else, but what if it's you? Why can't it be the guy from the strip club inappropriately at some Halloween events giving out free stuff to kids? That's any community's worst nightmare. He thought of it, and he knew that I would like to wear the makeup, and then he could incorporate that makeup when we reshot it. My first time being killed, when we shot the kill in Atlanta, Tyler wasn't wearing the mask. Then we reshot it in Connecticut with Tyler wearing the mask, and it was much more effective. My death became a much bigger part of the movie.

AG: Your cut scenes from *Halloween* did live on. They're not in the theatrical version, but they are on the home video release. Any stories or recollections you wanted to share about those scenes that weren't as widely seen by audiences?

Daniel Roebuck: That was the first time I got to work with Sheri specifically. I like that because I kind of knew her, and we had never acted together. The Rabbit and Red Lounge set was really terrific. That would have been my second time working with Rob, so I knew that he liked when I went off script. We probably shot one the way it was written, and then he probably said, "Just have a conversation and have the cameras rolling."

I think because he's an iconoclast to some extent he's always gonna come up against the man. I think he thinks way beyond what they could think. Harvey Weinstein and Bob, these guys did not have couth. They're without couth, and they had the hubris of their success. Wouldn't it be great to go, "Jeez, we got this guy. He does things his way. Let's see what he does." They would have never had that same attitude with Quentin Tarantino. But Rob wasn't Quentin in their eyes. They were the worst of what Hollywood had to offer for that period of time. We could argue that great things came out of it, but at what cost to the moral fabric of Hollywood? At what cost did those Oscars come? All those movie stars that looked the other way so they could stay in their good graces. I condemn all of them.

AG: Were you surprised that Rob made a second *Halloween* film?

Daniel Roebuck: I was surprised and elated. I was elated because of my narcissism. I was saddened that I didn't get to have more of an impact in the first movie, but how wonderful that I got to be twenty years older in the second movie. My dad and brother came to the set, and once they put me in the makeup, I looked as old as my dad, who's twenty-one years older than I am.

AG: Would you describe the second film as being pretty comparable in terms of atmosphere while making the movie to the first?

Daniel Roebuck: Creatively, they were the same because Rob is Rob. What was kind of fun about the second one was that it wasn't made in Los Angeles. They were shooting down in Atlanta. So that gave Rob the ability to make the town a little more alive. When you're in Los Angeles, you are limited by how much small-town America you can really shoot. California, it's just too new of a state to have the old courthouses or whatnot unless you go to the hinterlands of California. I think it gave him a much bigger canvas on which to work. You'll note that the movie is wider, bigger.

-CHAPTER 6-
THE BLUMHOUSE ERA

Following Rob Zombie's *Halloween II* in 2009, there was a nine-year gap between films. Those were messy years for the Brothers Weinstein, and as their empire crumbled, Blumhouse Productions stepped in and acquired the rights to the franchise. While it came as little surprise that the series would again move into a new timeline, the hiring of comedy heavyweights Danny McBride [*Pineapple Express, The Righteous Gemstones*] and David Gordon Green [*Pineapple Express, Your Highness*] to spearhead the return to Haddonfield was a shock to many. In *Halloween* (2018), Jamie Lee Curtis returned to the franchise that had launched her career, once again. Narratively speaking, Laurie Strode suffering from PTSD as a result of what had happened to her on Halloween night 1978 was becoming the norm for the franchise. We saw it in *H20*, and then Rob Zombie used the formula as well. The Blumhouse trilogy embraces the same theme, though its execution looks drastically different.

The glaring difference here is that *Halloween* (2018), the first of the Blumhouse films, ignores everything that came before except for the first film. This means Michael and Laurie are no longer siblings. While I can understand retconning out large portions of the series, why would Michael come back after some random girl he hadn't killed forty years later if she's not his sister? On the other hand, David Gordon Green and team have a very specific view of the Shape and what exactly he represents. In this trilogy, he is the pain and suffering of society. He is our collective torment. He is more the Shape and less Michael Myers, summoned by people through their actions, through their fears. In this context, it makes perfect sense to ignore everything but the first film.

The Blumhouse trilogy really leans into the *Choose Your Own Adventure* modality that the franchise had adopted over the years. By this point, we had had four distinct timelines, and really, why not create a fifth? Why be beholden to previous filmmakers' visions if you can just start over? Of course, this doesn't sit well with everyone, and that's okay. Pivoting and telling new stories with new versions of the characters allows Haddonfield to go on and on. In the films that focus on the trauma of Laurie Strode, she is presented in different ways: battling alcoholism as she tries to hold it together for the sake of her son and career in *H20*; succumbing to mental illness in Rob Zombie's *Halloween II*; and here evoking Linda Hamilton in *Terminator 2*. Changes like this make each era or timeline feel distinctive.

Halloween Kills, the second film in the Blumhouse trilogy, is extremely fascinating. It works best when you view it as the middle chapter of a trilogy instead of as a stand-alone film. The body count is over thirty people. Killing is practically the point of the film: Michael didn't get Laurie and goes on his most bloody killing spree yet in Haddonfield after she escapes him. Death after death after death: this film is solely about the brutality of Michael Myers. Whereas *Halloween* (2018) presents Michael Myers as a flesh-and-blood killer for the most part, *Halloween Kills* poses the idea that perhaps Michael is more myth than man. We see his decades-long impact on the town. We see how the trauma he's caused has defined the lives of the people who live in Haddonfield. His 1978 murders have had the type of impact that a large-scale, mass shooting would have on a community, or a devastating natural disaster. Of course multiple homicides in one evening are painful and will forever leave an impression on a community. But this was . . . more than just lasting grief. Michael's mayhem had cast a permanent spell on this town. When he came back four decades later to kill again, his damage was much greater than the first time, forcing those who survived to figure out how to move forward. Do we band together as a community or are we irreparably broken? Are we left pointing fingers or trying to heal? In many ways, that's the theme of *Halloween Ends*, the film that followed: How does this particular community respond to the destruction in its midst? If we extrapolate, what does that say about humankind?

Halloween Ends is still frequently debated on social media. Much like *Season of the Witch* decades earlier, it operates outside the box. It's a tale of Haddonfield a few years removed from Michael's rampage. The town's spirit is broken; the people are judgmental and cruel. There's no collective healing. Hurt people have been left behind, and hurt people hurt other people. Fingers point at Laurie, accusing her of being responsible for all of this. Kids bully local teenager Corey Cunningham, and the whole town turns on him after an accident results in the death of a child he is babysitting. It isn't Corey's fault, but the townspeople want someone to blame, and Corey, already an outcast, is an easy target. He will pay for the pain caused by other people. This broken kid's surrender to the darkness and his aspirations of learning from Michael are a plotline few saw coming. It drew intensely negative reactions because it seemed unfathomable that the Shape would be as weak as depicted here or that he would ever train someone to become his heir apparent.

But these things do make sense under the pretext that Michael is more myth than man, as *Halloween Kills* wants us to believe. This was David Gordon Green and team establishing their own mythology. Whereas the franchise once used an ancient cult to explain the horror in Haddonfield and Rob Zombie then pivoted to mental illness and a traumatic family dynamic, the Blumhouse trilogy opts for a more metaphysical explanation. They never beat viewers over the head with exposition, but the subtext is there. *Halloween Ends* really functions on two levels: on one, a copycat killer fails to usurp the original, but a more sophisticated reading impresses upon us the notion that society creates monsters all the time, only some of whom rise to status of urban legend.

While the Blumhouse trilogy attempts to separate itself from the rest of the franchise, it cannot be ignored how closely these films follow the pattern established in the first three titles in the series. Much like *Halloween*, *Halloween* (2018) is the story of Michael wreaking havoc on Haddonfield, killing numerous people but failing to kill Laurie. *Halloween Kills* evokes *Halloween II* in that both are set on the same night as their immediate predecessor, both are set largely in a hospital where Laurie is recovering, and both feature a Michael who is more vicious than he appeared in the film that came immediately before. Then *Halloween Ends* follows the pattern of *Halloween III: Season of the Witch* by veering from the formula and trying to steer the story away from Michael Myers. *Halloween III: Season of the Witch* takes a heavy-handed approach by radically pivoting and removing Michael, whereas *Halloween Ends* deemphasizes Michael, demonstrating that his brand of evil can come from more than one source. The Blumhouse team claims that none of this was intentional, which makes the similarities even more fascinating.

Although *Halloween Ends* was always planned as the exit for David Gordon Green and team, they did leave a blueprint for whoever picks up the story, leaving behind a world without Michael (and Laurie) if the new creative team so chooses. But given the *Choose Your Own Adventure*-style world that *Halloween* and Haddonfield inhabit, any future filmmakers would likely have had that freedom anyway.

Interview: Jefferson Hall (Aaron, *Halloween* 2018)

AG: What was the casting process like for this film?

Jefferson Hall: The casting process was pretty ambiguous. I can't remember what they put it under. It was different, like an alias. They do that a lot. Most shows and films with that sort of level of infamy when they come in, they'll have a silly name. You wonder what you're really auditioning for. I can't remember if that was the case. But I knew it was David Gordon Green. I was a huge fan of David Gordon Green from *Eastbound & Down* and his comedy work. So I got asked to do a self tape, and I did one in my ex-girlfriend's living room with a leather bag over my shoulder. She read it, and we did the tape. I think we just did one tape. Maybe they were pushed for time, I don't know, but I think that was it. It was pretty straightforward.

Then I spoke to David on the phone. David's the sort of guy, he doesn't really bullshit or fuck around. He was very forthright. You know, "I want you to do it correctly." It was very exciting. I wasn't a fan of the movies at all. I don't really like horror movies. I don't think I'd ever seen *Halloween*. I think it's kind of a good thing to do, to go about castings that way. Otherwise I would have started thinking within the genre and playing those moments.

It was incredibly exciting. It was my first real, small part in a movie. I was like, "Wow, I'm going to America. I'm going to be in a film, and it's *Halloween*." So I watched the first *Halloween*. I was like, "God, I don't know about this movie. It seems pretty old to me." And like I said, it's not my genre at all, but I could see why he was doing it. The immediate sense was like, "Wow, this guy's really going to respect that original and approach it with some real authenticity with regards to how the original was made and tonally," similar to the way I think J. J. Abrams did with *Star Wars*. I remember having a feeling like *You've dug up the body and you're going to bring it back to life*, rather than like, *Oh, fuck the body. Let's just make a robot pick up some franchises.* He Dr. Frankensteined it. He cleaned it up, gave it some new eyeballs, and gave it a new brain. That was very exciting.

AG: Your character, Aaron, and his partner, Dana, open the film. Having true-crime podcasters open the film, seeking a conversation with Michael Myers, immediately roots the film in a modern setting and feels appropriate. Almost as if "Of course this should be happening in 2018." Did you draw from any specific sources or inspirations for this opening scene?

Jefferson Hall: No, not really. I don't really work particularly like that. I've lived a pretty varied life, so you just sort of say *I got it.* Had it been something that was really obscure to me, I'd probably do some research and go, *All right, how does this affect you?* But you start with yourself and then build up from there. And it's not just me wanting to sit around in a different costume. Maybe sometimes it is, actually depending on whether I care. But I did care about this; I could feel it in the writing and having watched the films. What I did do is watch the first two movies before this to get the flavor of who Michael was. That was more than enough for me.

I'm an actor. I'm pretty programmable. Haddonfield is a real place. He is a real dude. He did these things. I've got his mask. I've got the mask in there. Now I'm gonna go and visit him. Because of what happens to them, I think it needed to be approached in a way that's quite front foot and a bit sort of Piers Morgan-y, a bit sort of pushing it, pushing your luck a bit. I think he did have that sort of ruthless streak as a journalist. Bringing the mask into the asylum was a very sketchy move and misguided. That's the sort of thing a journalist like that would do to provoke a reaction.

AG: Visually, this scene in the courtyard is unsettling. The wide-open space, daylight setting, and the unique patterns on the ground are all striking. It's almost in direct opposition to most slasher films, which are set at night and in tight, enclosed spaces, where characters can't run or escape. I wanted to ask about your recollections filming this scene.

Jefferson Hall: There are times as an actor where you go into a job and you're like, *Yeah, just imagine it's like that.* And you're like, *This set's kind of shitty.* But this was like, *Holy fuck.* We went through all the iron bars. We went to a penitentiary to film the walk-through through the iron bars and stuff. There was a wire fence with all the inmates and stuff. So we were already on edge. We had to go through all those cages, which really primed you. But walking out into that square and seeing Michael with his back turned, it couldn't have been easier to sort of get into it. It's so intense, and it was a great start. I think we started with that as far as the structure of the shoot was concerned. That was our first thing we did, if I remember correctly. You really felt in that moment, that spacial thing you talked about, but you felt that as the character, standing there. You're like, *I'm so fucking vulnerable right now. This is crazy. What am I doing?* It's like those guys with the chicken carcasses on a grabby stick and hanging it over a crocodile's fence. It's like doing that without the fence.

I think it was James [Jude Courtney] that day. We did most of our stuff with James. He actually didn't wear the mask for all his bits, because he gets masks from us. So we hung out with James, and he's totally laid-back, like a surfer dude—really cool, laid-back guy. But then, when the action came, his physicality was so incredible. I went to a convention with him in Cincinnati, and I was thinking, *Cool, we're gonna sign some autographs, meet some fun people. It'll be a good time.* And James's fucking line went out the door around the building like he was part of the Beatles. I was like, *You can't even see his face in the film. I was so pissed* [laughs]. In hindsight, what he did physically in that first take was remarkable to me. It makes my hair stand up now because it was like there's something about this person that's not quite human, which is really spine-chilling.

AG: You had another scene with him, your death scene. It is memorable in the sense that it really begins to propel the story into a higher gear. Let's dive into that.

Jefferson Hall: That was in a studio that was in a hangar or something. They built that toilet. David was saying, "You know, you come back. You're gonna come back in *Halloween Kills*, and we'll have a scene with you in hospital," and there was talk about that. There was actually a scene that I read where I was like, "Kill the motherfucker!" Have you ever seen *Friends*? Remember Joey plays Dr. Drake Ramoray, and he gets killed off by the writer, and he gets pushed down an elevator shaft? There's a moment when he does it and they're filming, and he's really not into it. He's like, *Yeah, whatever, fuck you.* I remember being killed being a bit like that.

When I pushed over, David's shouting in a megaphone or something. I'm on the floor, and my eyes are flickering. If your eyes flicker a bit, there's still some life in you. There's still a chance that maybe they could change their minds. They might look at the dailies and say, "He's not so bad. We can get him an acting coach. He can come back in the second one." I wanted that so badly. And I was lying there with my eyes flickering, and David's shouting, "Shut your eyes!" So I shut them, but I still twitch them. He yells, "No, completely. Shut your eyes like you've been asleep for an hour." I was like, *You motherfucker*. So I did that.

Rhian [Rees, who portrayed Dana Haines] was amazing. She was really freaking out. It was really disturbing. The environment they created is very small. James was cool, but before he got into that, that was his thing, stunt violence. I think he's a very mild-mannered guy, but he puts on the mask without putting on the mask, if you know what I mean. Before the take, he would be getting pumped up, and I'd be like, "Come on, the fuck, just chill out." And he'd be like, "Yeah, yeah, yeah, yeah. I want to kill you." I was like, "Yeah, you know, like, you gotta pretend to kill me." And he had to like bash my head in, right? He's very professional. Every time he did, you know the small hairs on the back of your neck? He would catch those small hairs. And it's kind of worse than being punched in the dick. Those small hairs being pulled on the back of your neck, they really bring tears to you. They really hurt. They hurt in a way that makes you sort of go "Get off me!" rather than "He is killing me!" Really want to make me scream more petulantly than desperately. But I felt safe with him, but I was terrified also, because he was terrifying. David's a very humorous guy, and Danny [McBride] was around too, so there was a lot of humor put into it, and there was nothing heavy or sort of method about the set. But you did stuff like that, and you couldn't help but feel the horror of it. I thought it was pretty remarkable.

AG: David Gordon Green has become a polarizing figure in the *Halloween* fandom. Tell me a little about his style as a director and your memories of working with him.

Jefferson Hall: That is interesting, because I thought tonally his *Halloween* films were the most authentic, in a way, since the original. I think he brought a level of humor. I mean, a lot of people have done it. You see it with *Stranger Things*. You saw it with *Super 8*. It was another good example. The way they made movies back then [in the 1980s], there was something about them, something endearing and charming. I thought David walked a really thin line between it being self-referential and self-aware but also authentic and sort of Easter egg-y to the first one. But he didn't get carried away with that. I think he's got a childlike way of directing, a very genuine way, and a fun way. I think if he got bored with the way you were doing it, and that can happen—you plan how you're going to say something, and in the moment maybe you change it—he'd always run the take and say, "Just do this, say this, or respond to this. Just bug your eyes out, and then take it." He would keep it quite light and fun. Having met people at conventions, the hardcore fans, they're not jokers. Those people take it really seriously. I think they're very reverential about how it should be. David was great. He was amazing.

I had a little apartment there. I covered the walls, and I really actually drove myself mad. I forgot about this completely until now. Before I went over for the shoot, I got every book I could on serial killers. I didn't listen to podcasts, but I read everything I could read on serial killers. Obviously, it's disturbing, but I did that for like three weeks before the shoot. While I was there, I had photocopied a bunch of stuff and had them in this little apartment all over the walls. I got really into it. I wrote and wrote and wrote. I wrote endlessly. I remember one night I was writing, and I'd written so much, and it was so in me. I think I emailed David around midnight before the shoot the next day and said, "Listen, I've written this thing about tomorrow." He got there in the morning, and he'd printed it out, and he's like, "Cool, here are your lines." It was like two pages of me waffling about zero killers and the likeness to animals. I probably got it somewhere. I was really into that side of it, and he was really collaborative with that. He gave me some freedom to explore the character in that way because that was pivotal to the character.

David's amazing. He's in my top five directors—his energy, his irreverence, but also his knowledge of film and knowledge of that film particularly. Horror is not my genre, but I thought there were some remarkable moments that were just so cool, so exciting, so terrifying. Like you said, a lot of them weren't in the dark, and the ones that were in the dark played the light, like the security camera in the garden with the kid. I just thought it was amazing.

All my memories with him were so lighthearted and so lovely, and he was just a nerdy, funny dude.

AG: Many fans were intrigued by Danny McBride working as a writer and executive producer on *Halloween* films, as he was mostly known for his comedy work. Did you get to work with him much?

Jefferson Hall: I've met some pretty famous people, but I've never been so starstruck as I was with Danny McBride. I watched all of *Eastbound & Down*. I can quote that endlessly. Danny came in, and he was like, "What's up, motherfucker? You're the new Dr. Loomis. You're Loomis." I was like, *Oh my God.* I was late to the read through and sat next to him. God, he's handsome in real life. I said to my friends, "Why can't I make friends with him? I'm gonna make fucking friends with him." Never did. But yeah, he was around. He was around as a producer. Filming there is where their offices are [Charleston, South Carolina]. It's pretty much where they come from. It really had an indie vibe to it and a real sort of family vibe to it. There were no big stars on the set apart from Jamie, who was there, but she was great. Danny was around a bit, but it just wasn't one of those movies where you felt there was massive hierarchy and it was closed doors. We went to David's house to rehearse a scene. It was just really chill.

AG: Any additional on-set memories that you could share with me?

Jefferson Hall: I just remember that the team that worked on it was incredible. I remember going to the set where Jamie's character lived, and it had all those mannequins that she'd shoot out. I remember having a smoke break there and looking at that set and how eerie that was. It was just really, really thorough. David liked to have real people from town in the film. Whatever scene we did, I always felt like there was someone from the area in the scene. David was like, "I've seen this cool person. Let's get them in." I know that he involved the landscape and the people of that area into the film so you didn't feel like you were like, "Oh, we're on set." You felt like no matter where you were, you were kind of in the world. He created that environment incredibly. It was very conducive to sort of not just relaxing, but feeling you're in something from the get-go, from being in that checker block yard of all that crazy noise, being in the cells, and being in that penitentiary to being at a gas station, some locals sitting in a car who I don't think acted before. Yeah, he did all that. Like I said, it wasn't my genre, but I didn't ever feel like I was stuck in some sort of nerdy horror world. I thought I was in a movie about people, about a place, about a crazy guy.

Interview: Paul Brad Logan (Writer, *Halloween Ends*)

AG: What's your relationship with the *Halloween* series like?

Paul Brad Logan: I saw *Season of the Witch* first, which is a strange way to get into it, but the box art compelled me. I think I was eight at the time. Then I saw *Halloween 4* in the theater. It frightened me. I was still relatively young, maybe twelve or thirteen. There was something about that first *Halloween* movie, much like *Texas Chainsaw Massacre*—I knew that once I saw those films, I would maybe not be the same afterward. I was worried about my psyche, I think. And it's true. It's the most unnerving movie of that genre. It gets under your skin and definitely stays with you.

AG: It feels very real, like this could happen to anybody.

Paul Brad Logan: But it also skirts that line. It's a strange supernatural thing that's not supernatural. I always loved that. The *Friday the 13th* stuff was fun to watch as a kid. I could watch that and not have nightmares. That could be a party movie, but there was something about especially the original *Halloween* that was inexplicable and ambiguous about what that entity the Shape was. That really had that lasting effect for me.

AG: How did this job on *Halloween Ends* come to be?

Paul Brad Logan: I've been friends with David Gordon Green for a good fifteen years or so. Over those years we had written screenplays together, and the first movie that got made of mine, *Manglehorn*, David directed. It came out in 2015 and starred Al Pacino. Ever since then, we've been collaborators and send each other screenplays of what we're working on. I remember he contacted me in 2016 after he got that initial email from Jason Blum asking if he would be interested in taking on *Halloween*. I was over the moon excited for him to do it because I love when sort of idiosyncratic directors with a point of view and a voice take on specific genre stuff like that. Out of morbid curiosity, I wanted to know what David was going to do with *Halloween* and Michael Myers. He sent me a draft of the script that he, Danny McBride, and Jeff Fradley had written early on, and we were always in communication throughout that process. I think even before the movie came out, probably the summer of 2018, he started kicking around the ideas for sequels. I think initially their idea was to make the back-to-back movies, *Halloween* and then *Halloween Kills*. Jason Blum said, "Why don't you just make the first one, and we'll see how it does?" So after he had made it, he started talking to me and asking me if I had any ideas for a sequel. He sort of had this loose idea for a sequel that was going to be parallel timelines. One timeline would be set in '78, and the other would be set in the present day. I pitched some ideas for it, and then he hired Scott Teems to work on that with him. I guess my ideas weren't right for that one.

Then, maybe a month later, he called me and his other screen screenwriting friend Chris Bernier to join him in Charleston and start brainstorming ideas for what our final chapter could be. The only sort of prompt that he had was that he wanted it to take place several years after the events of 2018. He wanted to see all the characters in a different place, and he wanted to have the Shape missing within this world. And that was really it.

AG: That's very interesting, that this wasn't always conceived as a trilogy.

Paul Brad Logan: I think David had ideas from the get-go—the way that *Halloween Kills* was going to be done and then the idea of the third one with Laurie in a different place. We wanted it to be an organic experience. David's so fun to work with. I wish everybody could work with him, because writing stuff with him is like a creative playground. Meeting together and brainstorming all of these ideas for what this movie could be was like a three-week writers' workshop where we just came up with every insane version of this story, just to see what was going to grab us and what was going to make us have a reason for telling the story. If you're just going to make a movie just to make a movie, it's pointless, and people can see through that. Or at least I can, and I don't wanna be a part of that. I want to do something I feel good about. I remember once we were brainstorming, and David was like, "Hey, Paul, why don't you go back to your room tonight and write *Halloween Ends* as if it were *Gummo*" [cult classic film from 1997]? So I did. I only cranked out like forty or fifty pages, but it was like my version of maybe what Harmony Korine would have done in '96 as a follow-up to *Gummo*. It sort of unlocked all these creative ideas and really gets everything moving. It all began with that opening scene, the babysitting scene. Once that happened, then we knew what story we wanted to tell, and we got very excited. Then the process moved pretty quickly once we had that first scene. That was sort of our key to unlocking what we wanted the story to be.

AG: Like most, I did not see the first scene coming. I was immediately caught off guard and felt uncomfortable. After the film ended, I had some time to process it. I started to think about how in slasher movies, there is a formula that they follow and the way that your film completely skirted that formula. It made me feel very uncomfortable throughout the movie because I didn't know what to expect. You totally removed all expectations after that first scene. I thought that was a brilliant stroke.

Paul Brad Logan: That's nice to hear. I can't even say that it was an intentional thing to subvert every expectation. We wanted to tell a story that we hadn't seen before, to be as organic, genuine, and authentic with that idea as we can. I've since heard people describe the opening scene in similar ways, but it was never something I was thinking about. For me, this is the opening scene, and this is what happens to this character and what sets him on this journey. It was definitely super exciting when that idea came to us. That was pretty much the one thing that sort of stayed the same. We worked on this damn script for I don't even know how long. That was January of 2019 when we started this. I was still doing drafts while we were filming, writing new scenes and stuff in the spring of 2022. That scene was the only scene that I could never change. It was always pretty much verbatim of the way it was conceptualized from the beginning. I thought that was the most interesting aspect because every other scene in the film, there's the other side of it that we explored, but that scene was always the same.

AG: Your film followed a lot of the social commentary that started in the previous film, where everybody in the town has almost this one-track mind, and we see the dangers of that. In your film, some of that bleeds over, but there's also a finger pointed at society, especially with the Corey character and the way that society treated him. And with Laurie too we see examples of everybody just pointing a finger at her and blaming her for things that perhaps she wasn't in control of. How important was this message to you as a writer?

Paul Brad Logan: It's one of those things that was organic to the story. It was never anything that I was thinking about like, *This is our comment on society or our comment on groupthink*. It seemed like such a natural part of this world that it has been overwrought with fear and grief. In the rubble of that broken spiritedness, it's an angry place, and you can't really pin it to anything. It's like this ambiguous, evil energy that's just infiltrated them. It's in the soil, it's in the water, and it's all created by this monster. Without that person to indict, you're looking at whoever else you can blame or for meaning for your existential rage, your existential grief, and all of those things. For me, it was always more of a character trait. I grew up in west Texas, a small oil town. It was a real boom-and-bust place. Most of my childhood was spent during the bust time. Sort of a derelict town, and I just grew up being very afraid of people. It seemed like there's a very sinister energy within a world that's broken. In the movies I grew up on, like the Stephen King movies and books, there was always this element that I related to within these small towns. Haddonfield fit that sort of mold. It was an organic part of what they had started in *Halloween Kills* and, for us, what this town was to us would look like four years later.

AG: One of the strengths of this trilogy was how the town of Haddonfield was handled. The setting was a character in a sense.

Paul Brad Logan: I love a sense of place, and the movies that always resonate with me and resonated with me since I was a kid were movies that felt almost regional or even like *Twin Peaks*, for example.

AG: That's exactly what I was thinking, *Twin Peaks.*

Paul Brad Logan: *Twin Peaks* was definitely something that we would talk about, especially with the sort of angsty teen delinquent, David Lynch's take on fifties, juvenile delinquency, but set in 1990. His perspective on that was so formative for me, someone who grew up loving *Rebel Without a Cause* and *The Wild Ones.* I just love teen-angst movies, whether it's *Pump Up the Volume* or even *The Wild Ones. Twin Peaks* was the perfect combination of all of those things, and that was definitely something we were very aware of. David Lynch is a hero of all of ours, but I worship him.

AG: I think there's a lot of comparisons between your film and *Twin Peaks: The Return.* Horror has moved into a place where it's more thoughtful and also less on the nose. But similar to [*Twin Peaks*] *The Return*, it wasn't always about concrete answers. To kind of tie it to the Corey character, I didn't need to know all the answers about the journey that he took. I saw the pain that he was in, and I saw what the end result was. I didn't necessarily have to know if it was a supernatural thing or an emotional thing. What mattered to me was watching his journey, and the actual explanation was secondary.

Paul Brad Logan: I agree. I think all of us that worked on it have our own ideas of what that specific thing is. But even when writing it, it was almost like we were very careful not to define it with one another. David [Gordon Green] is great about keeping things open so he can explore them even as he goes into the film. It's not so completely definitive that we have to nail this story beat and get to this point and get to this point. As things present themselves in one scene, it might open something up for a moment later. He's very open and immediate in letting real life come into the filmmaking part of it, and following the instincts and inspirations is a big part of what makes his movies the way they are. Same with me, growing up being so inspired by filmmakers like Hal Ashby, Robert Altman, and John Boorman, those filmmakers from the seventies who made you feel like you were watching real moments happen. Even with big cinematic set pieces, they still had enough real-world emotions in it to feel like it was really happening and you were watching it as it happened.

AG: It just dawned on me that I will never look at the motorcycle scene with Allyson and Corey the same. I will always correlate that to *Twin Peaks* and James Hurley.

Paul Brad Logan: I've got a sticker that our makeup person on the movie made of them on the motorcycle. I was like, "Oh man, I am sixteen all over again watching *Twin Peaks*." I just totally geek out at that moment of seeing them on that motorcycle, just the energy. It's just so cool: a guy on a motorcycle at night with a girl he's really into on the back of it.

AG: There's a forbidden love feeling to it too. It's dangerous, and then the mood, the lighting, and the music—it was special.

Paul Brad Logan: I totally agree. I just love it so much. I can even separate myself from it as someone who worked on it and just appreciate it as what it is. I remember watching the first cut I ever saw at a test screening in Las Vegas a few months before it came out. I didn't know what music was going to be playing over the motorcycle scenes, and then when I saw it, I just wanted to live in that moment.

AG: I don't want to assume that this was deliberate, but I have to ask about the homages to *Halloween III: Season of the Witch*. There's visuals that are definitely linked, such as the title card, but also in a sense, the story seems to almost be a response to *Halloween III*, almost like saying, "This is how you move away from Michael Myers." Was that deliberate at all?

Paul Brad Logan: I don't know if David had any deliberate intentions. I just think it's very strange, and I don't think this was intentional. I think this just happened. I'm going to stand by my narrative that this just happened organically because it wasn't intentional on my part, even though I love *Halloween III*, so much. But it's very strange how David's three movies sort of follow the first three *Halloween* films.

It's just a very strange thing. Even when I'm reading the first outline for what *Halloween Kills* was going to be, it didn't even dawn on me all the similar stuff between that and *Halloween II*. It didn't dawn on me until I watched it. Even without trying to do it, you made some sort of response to *Halloween II*. For *Halloween Ends*, I didn't think the font would be used for the credits. That wasn't something that was in the script. Then when it happened and I'm watching it, I was unable to not think of how this is like our crazy version of *Halloween III*. It's something I just never thought about when writing it, and it just sort of happened naturally.

AG: My takeaway right after seeing the film was that they have set it up for future filmmakers to come in and take over the series but without Michael perhaps. You had given the gift of moving away from Michael but still having the *Halloween* name to whichever filmmaker was next.

Paul Brad Logan: I'm a sucker for watching Michael Myers or Jason

Voorhees or Leatherface or Norman Bates walk around and murder people. So fun. I know I've got a paralyzing problem when it comes to ideas. If something has already been done, I can't really do that again. I would be distraught if I was sitting there just trying to write him going from this place to this place and killing this person. There's so many movies like that, and we can all enjoy all of them. I wanna see different stories within this world, within this mood, within this energy. I want to ask questions like "What is the mythology of this town and how can that play a role?" I always like to come at things a little bit like thinking about things like a book or a novel that can cover more ground. That's what interests me. I just wanna see the world open up a bit, and I wanna see what's going on in the corners of this place that haven't been explored before—what this town feels like, what it smells like, what it looks like. Those are the things that interest me. *Halloween Kills* is all Michael Myers. It's so much. I'm not dismissing him. I think he's a natural part of this world. He's what creates this world. I remember saying to David, "He's gotta be living under the bridge. Almost like a storybook monster, he's mythology at this point. He's the bogeyman." That was one of the big ideas in these other movies—what is the bogeyman? Is he the bogeyman? This movie is like, "He is the bogeyman. That's what he is." If the bogeyman exists in this world, what is that going to do to the people within that world? That was something that I felt very compelled to think about when writing this.

In our early drafts, there were direct references to *Halloween III*. There were scenes where the commercial is playing on TV because the Silver Shamrock Factory is alive and well. I think the reason it got pulled was some sort of copyright bullshit. One day the stuff wasn't in there anymore. I don't really remember the answer why. The industry is so boring. You just wanna go make stuff that you feel good about, is fun, and you feel passionate about, and then at every turn there's somebody else who owns this part of this thing and . . . yeah. I'm so naive in my approach to that stuff. I just want to be completely pure and unadulterated by lawyers and studios.

AG: There was a heavy marketing push for the final confrontation of Michael and Laurie.

Paul Brad Logan: You can't do anything about the marketing, but my God, it was good. It's a complicated thing, and I try to stay out of it. But the confrontation between Laurie and Michael, there were all these different versions of what happened in that last part of the movie. I would propose a cat-and-mouse, sort of like a hide-and-seek situation. Again, you're just going to do what they've done in so many other movies and what David already sort of did in 2018 with his climax. If they're going to come face-to-face one last time, it's just gotta be intimate, stripped down, and brutal. It's gotta be emotional and psychological. That's where we went. It's a weird thing when you're working on something. You're so into the making of it. The expectations are there. They're never not there, but it's not the only thing you're thinking about. If it were, it would be such a paralyzing proposition to even do anything. At a certain point, you just have to follow the story, believe in it, and be okay with it. It wasn't until *Halloween Kills* actually came out that I started to wonder what people will think of the movie we've written. That was the first time I actually started thinking about it in terms of a vocal minority who will have a lot of things to say about this. To be honest, when I saw *Halloween Kills* for the first time, the test screening was one of the best screenings I ever saw in my life. I was like, "This is the greatest thing ever. My God, it's so entertaining and it's so exciting, and it just races by." I just thought it was so fun. Then, when it came out, I heard a lot of chatter about it. I just knew that *Halloween Ends* would have a louder chatter around it. I don't know if it did or didn't because I sort of tapped out. I did get a lot of messages sent to me that let me know that there were a lot of people who had strong opinions about it, to put it lightly. It is fun, though, to have something that people feel something about, and that's great.

So much credit is due to Rohan [Campbell, who played Corey]. He's just a force of nature. He's so good. I wrote fake dialogue for him to perform in auditions, so he didn't know what the movie was that he was auditioning for. He just knew that David was directing it. Maybe he had some suspicion it was *Halloween Ends*. After hearing this dialogue a couple of times with different people, Rohan came in and was making every single thing work. I can't say enough incredible things about him. It was just a really fun experience getting to watch him perform. I wish there was more time spent with Allyson and

Corey's characters, especially Allyson. I wrote the novelization, so I got to live in the world a little bit longer and go deeper into their characters, and Allyson in particular is a character I love very much Their relationship does so much for the movie, and it's almost a little unfair because we wrote this and then they're making it like a million times better.

AG: Was there ever any consideration for Corey to survive and maybe leave him ambiguously out there?

Paul Brad Logan: That's interesting. I had about four hundred drafts of the screenplay—every iteration of everything you can think of, especially that last ten to fifteen minutes. We went through every single idea you could possibly have. I can't really speak too much about it other than I think we all knew that this was going to be David's final movie within this series. I don't think any of us felt that anybody was going to pick it up and carry that story along. Whoever owns the rights, they're going to do whatever they're gonna do with it. Let them be free to tell their stories any way they want to, and hopefully they will feel as compelled to do something. I just want people to tell the story that means something to them, that they have a reason for telling and not just like, "Okay, we've got this thing that'll generate money. Let's crank out another version of it." I think that's what happened to so many of those sequels, and they just get so watered down and commercial. Hopefully people will start looking at these things like, "Oh, this might be a place to explore a certain characterization, a certain mood, a certain tone, a certain emotion," which is, I think, the great thing about horror movies in general: they give you that room to explore those things.

AG: I do need to ask about the finality of it all. In the scripts and the final version, you went to great lengths to show that not only was Michael dead, but Michael was disintegrated. What was the thinking behind that definitive of an ending?

Paul Brad Logan: We always knew that this was it; this was the period in our story. David did not want any ambiguity with that character. I think he just could hear the groans if there was something, if you see Michael's hand twitch or if you see his chest move or if you hear him breathe. David could almost hear the groans in the theater. Once he said this is going to happen, there was not really much discussion about it. We know where we're going with this, and we're just going there and that's going to happen. I think he just really wanted definitive closure on it for his version of this movie. I don't think he was necessarily looking at it like the end of everything, you know. In a year or two, somebody else is going to own this, and they're gonna go do their own thing, and let's see what they do with it. That was sort of it. It was a definitive ending for our story. We had different variations of the ending. The junkyard scene with him was a rewritten scene that David went and filmed after we made the movie. There were other variations, but in every other variation, he was killed definitively. In every single version we ever did, that was something that never changed.

-CHAPTER 7- THE TIMELINES

While retcons, sequels, and even requels are commonplace these days in the horror film genre, *Halloween* is different. Across the thirteen films in the franchise, there are no fewer than five timelines. For some, this might be a source of frustration. Others might welcome the *Choose Your Own Adventure* type of feel. And then there are those who simply go along with whatever the story might be as long as Michael is there wreaking havoc. In many ways, this Michael-verse is a testament to how strong this franchise truly is, that it can keep reinventing itself. People want *Halloween* to last forever. In this chapter, we are going to analyze the five timelines. We'll look at what makes each timeline unique and explore the possibility of a future for each of them.

Timeline 1: *Halloween, Halloween II, Halloween 4, Halloween 5*, and *Halloween: The Curse of Michael Myers.*

It would be fair to call this the original timeline save for a brief detour with Season of the Witch. In this timeline, Michael kills his older sister, Judith, when he is six years old and then returns fifteen years later to come for his younger sister, Laurie. After successfully fighting off Michael and leaving him in a fire-induced coma, Laurie has a baby [Jamie Lloyd] with an unnamed father and then dies in a car wreck when that baby is still young. Ten years after he failed to kill Laurie, Michael once again escapes, and this time he's coming for his niece. A larger mythology unfolds, revealing that an ancient cult had claimed Michael as a child, and now he is looking to pass down this curse. This timeline ends with Michael killing the remaining cult members, in effect ending the curse, including an ambiguous off-camera scene where Michael, nearly dead himself, finally kills Loomis. It's unclear if Michael also dies or not. He has been subjected to a beatdown from Tommy Doyle [Paul Rudd], and had the franchise not changed course after this film, he surely would have lived. But there is an argument to be made that with the Thorn cult decimated, maybe Michael, without his powers, succumbed to the Power of Paul Rudd.

This is the timeline longtime *Halloween* fans are used to. A complete story is told. An explanation for all the violence and madness is given, and the cycle appears to be over. Up to this point, there have been no reboots. With the exception of one stand-alone film, the first six entries in the *Halloween* franchise build off each other, carrying plot points forward. It's one cohesive story. Messy and convoluted at times, yes, but still cohesive. Obviously, the first film is universally loved, but the second and fourth films also rank high on the list of franchise favorites for many. The fifth and sixth *Halloween* films have their cult followings (pun intended). This is the *Halloween* timeline many people grew up on, and they had mixed feelings when it was disrupted.

Timeline 2: *Halloween, Halloween II, Halloween: H20*, and *Halloween: Resurrection*

When *Halloween H20* came out in 1998, people were confused. Back then, film franchises didn't retcon multiple movies out of a franchise, but that's exactly what happened here. For the big twentieth-anniversary return of Jamie Lee Curtis, the writers and producers deemed it necessary to change the canon of *Halloween*. The first two films, which Curtis had starred in, still happened. But everything that came after no longer did. Now it turned out Laurie Strode had developed a drinking problem after her hellish encounter with her older brother, changed her name, had a baby, and gone into hiding. Jamie Lloyd, who had carried the previous three installments in the franchise, was replaced by a son and never mentioned again. This, arguably, is what bothered many fans the most. Jamie had in effect replaced Laurie. Now we're supposed to act like she and her films didn't exist? Back then especially, it was a lot for fans to wrap their heads around and get behind.

On one hand, it could be argued that this reboot/retcon was inevitable. *Halloween 6: The Curse of Michael Myers*'s dark, detailed mythology suggested the franchise would center on Michael moving forward. Reintroducing Laurie in this timeline would have been difficult. This was now a story about an ancient cult rather than Michael's obsession with killing his younger sister. This dark subject matter also made it difficult for future films in the franchise to resemble typical slasher fare: teenagers being teenagers, running from a masked killer hell-bent on death and violence. How do you step back from the Cult of Thorn and return to a prototypical slasher?

Timeline two gave us the return of Laurie, the death of Laurie in the franchise's eighth film, and a reboot of sorts as a result of removing the previous three films from the franchise canon. What would Michael do now that his sister was dead? Go home and kill anyone he came across. It was a simple yet effective strategy that set the franchise up to keep going without the heavy baggage of a complex mythology. After *Halloween: Resurrection*, the franchise found itself in an interesting place of not knowing where to go next; the board had been cleared, so to speak. Timeline two abruptly ends however. The closing shot of *Halloween: Resurrection* shows us Michael is very much alive, so this timeline can play out in our minds however we would like it to.

Timeline 3: The Rob Zombie Films

Despite the second timeline's removal of legacy characters and complex plots, the franchise's producers never found a new direction to take the series in. It's a shame, because they had a clean slate and could have done anything they wanted. To cash in on the remake craze of the early 2000s seemed aberrational for a franchise that was known for being bold and trendsetting, not trend following. But rather than the producers committing to any of the pitches on how to move forward, *Halloween* joined the list of modern horror classics that were being remade.

Group photo on set of *Halloween* 2007. Image courtesy of Phil Parmet

Rob Zombie, in his two *Halloween* films, had imprinted his own identity on the franchise, despite major studio pushback. Michael was no longer cursed by a cult or even killing randomly; he had endured years of childhood trauma. This Michael was much more like the real-life serial killers of that era: less supernatural, more Richard "Night Stalker" Ramirez. This was shocking to some longtime fans, whereas others appreciated the psychology. Zombie's films were grittier and more overt than the franchise films that preceded them. They had the "Southern sleaze" feel of many seventies and eighties horror films; suddenly it was as if Haddonfield had been dropped inside *The Devil's Rejects*.

This timeline is fairly cut-and-dried. Michael kills his older sister, Judith (again); her boyfriend; and his stepfather. He's locked away for many years (again) and returns home for his sister, but this time not to kill her. Rather, he seems to want to reunite with her as brother and sister. When she rejects him, he snaps. Laurie fights him off (again) and suffers severe mental-health ramifications as a result. In the end, Laurie snaps and, depending on how you look at it, either gives in to the darkness within her (as her brother did with his) or suffers a complete mental collapse due to severe trauma. Could this timeline have continued? Possibly. But how fascinating would it have been if Rob Zombie had followed John Carpenter's original path and made a third film not involving Michael or Laurie at all? What if Rob had been empowered to pull a *Season of the Witch* and make films about terrible things that happen on Halloween night? Think of the potential. Rob Zombie is a talented filmmaker who felt shackled by the constraints of a remake and by fans pushing back against stylistic changes.

There was also room to continue with Laurie and Michael in this timeline. While the ending of *Halloween II* (particularly the director's cut) feels definitive, is anything ever definitive in the Michael-verse? While I'm sure a segment of fans would have revolted, another film showing Laurie wrestling with her dark side with Michael appearing to her the same way their mother had appeared to him in *Halloween II* would have been captivating. While this is easily the most polarizing timeline, the entries that unfold here are good horror films for the most part, and they do add value to the franchise. The likelihood of this timeline ever being revisited is next to none, though, as the franchise went on to reinvent itself yet again.

Timeline 4: *Halloween, Halloween (2018), Halloween Kills*, and *Halloween Ends*

The David Gordon Green trilogy might not be as divisive as Rob Zombie's two films, but it's close. The franchise had already retconned out three films and produced two remakes (perhaps better described as reimaginings) by this point. The idea of once again removing multiple films from the franchise narrative seemed slightly preposterous, yet not out of the question. At this point, *Halloween*'s producers were clearly fine with clusters of films telling a story, then another cluster of films telling a different story. Why not introduce a new timeline that removes even the beloved 1981 sequel, *Halloween II*, as well as the two latter Jamie Lee Curtis entries so that a new generation of horror fans can have their own timeline?

The David Gordon Green trilogy told fans to ignore everything but the first film. Michael was just an evil babysitter killer, not Laurie's brother. She's lived through forty years of trauma, and what happens when untreated trauma resurfaces? The concept was intriguing. There's an emphasis on telling a sustained, cohesive story here. And for those people who loved the first film but fell off over the years due to how many films there were and how many times the timeline had been altered, this was an easy sell: none of that had me happened except that film you really liked back in the day.

Whether you enjoyed this trilogy or not, David Gordon Green and team should be given credit for telling the story they wanted to tell and seeing it through. They provided their own answers, albeit sometimes abstractly, in ways that didn't tell viewers how to interpret the material. Draw your own conclusions. These three films came out during turbulent times and offered heaping doses of social commentary, which was unique for this franchise. For some, that was a turnoff. It wasn't what they wanted from a Michael Myers flick. Others, myself included, felt that it added interesting layers to the narrative. Many fans were simply happy to have new stories involving Laurie Strode and Michael Myers and either embraced the new timeline or tolerated it as the price paid for getting two of their favorite cinematic characters reunited. *Halloween Ends* posed questions about the mythology of the Shape and laid the groundwork for future filmmakers to build on, in a few different directions. There's a path for someone else to be the Shape and take the reins of terror from Michael Myers himself. There's also a path to be taken without the Shape at all. The future of this franchise was left wide open, a generous gift to whoever takes over from here.

Timeline 5: *Halloween III: Season of the Witch*

Yes, the stand-alone third film in this franchise is set within a timeline all its own. In this world, *Halloween* is simply a movie, as evident by the fact that the film plays on TV early on in *Season of the Witch*. The "meta" concept wasn't common in horror back then, but credit for this innovation, typically attributed to Kevin Williamson and Wes Craven because of the *Scream* movies, should go to Tommy Lee Wallace and John Carpenter as well.

Could this timeline have continued? Well, I suppose that depends on how you interpret the ending of this film. Possibly yes. There was the potential for more story within the *Season of the Witch* universe. This also could have launched an anthology of stories connected only by transpiring on Halloween night, as John Carpenter and team intended. Perhaps television is the better place for the anthology concept if it were to resume now. It would provide a clear distinction between the Michael Myers entries and the anthology entries: the Shape on the big screen and other Halloween-themed stories on the small screen.

Conclusions

One could argue that *Halloween*'s fractured continuity and multiple timelines are a strength of the franchise. For a series to span four decades, reinvention is a must. Finding new fans is a must. We can each have our own *Halloween* story. Maybe we cling to the Cult of Thorn arc, or maybe the mythology was too much for us and we found comfort in Laurie returning in *H20*. For others, Rob Zombie's stylistic changes or David Gordon Green's simplifying of the mythology (by removing large parts of it) might be of more interest. There's beauty in choice in the Michael-verse.

This also leaves us with a wide-open future. It's highly improbable that any of these timelines are returned to at this point (except perhaps the David Gordon Green trilogy), given the franchise's penchant for reinvention. Fresh, new voices can sign on to this film series with the freedom to tell the stories they want. The precedent has been set. *Halloween* isn't afraid to be bold. The horror genre over the years has become more artistic, more daring, forcing filmmakers to move away from dated tropes in order to be recognized. While *Halloween* films are unlikely to ever venture too far into the art house realm, boundaries can continue to be pushed. and the sky's the limit for a franchise that isn't afraid to explore new directions and take creative risks.

-CHAPTER 8- THE *HALLOWEENS* THAT NEVER WERE

No look at the *Halloween* franchise would be complete without reviewing the deleted scenes and many unmade scripts. This is quite the daunting task. As part of my research for this book, I read *Taking Shape* and *Taking Shape II*, written by Dustin McNeill and Travis Mullins. McNeill and Mullins tirelessly examine every unmade script and deleted scene they could find, resulting in two treasure troves of information that every horror fan needs to read. I became fascinated with these authors and their obvious labors of love. It dawned on me that interviewing them would be far more interesting than trying to cram as much information as possible into one chapter. McNeill and Mullins are not only incredibly knowledgeable, they're also really great guys. Befriending them has been a highlight of the *Horror in Haddonfield* experience for me. Below is a conversation I had with both Dustin McNeill and Travis Mullins through email.

AG: Do you recall when you became fans of the *Halloween* series? What was the journey like from fans to authors of must-own books detailing the franchise?

Dustin McNeill: I came into the franchise around the time of *Halloween: The Curse of Michael Myers*, which I vividly recall seeing advertised at my local video store. That iconic poster of the mask bathed in eerie blue light and the gloved hand clutching a knife, it's seared into my memory. I would study with wonder and fascination the covers of the videotapes for *Halloween* one to six at the store, but I couldn't yet rent them, as I was only twelve. I could, however, catch them on television, which I did, scouring the weekly listings for broadcasts until I'd seen all the earlier installments. My first theatrical experience with *Halloween* was *Halloween H20*, which was so massive that year. It was on all the magazine covers and newspaper front pages, even *USA Today*, and it even had its own half-hour prime-time making-of special on the Syfy Channel. I'm probably the world's biggest *H20* cheerleader.

Online, the fandom commotion for *H20* was like nothing else I've ever seen. The official site did almost daily updates right up until the day of release. It was so exciting. Like everyone else, I had my own fan site hosted on Geocities, which had an image gallery, movie descriptions, MIDI files, and a guestbook, of course. It was among the hundreds of fan sites listed on the HalloweenMovies.com links page, which was the honor of all honors. This gigantic online community is, in large part, what influenced the direction of *Halloween:Resurrection*.

I should skip forward some. Twenty years go by, and I'm still an ardent fan, having enjoyed the Blumhouse reboot. Sensing the revitalized fan base in the wake of *Halloween* (2018), I suddenly had the itch to document the franchise's history in a massive book, which was long overdue anyway. It was certainly a franchise worthy of having a making-of book, and the readership was beyond ready for it. I'd already written and published well-received books on *Phantasm* and *Freddy vs. Jason*, so I felt adequately prepared to tackle *Halloween*. There's no way I could've started with a franchise as top shelf as *Halloween* is. You've got to build up to it, and I did.

Travis and I shared a strong interest in the unproduced *Halloween* movies, which we'd always planned to cover in an appendix section. At some point, that appendix grew to the same size as our coverage of the eleven actually produced movies, which led me to spin it off into a second book: *Taking Shape II: The Lost Halloween Sequels*. I'm proud of what we were able to uncover in the first *Taking Shape*, but *Taking Shape II* was really envelope pushing in how much new information it contained. We got writers, directors, producers, and even studio execs to open up about unmade projects that no one had ever heard of. The wild thing is that *Taking Shape II* turned out to be substantially longer than the first *Taking Shape*. Not bad for an appendix!

Travis Mullins: It's fun to look back on this. I first became aware of *Halloween* when I was ten. I had stumbled upon a showing of *Halloween 5* on AMC as part of the channel's annual FearFest programming, then called MonsterFest. I really knew nothing about the franchise other than it was a series of horror films and they starred Jamie Lee Curtis. I knew her from *Freaky Friday*. I was expecting to see her in this particular sequel. Little did I know that I was also very familiar with Danielle Harris from her other work. Movies have always been a huge part of my life, and by this point, I had access to a computer. One of the most fun things for me then was perusing IMDb and its message boards, learning movie trivia and making connections between films and actors. I was not a horror fan, though—too young, and I was raised on a collection of Disney VHS tapes, so I was a bit of a fairy princess at heart. I didn't have a lot of restrictions placed on my TV viewing, but I never wanted to be scared and had enough sense to back away from anything that felt like it was going to affect me in that way. Growing up, though, I had stumbled upon a couple of shocking images that stayed with me—mostly from Stephen King's *It*—and I guess there was a bit of a thrill there, because I then bought the book and started carrying that around in elementary school like it was nothing. But I'll say it was *Halloween* that was really my gateway to horror.

By the time you get to *Halloween 5*, you're already so far down the rabbit hole in terms of the series mythos that after watching it, I felt like I needed to know what came next and what came before. At the time, we had a neighbor whose ex-husband must've been a huge horror fan, because he left behind a huge collection of horror tapes, and it was from this collection that I discovered the first two films. Soon enough, I began seeking out the other films and branching out with the other franchises. This all began in October 2006, and it was in the early stages of Rob Zombie's remake getting off the ground. It was an exciting time to become a fan, having a new movie right there on the horizon. I was glued to the early development of that film. I remember the fan debates and casting announcements. I was constantly on the alert for updates via the official MySpace pages and message boards. I vividly remember the excitement of the first teaser trailer dropping and even obtaining the infamous leaked script prior to that. I was so young it's ridiculous. Rob Zombie's *Halloween* was actually my first horror film in theaters and the last film I saw with both of my parents. To look back on this, "awkward" is an understatement. Of course it was my idea, and I still remember the ticket usher's judgment. "Two adults and . . . a child?"

Taking Shape was a dream, and I still question whether it actually happened. To put it into perspective, I was twenty-two when I began collaborating with Dustin. I had written a couple of articles for *Dread Central*, the first of which was an interview with Robert Harders, a screenwriter who had once pitched an alternate take on *Halloween 5*. It was this article that piqued Dustin's interest, as he wanted to license it for his book on *Halloween*, which he was already knee-deep in writing by the time I got involved. It was October 2018, and there was a lot of fervor around the David Gordon Green reboot with Jamie Lee Curtis. At that point, I had recently conducted the first interview with Sandy Johnson, who played Judith Myers in the original, so it was just another exciting time to be a *Halloween* fan. Dustin reached out to me via social media, and we began chatting. I had a couple of unproduced scripts that I was willing to share, and he was kind enough to shoot over a couple of his rough drafts for input. I expanded upon them a bit, most definitely the *Halloween 5* chapter, and soon enough, he extended an offer. Suddenly, I was a coauthor.

My fandom aside, it wasn't anything I could've predicted. It's not a gig that I recall as really fighting for, which wasn't always the case, as I practically pestered my way into briefly assisting with the special features for the *Texas Chainsaw Massacre* 4k Blu-ray, another byproduct of my time with *Dread Central*. That experience was coming to an end when Dustin reached out to me. I'm still very incredulous about it. It's never lost on me that my very first article for *Dread*, which was orchestrated on a whim, really, somehow proved very advantageous for me on a creative and personal level. With *Taking Shape*, I just started providing more material, more scripts, more interviews and expanding upon the text in any way I could. Funny enough, when the decision was made to split the book into two books, most of my interviews were relegated to *Taking Shape II*, which was kind of a kick for me to have the majority there, as I was always more interested in focusing on the unmade takes and discovering new things.

It was a really fun time. To be presented with the option of helping to cowrite a book on my favorite franchise? I was ecstatic. Here I was a walking *Halloween* encyclopedia trying to do big-boy things. I was still in college, majoring in journalism, and already getting the chance to do something in that realm on the side. I was emailing and scheduling interviews in between classes and probably felt like a secret little rock star. It'd be hard to judge my interview skills, as they're probably poor, and I think my youthful naivete and chutzpah have granted me a certain level of support. But I love a good trip down memory lane, and I always try to approach things with an eagerness and a readiness in terms of having a ton of prepared questions. It's always cloaked with an undeniable nervousness, though. That's just me. But I think the experience of working alongside Dustin has helped with that. It really granted me the opportunity to speak with people that I just wouldn't have otherwise, and I'm always grateful for that.

I feel a bit sheepish in saying this, but Dustin and I have probably only ever had maybe two phone calls in the seven years we've known each other. We've also only met in person just once, which was a rapid two hours of just chatting over dinner. I'd bet it sounds crazy to think we could've collaborated on such an endeavor without much of a serious connection, but we really were in constant contact through social media, just messaging each other every day about anything under the sun. Very modern. Talk about a fluke. He was incredibly generous with my input. He had never had a coauthor before, and I had never written anything of great substance, so it was a marriage that probably shouldn't have worked out. But it did, and we were able to manage any creative squabbles fairly easily. I'll always defer to him as the main man in charge. On the whole, I don't think *Taking Shape* is intrinsically linked to the franchise in any great way, but we brought a lot of previously unshared knowledge to the table that we'd hoped fans would enjoy. And I'd like to think we succeeded in that. They're not perfect, but I'm proud of that time and grateful for Dustin. For better or worse, we were as independent as the original *Halloween*, just fans trying to do something cool within our means. Huge learning experience. And it was a lot of fun.

AG: Throughout the course of your two very extensive books, what was the biggest "Oh, wow" moment for you both?

Dustin McNeill: We came across several holy grails writing those books, but my biggest "wow" moment came when we got our hands on Nigel Kneale's original draft of *Halloween III*. No one we'd been speaking with still had their copy, not even Tommy Lee Wallace. It wasn't necessarily better than the final film we got, but it was longer and had an expanded characterization for Conal Cochran, who was far more evil as originally written. Some of Nigel's concepts turned up in the film's novelization, but many were simply discarded along the way.

Travis Mullins: For me, the greatest joy was always uncovering new details about an unproduced sequel and, if we were lucky, a script to go with it. Managing to track down a copy of Nigel Kneale's original *Halloween III* script was a huge thrill. But without a doubt, the biggest thrill for me was scoring an interview with Shem Bitterman. He had written the earliest version of *Halloween 5*, which more heavily toyed with the idea of having Jamie Lloyd become a killer. At the time, Mr. Bitterman was incredibly elusive in talking about his work, and we had never heard the exact details of this pitch, but somehow I was able to make it happen, which still surprises me. He had also scripted an alternate version of *Halloween 4*, which only added to that "Oh wow" factor.

Really, I enjoyed any chance I had to dive deep into the making of *Halloween 5*. My conversation with that film's director, Dominique Othenin-Girard, was an utter delight. At the time, my home was in the process of being remodeled, and here I am having a transcontinental phone call with the director of perhaps my favorite *Halloween* sequel. All the while table saws are screeching in the background. Dominique was brilliant and very open, and it was such a fun chat. He really had a unique vision, one that might not have gelled with all of the fans, but as is usually the case, he was trying to juggle bringing that vision to the screen while dealing with things outside of his control. I understood and appreciated his rationale for the film's more polarizing elements. It was fascinating to learn more about his connection to Debra Hill and how she was briefly involved in shepherding some of the sequels.

AG: How many unmade *Halloween* scripts are you aware of? What's the one you most wish had been a reality?

Dustin McNeill: We covered twenty-four unmade sequel scripts in *Taking Shape II*, but there were at least a dozen more that I can recall, probably more. Some were never developed beyond the treatment stage. Travis and I tried to only consider scripts that were official or semiofficial, because there are countless unsolicited spec scripts out there, some by fans and some by professional screenwriters.

It's a really tough question to answer, but I'm especially partial to *Halloween* comic writer Stef Hutchinson's reboot trilogy pitch, which would've been an extreme reimagining of the series. The three chapters of that trilogy were titled *Rise of the Boogeyman, The Witching Hour*, and *Fires of Samhain*. I think Stef would've given fans the most intriguing characterizations of the Shape and Loomis we've seen yet. He developed the Shape far beyond being just a slasher and Loomis beyond being a mere Captain Ahab archetype. His ideas were a complete reinvention of the series formula, which I tend to enjoy.

Travis Mullins: Like I mentioned, getting ahold of Shem Bitterman was a thrill, and I would've loved to have seen his version of *Halloween 5* become a reality even though I'm pretty partial to the film we received. For someone who admittedly didn't have much of a fondness for the genre, Shem's scripts were incredibly nuanced, above and beyond what is typical for a *Halloween* sequel. Getting a chance to read them, my imagination was on fire. The visuals were just jumping off the page, from Jamie's hallucinations to Rachel having a more active role, conflicted about Jamie's innocence, to Dr. Loomis going off the deep end and wanting to kill Jamie himself. There were some great set pieces, from Rachel going back to the mineshaft to the entire farmhouse finale. The fact that this all would've taken place on the same night as *Halloween 4* is pretty nuts. Would it have been successful and popular among fans? I really doubt it. But it would've been supremely·interesting.

Funny enough, I want to say that it actually occurred to me during writing that my standards and expectations for a *Halloween* film have vastly gone downhill. You really have to give props to the Akkads and the filmmakers for trying their best to make smart decisions and to make the best movies, because you can easily read so many bizarre takes. After a certain point, it's like, "Perfect! I want to see that!" After hearing of a new concept proposed, I might think it's awful, but I'd probably still see it. I just don't want to place too many fan demands on the material anymore. I think the franchise might be a bit inhibited because of that. It's not the most polished franchise in terms of continuity, but there's a lot of prestige bestowed on it because of the weight of the original, and it'd be really difficult to conjure up something that doesn't feel like a retread or like it's playing it safe. If a *Halloween* TV show ever comes to fruition, I'd be excited because it really would be a chance to do something entirely fresh.

AG: What's an example of a deleted or scripted-but-not-filmed scene that you wish would have been a reality?

Dustin McNeill: Can I answer with a deleted plotline instead? I'm a huge *Halloween H20* apologist because I really love that entry, but it's sorely lacking something without Loomis. There was originally a wonderful detective subplot that ran alongside the main story that I think would've greatly enriched the material. In one scene, the detectives would've visited Keri Tate at Hillcrest Academy with suspicious intent. "Has anyone ever told you you bear a striking resemblance to Laurie Strode?" The detectives would've also found Laurie's headstone missing from her fake grave in Haddonfield Cemetery, echoing Michael's actions in the original film. In a nice touch, the script mentioned that Jamie Lloyd would've been buried in the adjoining plot. It's scenes like these that I would've loved to have seen in the film.

Travis Mullins: It was fun to dive into all of the unmade *Halloween*s, but it was really just as much fun to pour over all of the scripts for the films that did get made. There are so many scripted moments that would've probably further enriched the films had they made it to the screen. I think back to the original and recall that we were intended to see what Laurie Strode is writing in her notebook when she sees the Shape outside her classroom ("LAURIE STRODE IS LONELY"). I also recall there being a scene where Annie was supposed to receive a phone call from her dad telling her to be careful that night. This is just before she enters her car to go pick up Paul, and, well, we know what happens next. There was another scene where Laurie arrives home from school, and we would've seen her mother making candied apples in the kitchen. I believe this scene might've even been shot. It really is the greatest pity that this footage, along with basically every take from the original, has been housed with a collector all these years, and nothing has been done with it. I'm holding out hope this will change in the future.

The sequel that suffered from the most script meddling is undoubtedly *Halloween: The Curse of Michael Myers*. There's a lot to like about the film, but it does suffer from being a bit of a jumbled mess in the final edit. That's really no fault of the screenwriter, Daniel Farrands, who was clearly a huge fan. It was incredibly ambitious on his part to try and expand the storyline while connecting the dots with the previous entries. Had his original draft been followed more closely, it probably would've resulted in a better movie. Anyways, one of the elements from his original draft that I wish had been retained was the fact that Jamie Lloyd would not only have survived her initial attack but would've returned in the finale. She would've offered guidance to the other survivors, helping them to escape Smith's Grove before sacrificing herself to the Shape. She would've died a hero, the most fitting conclusion for that character.

I don't think fans tend to remember the *Halloween 4* deleted scenes as much because there's only a small handful and they're rather inconsequential. There was a scene in which Rachel and Jamie are driving around town with Lindsey—who as far as I'm concerned is Lindsey Wallace from the original—and the Shape is trailing them in his stolen truck. At one point, he was supposed to cut them off, which would've led to Lindsey calling him a "stupid jerk." Later, we would've seen Rachel and Jamie walking the streets of Haddonfield, where Jamie spots her uncle lurking from around the corner of a building. Rachel goes to investigate, but of course he's no longer there. Both of these scenes were callbacks to the original, which would've been very fun, and it's been confirmed that the second scene was actually shot.

For *Halloween 5*, there was a scripted scene where Dr. Loomis and Sheriff Meeker visit a cemetery where they encounter the desecrated grave of a nine-year-old girl—the coffin is missing, and of course this is the same coffin that later appears in the Myers house attic. There was some classic Loomis dialogue here, and it could've made for a chilling daytime scene. I don't believe this scene was shot, but there's actually a lot of deleted material from *Halloween 5* that has never been released, including a sequence where Michael kills a bunch of officers outside the children's clinic.

It's always been a dream that we might one day see Rick Rosenthal's original cut of *Halloween II*, before John Carpenter insisted on cutting a number of sequences and shooting a few additional scenes. Of course, we've seen several of the deleted scenes that were featured in the TV cut—unfortunately cropped to the 4:3 aspect ratio—but there are still a couple of scenes that have never been released. The most notable would be the death of the blonde news producer that we briefly see outside the Wallace house. Her throat was slashed and her car stolen while en route to Haddonfield Memorial to get a statement from Laurie. This would've led to a scene where a news crew arrives at the hospital only to be dismissed by Mrs. Alves because the producer hasn't yet arrived to work things out.

AG: On the flip side, what's something that didn't make the final theatrical version of any of the films that's ultimately for the best?

Dustin McNeill: There were some especially barbaric moments with young Michael that Rob Zombie considered for his remake that I'm glad were never realized. I don't know if someone talked him out of these ideas or if he removed them on his own, but nixing them was definitely the right call. There are some things we just don't ever need to see Michael doing.

Travis Mullins: So many. I agree with Dustin that the early leaked draft of Rob Zombie's remake contained a number of depraved passages we should be grateful did not make the final film. On a lighter note, there was a sequence in *Halloween 5* that was indeed filmed but didn't make the final cut. It's when Jamie manages to sneak out of the clinic to reach Tina at the Tower Farm party. We never actually see how she leaves the clinic. If you'll notice, the editing is a little shaky in this sequence, and before we know it, Jamie is out on the streets, where she soon bumps into Billy. But there was a scene where in order to avoid detection, she actually disguises herself with the garb of a medical worker, giant headgear, stethoscope, and all. She almost blows her cover when she bumps into one of the stationed officers, and I think he was to make some sort of humorous quip about her. There's some behind-the-scenes photos and footage of Danielle Harris wearing this garb, and it frankly looks ridiculous—such a cheesy little bit you can almost imagine the infamous clown cop music playing in the background. It'd still be a kick to see this scene one day.

AG: There's a lot of lore surrounding *Halloween 4*. Any particular unmade scripts or ideas that you favor over others?

Dustin McNeill: I really loved in Shem Bitterman's *Halloween 4* how different the characterization of Jamie Lloyd was. She wasn't fearful of her uncle in his original draft, but instead desperately sought a relationship with him as her last remaining blood relative. This sad longing for familial connection blinded Jamie to his true nature, which led her to make excuses for his murderous ways. It's not until late in Bitterman's original story, when Michael attacks Rachel, that Jamie finally realizes that yes, her uncle is pure evil. Jamie's childlike naivety towards Michael puts her in danger throughout the story, making it all that much harder for Loomis, Meeker, and Rachel to protect her. I thought that was a neat story turn.

Travis Mullins: Call me crazy, but I can't tell you how much I would've loved to have seen the *Halloween 4* that was written by Daniel Kenney and Marc Allyn Medina. It's just wild to consider. And the story of how those writers became involved was fun. They were fans but weren't really involved in the film industry, and I want to say they were approaching things from the mindset of the general public. And it's exactly the kind of direction you might've expected *Halloween* to take if the brand had been as much of a pop culture fixture as *Friday the 13th* or *A Nightmare on Elm Street* at the time. It would've been awesome to have another movie with Jamie Lee Curtis and Donald Pleasence, now deep into the 1980s, with a Chicago backdrop, a rock star cameo, and Michael in a leather jacket. Had this happened, it very well could've changed the trajectory of the series. For better or worse, who knows? It's such a bold shift, it would never be considered now. But it's cool to look back and think we almost had a *Halloween* that was just pure popcorn flick, similar to *Nightmare 3* and *4* or *Jason Takes Manhattan*. Not everything has to be high art, and as a product, it could've been very fun. From that perspective, it's also a shame we never received that *Hellraiser* crossover.

AG: In your second book, you look at three potential sequels to *Halloween: Resurrection*. How close were those films to being made, and which ideas did you personally prefer?

Dustin McNeill: I think *Resurrection* came fairly close to getting a direct sequel. It was so seriously considered that former Halloween Movies webmaster Anthony Masi revealed that Busta Rhymes had personally met with Moustapha Akkad at the Trancas [International Films] offices about returning as Freddie Harris.

Of the three official scripts put forth, my favorite was *Halloween: Retribution* by Dudi Appleton and Jim Keeble, which tried hard to get the franchise back on track by returning to its roots. I know every sequel director says that phrase at some point, but it was really true with *Retribution*. This is the one where John Tate and Sheriff Brackett get snowed in at an abandoned Smith's Grove Sanitarium with a group of nosy teenagers. It was also one of two *Resurrection* sequel scripts that killed off Freddie Harris in the opening scene. Busta was still under contract with Dimension at the time, so it's likely he would've appeared here.

Travis Mullins: It's hard to say how close each potential script was to being greenlit, but the fact that there were multiple takes considered before it was settled to go the remake route, it seems they were initially intent on following up with another sequel. And it was decided early on that the Smith's Grove Sanitarium would be featured as a main setting. There were three official scripts developed, but we covered at least four or five different takes with reference to a couple more. That includes the *Hellraiser* crossover. There must've been a lot of internal debate, since *Resurrection* wasn't the biggest success. Getting a chance to chat with Nick Phillips, a former Dimension exec associated with the project, was great. He oversaw the development of what was then called *Halloween 9*, and he was a hardcore fan and passionate about his job, super insightful and one of the most fun chats for sure. I think it's interesting that at the first *Halloween* convention back in 2003, it was publicly suggested that Charles Cyphers should reprise his role as Sheriff Brackett, and lo and behold, that was soon developed with *Halloween: Retribution*, which is probably my favorite of that lot. There he's intent on avenging his daughter's death, and it's cool to think that the Akkads were receptive to that idea, even if it wouldn't come to fruition until *Halloween Kills*.

AG: Let's shift to Rob Zombie's *Halloween* films. For those who haven't read your books yet, there's a treasure trove of information on his two films. In particular, his second film feels drastically different than originally scripted. Do you think the ideas reserved for the director's cut/discarded ideas would have made for a better film, as Rob is on record saying? Or do you think *Halloween II* theatrical cut made for a better film?

Dustin McNeill: I'm in the minority camp that thinks Rob's *Halloween II* is a dark masterpiece, far better than his first *Halloween* effort. I also much prefer the director's cut on his follow-up for better exploring both Laurie's mental deterioration and Loomis's moral deterioration. Still, not everything Rob originally wrote or shot made it into his director's cut. One interesting scene that was shot but discarded and never released took place during the finale. A distraught Laurie begins to hallucinate multiple doppelgängers of young Michael who are running around the rundown shack where she's being held captive. Can you imagine it? What a complete vision of madness! I'd like to see that scene someday.

Travis Mullins: To be honest, I've not seen the *Halloween II* theatrical cut in so long. I almost never watch it, so there's never much of a distinction in my mind between the two versions. To me, the director's cut is the final film, which is funny because I can more easily distinguish all the various cuts of the first remake. From what I recall, I do think the director's cut benefits from having those extended moments in the order they're presented. It might not be one of my personal favorites, but there's a lot of newfound love for that entry, and I get it. And because it's truly his own unique interpretation, it's terribly hard to put demands on the material. I love the visuals. I love the performances. I love the relationship dynamics. I love that it's such a dark and depressive look at trauma and that every character is affected in one way or the other. I think it's known that it was a pretty difficult production, and there were a number of sequences cut before and even during shooting. The sequence that comes to mind is where two cops investigate the Myers house only to be slaughtered. I doubt it would've changed the overall story in any way, but it would've been cool to see more of Rob Zombie's unfiltered vision.

AG: There are a lot of what-ifs with this franchise, from unmade scripts, continuing different timelines or plot threads, or even potential involvement from Hollywood A-listers like Tarantino. This franchise could have gone in countless other directions. After all of your extensive research, what is the one what-if that most intrigues you to this day?

Dustin McNeill: I always go back to "What if the producers/execs/director had respected the artistic vision of Daniel Farrands on *Halloween 6*?" and also "What if Farrands had been allowed to do *Halloween 7*?" As most fans know, his script was endlessly screwed with on the sixth movie, which kind of wrecked that production. I'm not saying the Thorn storyline would've been the greatest *Halloween* story ever told, but I've long wanted to see what Farrands originally envisioned because I think he's such a sharp talent with strong creative sensibilities for this kind of stuff. And, you know, he just never got to tell his story properly. Hell, even on the reshoots, they literally ran out of time and were unable to finish the ending. That final shot of the mask and syringe on the floor was a total cop-out, hastily completed before everyone packed up the gear and went home.

Travis Mullins: I've harped on *Halloween 5* so much, but had it been more clearly established that Jamie Lloyd was destined to become a killer in the mold of her uncle, there's really no telling how that would've affected the franchise moving forward, so that's always a fascinating what-if. Something else that comes to mind is "What if the producers had really committed to following the commercial trends of the early 2000s with things like the *Hellraiser* crossover or a sequel in 3D?" It's just interesting to ponder where the franchise would be in the eyes of the public. For the record, I really loved both of the *Halloween 3D* pitches that we covered, and I'd be hard-pressed to choose my favorite.

AG: Which film in the franchise do you think has the most interesting story surrounding it when taking into account other script ideas and other possibilities?

Dustin McNeill: I've got to go with *Halloween 4* on this one because the earlier scripts were just so wildly different from the film we eventually received. You start out with the Dennis Etchison draft, which is filled with side characters from the original movie and written under the guidance of John Carpenter. Despite his endorsement, that particular draft is shot down for being just too different from the earlier films. Then you've got the draft by Marc Allyn Medina and Daniel Kenney, which brings back Laurie Strode and Dr. Loomis, shifts the action to Chicago, and makes Michael into a rock 'n' roll slasher. That one dies presumably because Jamie Lee Curtis refuses to return. Even still, you've got Shem Bitterman's original *Halloween 4* script, which is a fascinating variation on the eventual film we got. The plot structure is similar, but there are notable differences in characterization and action.

Travis Mullins: I have to agree with Dustin here. *Halloween 4* was a pivotal moment in the history of the franchise, and it's kinda fitting that our second book begins with the development of those lost sequels. It's arguably when *Halloween* became a franchise, at least in terms of the way we view franchises today. Not everyone involved wanted another sequel after *Halloween III*, and the series could've very well have ended right then and there. There were a lot of concepts tossed around, certainly more than we covered and most of which I don't think we'll ever be privy to. It was a world of possibilities then, and the producers really had the freedom to go in any direction they wanted. By introducing Michael's niece as his next target, they might've boxed themselves in, as it really cemented his motive as going after his bloodline. The filmmakers set it up nicely for the next sequel, but of course that approach was reconfigured, and a huge can of worms was opened with things like the rune tattoo and the Man in Black, which honestly damned *Halloween 6* from the start. You could argue that with all entries in the Thorn trilogy, the producers and filmmakers were really testing the waters to get a handle on what *Halloween* as a franchise even was or what it was really about, and that began with *Halloween 4*.

AG: Fun question for last: What's your favorite version of Michael's mask from any of the sequels?

Dustin McNeill: Okay, time to lose all credibility. I really love the mask used in *Halloween: The Curse of Michael Myers*. Not only is the design great, but they also light it really wonderfully. It's dark and shadowy in the barn scenes, sterile white in the endlessly long halls of Smith's Grove, bloodred in the underground tunnels, and coldly blue in the reshot ending. I'm also a big fan of the Stan Winston mask from *Halloween H20*, more so when the eyes aren't as visible. I also dig the Phantom of the Opera-style torn mask from Rob Zombie's *Halloween II*. Within that particular film, I just think it works!

Travis Mullins: I've always been a *Halloween 5* apologist. Considering it was my introduction to the series, I have to say I'm a sucker for that particular rendition of the mask. And I'll happily take all the pitchforks for it. Long hair, don't care, I love it. There's something about the furrowed brow that just registers as menacing. The only mask I'm not that fond of has to be the one from *Resurrection*. In general, though, I don't really have any major quips or qualms with the masks. Most are pretty passable for me. I'll agree with Dustin that *Halloween: The Curse of Michael Myers* and *H20* are standouts. There's a huge subculture with the masks, and I do enjoy the fact there's room for debate, because how boring would it be if it was the same mold in each sequel?

-CHAPTER 9-
25 YEARS OF TERROR

In 2006, the documentary *25 Years of Terror* was released. It's certainly a must-see for *Halloween* fans, as it features both new interviews from a convention for the twenty-fifth anniversary of the franchise and previous interview footage. While *Halloween* is known for having a lot of great featurettes and special features on home video releases (more on that later in this chapter), this documentary was the most complete look at the series up to that point. It feels special even if you watch it now, as John Carpenter, Jamie Lee Curtis, Danielle Harris, and many other loved and respected names from this franchise appear. It has a big, official feeling to it. The documentary was directed by Stef Hutchinson and produced by Anthony Masi and the late Paul Swearingen. Sean Clark, a name known by most horror fans and certainly by most personalities within the genre, was also a part of the convention production.

Below are my conversations with Sean Clark and Anthony Masi, two men who have both contributed a lot to this franchise and the genre as a whole over the years.

Interview: Sean Clark

AG: What's the dynamic like between the fans and the cast and crew of the *Halloween* films when they see them at conventions?

Sean Clark: I'd say *Halloween* fans are probably the most rabid of the horror franchises. I think that's evident just based on the fact that it's really the only horror franchise that's been able to sustain a stand-alone convention based on the franchise. I know there was a *Friday the 13th* convention for the twenty-fifth anniversary years ago that I attended, and it was okay. They had a great lineup, but the fans just didn't turn out for it, really. *Elm Street* has never really had a stand-alone convention. I think a lot of that has to do with only really having one guy who's played the killer, Robert Englund, not counting the remake. At least with *Halloween* and *Friday the 13th*, you've had various people play the part of Michael or Jason. I just don't think that *Friday the 13th* or *Nightmare on Elm Street* could have a convention or stand-alone event that would be nearly as successful as the *Halloween* ones have been. I think that's showing just how strong the fandom is for *Halloween*. The fans are just much more passionate, I think. Because of that, there's a strong connection between the cast and the fans. A lot of them have come to so many of these events that they become almost on a first-name basis with some of the actors, which is really cool.

AG: Your name has come up a few times in my research for the book, as well as in some conversations. It really led me to believe that you have a pretty special relationship with a lot of the cast and crew. What's that like for you? Not just professionally, but also personally?

Sean Clark: It's an honor. I never thought in a million years I would be in the position I'm in. It's kinda crazy. It all happened by accident, to be honest with you. I was a passionate fan. I am a passionate fan. Weird circumstances kept happening in my life that would open doors, and I just kept passing through them. It's bizarre to me that I have the relationship I have with all these people and that they all know me. I consider all of them friends. I could text Jamie Lee Curtis right now and she would probably respond to me. Do I text with her often? No, but if something happens and I was to reach out to her for something, she would absolutely get right back to me. The fact that I've been to her house, it's kind of crazy. It's a pretty surreal thing. I have a pretty special relationship with Nick Castle [Michael Myers from the original *Halloween*]. He and I have become pretty close. We're friends, but there's sort of almost a father-figure kind of thing there in a way. It's really cool.

AG: I was told off the record to ask you the story of how you got Jamie Lee Curtis to appear at a convention.

Sean Clark: The story is pretty unique. I attempted to get her to do a convention years prior. I went to one of her book signings, and she shuffled me off to her publicist, who to this very day is not a fan of her doing those sorts of things. I was getting lip service at that time, like, "Talk to this person, who's gonna eventually tell you no." That's pretty much what happened, and I got the hint. I didn't push it. I was doing the *Halloween* conventions at the time, and I had already done the twenty-fifth-anniversary convention. I think I was trying to get her for the thirtieth or something. Anyway, one day my phone rang, and when I answered this voice goes, "Sean." I immediately recognized the voice. My heart dropped, like *Holy shit*. I said "Hi, what can I do for you?" She basically told me that she's doing this thing for the children's hospital in Los Angeles. She's getting all of these Michael Myers masks signed by all the cast for a charity auction. She's trying to track down the various cast members but didn't have their contact info. Every time she talked to one of them and asked them how to get in touch with these other people, my name kept coming up. She said, "I decided fuck it. I'm just gonna call this guy." That's literally what she said. So we started talking about it, and she says she knows that I book cast and crew for conventions. She says, "Let me ask you a question. Do you think I would raise the most money for charity if I sold them online in an auction or if I auctioned them off at one of these conventions?" I said, "As much as I would love to get you to a convention, honestly you would make more money if you did it online. At a convention, say you have ten thousand people there. It's basically those ten thousand people that can bid on it. Where if you did it online, it could be a million people that could bid on it. So obviously your best bet would be to do it in an online auction of some sort." She says, "I appreciate your honesty, but tell me about these conventions anyway."

I think my honest answer to her opened the door there. She asked about which conventions she should think about hypothetically going to, and I gave her a few shows I would recommend. I think I picked five shows, the top five in the US. She told me to reach out to each one of them, tell them to give you their best pitch, and we'll pick one. "I'll do one and one only." That's how it started—literally just a random phone call I picked up one day, and it blew my mind. Then there was the documentary *The Night She Came Home*, which was filmed by her sister and her sister's husband. She called me I think the day or two before the convention and said, "Hey, my sister and her husband are gonna come and follow us around and film us all weekend. Are you okay with that? Do you think the show is okay with that? We're gonna do some sort of little documentary on it." And I said, "I'm sure they'd be thrilled." I was fine with it, not ever thinking it would ever go anywhere. They followed us all weekend: Kelly, her sister, and her husband, John. I would say within a month of that convention, I was sent a rough cut. I watched it, and I was like, "This is really good. This is really entertaining." I was thinking to myself, *Fans would love to see this*. This is like a behind-the-curtain look at not only her first convention but also a behind-the-scenes look at how conventions are run.

At that time, I was working on bonus features for the thirty-fifth anniversary release of *Halloween* on Blu-ray. I called up Malek Akkad and said, "Hey, man, Jamie and her sister did this thing, and she sent it to me, and I'm blown away by it. It's like a love letter to the fans. I think this should be on the Blu-ray." We sent him a copy and he agreed, and it ended up on the thirty-fifth-anniversary Blu-ray and ultimately in the box set that came out. It's just really a cool thing to be a part of, and now I'm immortalized in the world of *Halloween* as well.

AG: Let's stick with bonus features and home video content for a minute. I wanted to ask about any additional experiences or memories from that work that you cared to elaborate on?

Sean Clark: Well, I've worked on a bunch of them over the years. My first was the very first DVD release of *Halloween*, through Anchor Bay, which came out in 1998, I think. I did have a small hand in that, as goofy as it is. When the first menu comes up, there's a mask that turns and does a camera close-up on it. It was a mask I made, and I lent it to them. I don't know if they digitally did it or if it was just filmed. I can't remember. I just know that when I saw it, I was kind of horrified because it looked terrible. The mask I made that looked great looks terrible because of the way they shot it. But I think I ended up getting credit for that on-screen somewhere, like "mask provided by" or something. So that was technically my first DVD work I did for anybody. Through that, I got invited to the release party that they had at the Egyptian, where they also had a screening of the movie. The whole cast was there, including Jamie. They had a little preparty across the street at this nightclub, I think. That was the one and only time I met Debra Hill. I never got a picture with her, but I did meet her that night briefly.

AG: You were involved with *Halloween: 25 Years of Terror*, right?

Sean Clark: I guess technically next would be doing *Halloween: 25 Years of Terror*. That documentary was basically made by four people. It was myself, Anthony Masi, Paul Swearingen, and the guy who directed it, Stefan Hutchinson. How that was conceived was the three of us minus Stefan put on the very first *Halloween* convention in 2003 in Pasadena. That was not the greatest relationship. Basically, there's a lot of drama that went on. Those two kind of took sides against me without my knowledge. I didn't know what was going on. Basically, our original idea was when we were doing the twenty-fifth-anniversary convention, somebody said we should document this event. I was like, "Yeah, that's great. We should do a documentary." So the idea was at the event to have a room set up where we could take guests in throughout the weekend and interview them on camera. Now Anthony, for whatever reason, decided that the person he was gonna hire to film this was from the UK. It was a really stupid move. I'm glad it happened, though, because Stefan and I have become longtime friends. He and I are very close. Every time I go to the UK, I see him. He comes here; he sees me. We are close friends. Paul Swearingen sadly passed away a few years ago, but he and I made amends.

What ended up happening was everything was filmed at the event, and one of the big hurdles with bringing in Stef and his crew to film this thing was first, a much bigger expense than finding somebody local, and second, they found out later the way he was shooting everything was going to cost a lot of money to transfer back then. So a lot of bad decisions were being made. I was kind of glad that the convention was over and not much had been done since, and it was kind of radio silence. One day I go on the internet, and on a horror site I see an announcement: Anchor Bay signs deal for *25 Years of Terror* documentary. I'm reading this going, *What the fuck?* So I called Anthony, and I said, "Hey, just saw this press release. Anybody gonna call me and fill me in?" That's when he let me know that him and Paul had decided that my services were no longer needed. So I told him, "That's not how this works. This was something we conceived together, something we built together. You can't just decide I don't need to be needed and walk away." I slapped an injunction on the project through a lawyer, and at that point, Malek Akkad said to them, "You guys need to work this out, because otherwise it's gonna kill this deal with Anchor Bay." Basically, an injunction means you can't move forward on a project until the legal issues are handled.

At that time, I was probably more in need of money than I was credit. They brought me an offer that gave me a percentage of sales. What Anthony was fighting for more than anything was just to keep my name off of it because he was on a power trip and he's a control freak. So I took the money and a cheesy bullshit credit that he made up called convention writer, which I think he came up with because there was a lot of footage of me onstage interviewing people, which he also painstakingly panned and scanned me out of every frame. Whenever you watch the bonus feature or any footage from the convention onstage, if I'm the one onstage doing the interview, he's made sure to crop me out of it. I'm actually shocked he didn't have my voice dubbed. I really am. But there's kind of a beautiful ending to this story. They wanted me just gone, but Malek knew that I had all these connections. He said he wanted me to work on this thing. "We're paying him; let's at least get some work out of him." Tony was fighting tooth and nail, but Malek said, "Look, man, he's in; deal with it." So I set up some big interviews. I got the interview with Clive Barker. I got the interview with Rob Zombie, which Anthony fought tooth and nail. "Why are we interviewing Rob Zombie? He has nothing to do with *Halloween*." Look who looks like a genius now.

I conducted a lot of those on-camera interviews. I think Stef put together the first cut of the doc, and then Tony went in without telling him and recut the whole thing. So actually, Steph hates that his name is on it because he doesn't feel like it's a representation of his work. So we're getting this thing done, and I went into Malek's office one day, and Malek said to me, "Hey, this is great what we have here, but do you have any other ideas for bonus features for this thing? I think it needs something else. Do you have any ideas?" I said, "Well, there's this thing I've been doing online for the past couple of years called Horror's Hallowed Grounds that has gotten pretty popular, and I've thought about doing a TV show version of it." I pitched it to him, going back to the filming locations, and he goes, "Dude, I love it. Do it." He said, "I need it in a week." So I called P. J. Soles [Lynda, *Halloween*]. She came out and did some of the stuff with me. We knocked this thing out in a week, and now it's being put on the disc, which drove Tony absolutely insane.

Two thousand and eight was the thirtieth-anniversary convention, and that's when I decided I was gonna move forward with it on my own. By that time I had built up a really good relationship with Malek. We're not like palling around together, but we're definitely friends. That started a great relationship between myself and him. I did the thirty-fifth, the fortieth, and the forty-fifth. I brought in *HorrorHound* magazine to help with the fortieth and forty-fifth just because I personally became so busy doing what I do, Convention All Stars and all my other stuff. There was no way I had time to put on a convention.

Now I kinda went off the topic there, away from the DVD extra stuff, because there is one story I'll tell about working on the box set. Now, when the box set came out, they had already had pretty stacked editions of certain films. The Rob Zombie movies had just come out with pretty stacked bonus features. *Resurrection* had a decent amount of bonus features. The ones that really didn't have anything were *H20* and *Halloween 6* for sure. So they brought us in. They asked me to do *Halloween 4*, *Halloween 5* and *Halloween H20*. When we were working on *Halloween 4*, *Halloween 5* and *Halloween H20*, what we did was we rented a hotel suite at a place in Studio City for three or four days and we scheduled all the interviews. There was an interview every ninety minutes. I was doing ten to twelve hours a day of on-camera interviews, and my eyes were freaking crossing. It was so much work, but we got everybody in there. We could have all the stuff set up that we'd normally have to break down, set up, break down, set up and go to people. We had them all come to us and it worked out pretty good. It was just very exhausting, but it was also fun. We did some on-location stuff. We went to Trancas [Trancas International Films, owned by the Akkad family] and interviewed Malek at his office and interviewed Paul Freeman there too.

One thing I loved about that box set and that I loved about working with Scream Factory was it was a lot of fun to create those minidocumentaries that are on those disks. I'm not tooting my own horn here, but they're awesome, and I'm really proud of them. I'm not proud of *25 Years of Terror*. I think it's terrible. I'm proud of the fact that it kind of started a whole trend of horror documentaries that followed soon after. But it's not a good documentary. The stuff we did in that box set I think was really high quality, and it's fun. It was fun and challenging to take all that material and actually put it together into a cohesive documentary. I'm really stoked that we won a Saturn Award for it, the 41st Annual Saturn Awards, Best DVD/Blu-ray Collection release 2014. When we got nominated, Malek called me and said, "Hey, man, I just wanna tell you we got nominated, and we couldn't have done it without you. You were so crucial to this. I just wanna let you know that if we win, I'm getting you a statue." I guess the way it works is you get one statue if you win, then you can purchase additional ones for people that worked on it. He kept his word and he got me one. So a pretty cool achievement.

AG: Let's go back to conventions again. I wanted to ask about any interesting stories with the *Halloween* cast and crew that you, remember whether it's humorous or just stuck out to you for any other reason.

Sean Clark: Here's one that is a funny story. You see this in *The Night She Came Home* documentary. When we were putting this together, I said to Jamie, "I have an idea." The event was actually in a hotel, and she wasn't staying there; she was staying off-site. I said, "What if I get a hotel suite, and before the convention we invite all the guests?" She had this idea of "Why don't all the guests at this convention be people I worked with?" So everybody that was invited, every guest that was at that show in 2012, had to be somebody she had worked with. That was the rule. For example, Danielle Harris was pissed off that she wasn't invited to the convention. She's like, "I'm her daughter." But she'd never met her, and she never worked with her. So Jamie's thing was it has to be "anybody from the *Halloween* movies I'm in," *The Fog, Prom Night, Terror Train*, etc. So we had people from all those movies, and most of them had no relationship with her anymore. Some of them still saw her occasionally, but most of them hadn't seen her in forever, and we're trying to figure out how we're gonna accommodate all these fans and get through the weekend. So I said, "I think the smartest thing to do would be let's get a suite and before the convention have a little meetup and invite all the guests. That way you can catch up with people. They can say hi, take pictures with you, and all that stuff, and we've got it out of the way, right? So that way they're not walking up all weekend and slowing down the autograph process for the fans, because believe me, that would take forever." She loved the idea. So we're up there in the suite, and people are coming in. She was really enjoying being the one who opened the door. So there's a knock at the door, and the door opens. Now, mind you, at this point there were probably already twenty people in the room. The door opens, and it's Charles Cyphers [Sheriff Leigh Brackett, *Halloween*, *Halloween II* and *Halloween Kills*]. She hadn't seen Charles probably since *The Fog*. He looked like Colonel Sanders. He's bald. He's got a white goatee. She looks at him, and he goes, "Jamie!" She says, "And you are?" And he goes, "It's me, Chuck," and she goes, "Jesus fucking Christ. What happened to you? Get over here! Give me a hug!" It was really funny.

Interview: Anthony Masi

AG: You, along with Paul Swearingen and Sean Clark, put on the first *Halloween* convention, in 2003, correct? How did that come to be and how did that turn into *Halloween: 25 Years of Terror*?

Anthony Masi: In the late nineties I was running a very popular *Halloween*-themed fan site called the Myers Museum. It built up a very large and dedicated fan base, and sometime during that time period I got the idea to create an all-*Halloween*-themed convention someday. I was living in New Jersey and had no idea how to put something like that together, so the idea just sat in my mind collecting dust. In 2002, the webmasters of halloweenmovies.com,, Brian Martin and

Bruce Dierbeck, contacted me to see if I could cover the *Halloween: Resurrection* movie premiere in Century City, California, because they couldn't attend and I jumped at the chance. Brian then informed me that he and Bruce were stepping down from running the official website, and they recommended to Trancas [Trancas International Films, owned by the Akkad family] that I take over due to the popularity of my fan site.

It was at the *Halloween: Resurrection* premiere, which is when I met Paul. To help promote the movie, I suggested to Trancas that we offer fans a chance to attend the premiere, so we ran a little contest on the website where we awarded tickets to lucky winners in an online raffle. Paul was the first person to win, and so that's how we originally connected. Although I didn't meet Paul at the actual premiere, he called me the next day to thank me for putting the contest together and then said that while he was at the premiere he got the idea to put together an all-*Halloween*-themed event, and I told him I'd been thinking of the same thing for years, and immediately we moved forward to try and put it together. Paul and I reached out to South Pasadena's city hall and hotels, and they were very excited to work with us. I signed the contracts for everything, which gave me incredible anxiety over the year we organized the event! We put together a bus tour, locked down the convention, and started inviting as many cast and crew from the movies as possible to attend. Since my website was popular, it was the most logical place to start selling tickets, so once I put up the PayPal "buy now" button, we were off and running selling tickets and locking down the guest list. Moustapha enthusiastically agreed to attend after sending me the most amazing letter, and he and Malek hired me to take over halloweenmovies.com from Brian and Bruce, and I felt like part of the *Halloween* family. It was euphoric to watch everything unfold so easily and wonderfully!

Regarding Sean, after we were selling tickets and locked down the venues, by chance I bumped into him and asked him to put our dealer room together because I had no idea how to do that. Sean also hosted a few panels, which we asked him to do, but other than that it was me and Paul that put the entire rest of the event together, including the bus tour, bringing on all the guests, coordinating the bus tour and movie screenings/parties, and all advertising, ticket sales, insurance, and bookkeeping.

AG: Obviously something as big as this production has to be stressful. What kind of difficulties did you encounter during the planning or making of *25 Years of Terror*?

Anthony Masi: There were many challenges, but I will point out two. First, our director, Stef Hutchinson, lived in the United Kingdom, and unfortunately he didn't attend any of the editing sessions that were taking place in Los Angeles. I was living in Los Angeles at the time of editing, and even though I was a producer and not the director, after my full-time day job, at Malek's request I would drive into Hollywood and sit with our editor until 11:00 p.m., and this went on three to four times a week for months. Since Stef only sent notes via email, it was difficult to keep that workflow going on a time crunch because when you're editing, a lot of things happen where you need to make on-the-spot decisions. Malek gave me a very strict deadline, so I was forced to make some executive decisions that I don't think Stef liked. Stef and I got along really well, but the day came when I told him he had to either fly out and finish the job or that I had to do it, and from that point on he was irritated with the situation, and I didn't hear from him again for years. I saw a few interviews Stef did where he said he wasn't happy with the documentary, and I would always think to myself, *But you weren't here with the editor, I was!* I was very disappointed by this, but we saw each other again at the H45 convention in 2023, and it was a nice reunion.

The second was the nervous breakdown that I very nearly had. I was driving from Los Angeles back to San Diego after signing contracts with the hotels, which basically obligated me to pay for all the hotel rooms during the convention whether they were empty or not. It was sinking in that I signed these contracts and that I may have ruined my life financially if the event didn't sell enough tickets, and I honestly don't remember the drive home. To make a very long story short, things fortunately worked out.

AG: Paul Swearingen passed away a few years ago. I wanted to ask about your memories of working with him. What's something that perhaps *Halloween* fans might not have known about Paul that you think is important to share today?

Anthony Masi: Paul was a big kid, and we would talk on the phone for hours, and there was a lot of laughter. I think he missed his calling as a talent agent. He had a very jovial way about him, and boy could he schmooze! He moved away from Los Angeles, and as people do, we lost touch, but we reconnected years later. He called to tell me he was sick, and of course that was very sad to hear. He suggested getting together one more time, but that didn't happen, and then I found out on Facebook that he passed away.

AG: How do you think *25 Years of Terror* holds up today? Any standout moments or memories that you care to elaborate on?

Anthony Masi: I haven't seen *25 Years of Terror* since 2006! I sat with it for many months in the editing room and knew every frame, so when it got released, I had my fill. It frequently makes best-of lists, and that's always satisfying to see. I've been asked a million times if I'd ever produce an extended version of H25 to include all of the other sequels, to which I say, "Noooo waaaaay!" Not because I'm soured or anything—I can talk about the *Halloween* movies forever—but only because every single entry has copious amounts of interviews and behind-the-scenes footage already that you can find on YouTube and on the home video releases. Doesn't Rob Zombie's *Halloween* DVD have a four-hour making-of documentary? So in my opinion, there's nothing new that could be added to an extended version of H25 that fans haven't already seen or don't already know.

But if I had to choose my favorite parts of H25, I would say it was anytime I saw footage of the convention and bus tour. The whole weekend was so magical in a hundred different ways, so every time some of that footage was shown, I would be so happy. Malek asked me to organize the thirtieth-anniversary convention after Sean asked him if he could coordinate it, and even Malek was giving me first dibs, which I truly appreciated. I turned it down simply because in my mind, there was no way to top the original event. I am very proud of the work that Paul and I put into that first event, and to this day I'd say it's been my most rewarding creative experience. It was the first really big thing I did in my producing career.

AG: I spoke with Sean Clark, and he alluded to your relationship being turbulent at best. Mentions of an injunction, him being removed from the project, which in turn lead to a change in title. When you look back at that situation, is there anything that you would do differently today?

Anthony Masi: "Turbulent" is a good word! The general shamelessness and backstabbing opportunism in the entertainment industry should be studied. As for Sean, I think I irritate his ego, since he knows he owes me a debt of gratitude for opening the *Halloween* door that he walked through. What does he say when someone asks him what he did on the H25 documentary or how the *Halloween* conventions started or how he met Tommy Lee Wallace? I'm certain he doesn't mention me. So what would I do differently? I wouldn't have asked him to put the dealer room together at my convention. The butterfly effect would have taken care of all of the subsequent headaches I've had with him!

AG: You're obviously well immersed in the world of *Halloween*, with meaningful relationships with many involved in this franchise. What's a memory from being involved with all things *Halloween* that's of significance to you?

Anthony Masi: I have so many, but I'll rattle off a few! My mother and sister attended the H25 convention as volunteers, and when Moustapha told them he was "very impressed with your son and brother," it meant so much to me. I visited Rob Zombie's *Halloween* set and got to meet Malcolm McDowell [Dr. Loomis], and when I attended Rob's *Halloween* premiere, Rob came to find me at the after-party to specifically ask me what I thought about his film and said, "Your opinion matters to me." Talk about amazing! I became good friends with some of the cast and crew from the films and still talk to them to this day. I was able to produce documentaries for *Friday the 13th*, *Psycho*, *Scream*, and *Paranormal Activity* because of my work on the *Halloween* documentary. I helped organize one of Moustapha's memorial services after he died and did the graphic design for his memorial page in *Variety*. Because of *Halloween: 25 Years of Terror*, I met Danielle Harris and produced the very first short she directed. I have endless memories that I cherish.

AG: Your company website shows several home video releases for *Halloween* films that you and your company have worked on. Let's dive into that for a moment. Tell me about the work you've done there.

Anthony Masi: I've produced bonus features and commentaries—even did one with Alan McElroy for *Halloween 4*—for some of the *Halloween* home video releases, and I also directed the fifteen-minute promo called "Halloween: The Shape of Horror," which was played before every screening when *Halloween* was rereleased theatrically in theaters in 2006. That was a very cool experience, to see something I directed on the silver screen! We interviewed P. J. Soles, Nancy Kyes [Annie Brackett, *Halloween*, cameos in *Halloween II* and *Halloween III*], Charles Cyphers, Malek Akkad, John Ottman [composer, *Halloween H20*], Alan Howarth [composer, *Halloween II* through six], and Rob Zombie and his manager for that in one day in Hollywood. That day was a lot of fun.

AG: Will we see you or your company enter the world of Haddonfield again?

Anthony Masi: Yes, but not in producing capacity. My main focus these days has been board games. In 2023 I started a company called Stop the Killer Games, and we released the officially licensed board game for *Halloween II*, and we have more *Halloween* titles coming!

-CHAPTER 10-
DANIELLE HARRIS

Danielle Harris's interview gets its own chapter, for several reasons. As Jamie Lloyd in *Halloween 4* and *Halloween 5*, she not only is a lead actress, she also helped carry the franchise away from its uncertain past and into a viable future. In Rob Zombie's two *Halloween* films, she goes from playing Jamie Lloyd to Annie Brackett, while also connecting the franchise's past to its future. Besides Jamie Lee Curtis and Donald Pleasence, nobody is more associated with this franchise. Harris became the second face of this series at the incredibly young age of eleven. Her story is one of passion and perseverance.

AG: I've never heard anyone involved with *Halloween 4* say a bad word about the film or the experience of working on the film.

Danielle Harris: It's true. We're still friends with one another. It's crazy. I'm writing a book as well, and I've gone to storage and taken out boxes and boxes of stuff. I didn't realize what a pack rat I was when it came to memorabilia. I thought, *I don't have much. Holy shit.* The amount of stuff that I found from *Halloween* would blow your mind: Polaroids and party pictures and my seatbacks and stuff. I just have so much stuff. It's amazing.

AG: Let's start back at *Halloween 4*. What's the experience of filming a movie about a masked killer running around after you like at such a young age?

Danielle Harris: I didn't know any better. I didn't have a gauge, as that was my very first time on a movie set. I'd only done a soap opera for a couple of years and one episode of a TV show. Being on location, working with a crew, and having to bank your school hours and work nights and all that stuff was the first time for me.

AG: This film was primarily night shoots. Talk me through working nights at that age, trying to sleep during the day, stay caught up on schoolwork, and then working throughout the night again?

Danielle Harris: I came to set a week or so before we went into production, so I banked all my school hours. I only had to do three hours a day at the time. I think it's still three hours a day for kids, actually. So I would do six or nine hours in a day leading up to the shoot for a week or so. I had all my hours already sort of banked, so I didn't have to do school when I was on set, which was great. From what I remember, people were talking about how Utah was a right-to-work state, and there were no labor laws at the time. I know for sure that I didn't have the normal experience of someone telling me I have to take a break. "She's only ten; we can't bring her around this." I don't think we had any of that. I remember my studio teacher and my mom sort of just being so excited to have me do these crazy, horrific sorts of stunts that I would never allow my kids to do ever. I didn't know any better. If I would have known then what I know now, oh my God.

Looking back at what I did as an actress and all that emotional stuff, I can't imagine how that process was for me as a kid. I worked with Dwight Little two years ago on a movie, and it was our first time working together since *Marked for Death*, when I was eleven or twelve. I was so curious as to how I was as a kid, how I was to direct, and how he went about directing me as a child. Obviously, it's different nowadays than it was back then.

AG: Ellie Cornell spoke about your work ethic at length to me. But Kathleen Kinmont told me a great story about how much fun you guys had at the hotel swimming pool each night after filming.

Danielle Harris: I have pictures of her throwing me in the air. I think that my whole career in general, everybody in the crew and cast really made sure that I was protected. I wasn't sheltered, but I was protected from certain things, I think. But nobody treated me like a child. Everybody hung out and made sure that I would have memories of going to the movies or going to the Old Spaghetti Factory and having my birthday on set. So I was still able to be a kid, I think, in the little bit of downtime that we had. That was thanks to the cast and them wanting to hang out with me.

AG: So you still had a lot of those childhood experiences despite being in these high-pressure environments?

Danielle Harris: Yeah, I loved it. For me, I think my home life was a little bit messy and kind of erratic. We moved around a lot, and my dad had passed away, and there was just a lot of stuff going on. It was a way for me to sort of harness all of that, which I didn't even know I was at the time. I think people sensed a little bit of that as well. I am such a type A personality. I'm still super disciplined. I've never been late for work. I always know my stuff. If I ever forget a line, I panic. Work has always been my safe place, and I never wanted to jeopardize that. I think that still carries over, even now. When I work on movies now and I see people who haven't put their time in and are a little bit negligent with their professionalism on set, it makes me crazy. It makes me absolutely crazy because it's not the way I remember it being.

AG: My next question was actually about your type A personality. You beat me to it.

Danielle Harris: Oh my God, yes.

AG: Ellie Cornell felt that the two of you had that in common despite the age gap. You two were on set for right around forty days—first ones there, last to leave—and that you both really took this opportunity seriously despite being so young in your respective careers.

Danielle Harris: I think we were so excited to be there, but yet I at least had no idea what I was about to get myself into—to be the leads in the movie and have everything sort of revolve around you as your first experience and being able to do it together, with it being Dwight's first movie too. To have all three of us sort of experience this for the first time together was something that I think we hold on to. The same with Kathleen and everybody. It's one of those movies that sort of started a lot of our love for making movies. If it wasn't a good experience, I don't know how many of us would have continued to do it.

AG: I wanted to ask about Dwight. What was he like to work with here?

Danielle Harris: I love him, love him, love him. He said to me when we were doing *Halloween 4*, and I'll never forget this, he said, "If I ever have another movie to hire Jamie, I'm gonna hire you." How many times have I heard "I can't wait to work with you again" or "I'll find something for you" blah, blah, blah, bullshit. Dwight has called me every time he's been able to. I think he's sort of like a quirky, creative father figure to me. I always thought that it was a little bit ironic how I had a lot of men around. All the characters I played, I didn't have mothers, so I had fathers or a killer, running from monsters or whatever. But the directors I always felt superconnected to. I think I'm still a bit enamored with directors on set or people in a creative power position, I'm enamored with it. I'm curious, and it's sort of fun to watch. I'm interested in who they are as people and what they're doing and how that mind works. Even from a young age, I was super into it. Not really growing up with a dad, they sort of all became my father figures. So I hold each one of them in that regard. It's kind of crazy. Literally every director. I would hang out with Tony Scott at his house. You would think it was something bad, but it was actually something that I think saved me over the years and allowed me to stay in the business and not end up on drugs or have a bad reputation or whatever.

AG: I spoke to Dwight two or three days after he did an interview where he made a backhanded joke about making *Halloween 4 Part Two*. That story blew up, and he was laughing about it to me but did admit that there was some truth to it. He's candid about not liking the direction your character and others went in after his film.

Danielle Harris: There's always all this talk about the new universe and how things will work out. Moustapha Akkad's daughter, Lana, was one of my best friends growing up. I would go and stay with them at their house in Brentwood during the summer. I spent two summers with them. I was living in New York and working, and then in the summertime, when Lana was out of school, Moustapha would fly me out, and I would live in their house for two months at a time essentially and just be a kid. I was such a bad influence on Lana. I was introducing her to VHS porn that I found at someone's house and making her smoke cigarettes with me around the corner where there were no cameras—just this horrible influence at like thirteen.

I contacted Malek Akkad when I heard they were doing these three new films with Blumhouse. I told him that I didn't think he's bringing back Jamie for these films, but I've got ideas for some TV stuff and also just a lot of things in my mind if you ever would want to bring her back that I would love to talk about with you. He pretty much said, "We have to kind of make these three movies, and then let's see what happens after." They're in a different timeline than my story was. So I'm still sort of hoping. I've gotten a whole story outlined in my head of exactly where Jamie is right now. I've talked to Dwight, and I even thought about getting Dwight and Alan [McElroy] together to go and pitch it to Malek and tell him that we all want to make the sequel to *Halloween 4* together. How can we make that happen? What would it look like if it were Jamie's story and where she is now?

I truly believe that was not my character in *Halloween 6*. That's my idea. That was another person that maybe Loomis placed there. Jamie is hiding somewhere, kind of how the Laurie character was hiding out. I'd love to see where she is now. I thought of making a sizzle reel myself. If anyone knows how to make a sequel to *Halloween 4*, I think it'd be the three of us. I think fans would go crazy, but we'll see what happens. I'm not holding my breath, but I'm crossing my fingers and my toes that one day we get to see where she is as an adult.

AG: I have heard so many different pitches and ideas myself that people wanted to take to Malek or already took to Malek. While fans are very divided on the last trilogy, one thing it did was open the door to anything happening after. The future of the franchise feels wide open.

Danielle Harris: I hear rumors, and I don't know if they're true. I could ask, but I feel like I don't really need to fight for it. I should just be able to sit back, and if it's meant to be and they're going to revisit that, then they'll come to me. For *Halloween 6* they were looking to recast me because I was a minor. My agent at the time heard that they were looking for someone over eighteen that looked like me, a lookalike to replace me. She called me and told me, and then I was like, "Why didn't anybody ask me to do it? I want to do it." I didn't know anything about the script, but I called them and offered to get emancipated for it if it was a matter of them needing me to be eighteen. I was seventeen, so it sort of seemed silly to me. I have a love-hate relationship with this franchise—more love than hate, that's for sure, but it's still a little weird. I don't know what's going to transpire. Every fan that I talk to tells me they really want Jamie Lloyd back. It's not like I'm not acting, you know what I mean? If I wasn't an actor anymore and they had to pull me out from the cobwebs, I think it'd be different. But I've obviously been working, and the continued support in the horror community has grown over the years too, which is from doing my own sort of stuff. Hopefully one day we'll be talking about it.

AG: Let's move back a little to the last scene of *Halloween 4*. Obviously it's a huge shock. Dwight Little and Alan McElroy both were very clear with what their intention was. Michael was gonna be gone. Jamie was going to be the new antagonist moving forward. That was their plan, and they felt like whoever took *Halloween 5*'s reins from them would have you as the antagonist. Take me back to filming that scene at such a young age and then how you felt about the next film going in a different direction.

Danielle Harris: I don't think I thought much of it. At that age, it's so silly, but I was excited that I didn't have to memorize any lines for *Halloween 5* for the first three out of five weeks we were filming because I was just mute. They taught me a couple of things in sign language. I just thought it was so cool that I had an opportunity to play a character that didn't speak. It was really interesting to me. We shot it so quickly after we did *Halloween 4* that I think I was just so excited to be going back to the hotel that I stayed at with the same people, or at least I thought the same people. I was just happy to be there. I didn't even really understand. I hadn't seen any of the other *Halloween* films until after *Halloween 4* came out. I don't really think I understood what was at stake and how cool it was until I got older. It was also 1989. I think it was just too soon for an audience to accept the child being this brutal to continue to kill people. I think now would be a different story. My interpretation was that I had become him. That's what they explained to me when I touched his hand in the field, when they shot him and I went up to him and I touched his hand at the very end of *Halloween 4*. They're like, "Jamie, get away, get away." Dwight explained that "his blood goes into your blood and you become evil." So that was sort of the way he explained it to me. The only thing that they would not let me film in *Halloween 4* was the actual stabbing of the stepmom in the bathroom. My stunt double did it for me, which is so funny. I could do all these other horrible things. Throw me on a slate roof with no wires or anything that's holding me up and let's see what happens, but don't let her do a thing where she has to fake stab somebody. I think now it would be different.

I love *Halloween 5* for what it is. I don't think that it's a great follow-up to *Halloween 4*. Obviously it's a very different movie, almost a stand-alone movie. It was a little eccentric and a bit out there for me. Rewatching *Halloween 5* as an adult, I was actually surprised how fucking ruthless Loomis was to Jamie. I had no idea. I have no idea what that would look like as an adult, watching another adult do that to a child. Fucking weird. He's holding me in front of Michael like a human shield. If I was an adult and saw that movie at my age for the first time, I probably would have been mortified. Donald was lovely to me. I don't have a ton of memories of him because we didn't hang out and talk on set or anything, but he was always superkind to me.

AG: How was Dominique as a director?

Danielle Harris: I love Dominique. I have had the best luck with directors just really connecting with me and me trusting them and being excited to be creative. Dominique was very eccentric. He was really careful, really animated, and he's really interesting. He really took the time to help me perform my craft. That's a hard thing to do with a child. I see kids now on set, and they just wanna make sure they get their lines right. They're not really going through the feelings of what's going on in the scene necessarily. But he did that with me, and I loved him.

AG: How did you feel at the time about not really getting to work with Ellie on *Halloween 5* after having such a great on-screen relationship in the previous film?

Danielle Harris: I was sad that she was leaving. I remember when she wrapped that I was sad that she wasn't going to be there. But I got superclose to Wendy [Kaplan] and Tammy [Tamara Glenn]. I actually think I got closer to Wendy than I did to Ellie at the time. It felt like I had a lot more emotional scenes with Wendy. Or maybe it was just that I had done it before with Ellie, so it felt like something new. Wendy's a free spirit. She was just like her character. Fun, quirky, loving, and goofy, and we had a bond right away. I felt that connection with her immediately, but I was upset that Ellie wasn't going to be around longer. I know she was upset. She didn't say anything to me at the time, but I could just tell on set that she was upset by what I would see now as being replaced. I don't know why they couldn't keep the Rachel character. Dwight always says that he gauges every movie that he sees in terms of if they have the Jamie-Rachel relationship. That's what makes the movie: our connection with each other.

AG: We covered some *Curse of Michael Myers* topics and questions already. What was that aftermath like for you? You didn't get the role. You went through all of these trials and tribulations. You emancipated yourself. They literally had your picture and said find a woman that looks like her. You go through all this. They cast somebody else in the role; they make the movie. It's a troubled production, as everybody knows. How are you, a seventeen-, eighteen-year-old woman, feeling after all this?

Danielle Harris: I did this Disney documentary at the time called

Hollywood Live. I'm going through all this stuff for my book, and I found this old VHS tape, and I watched it. It was a reality show that followed Jamie Kennedy, myself, and a bunch of other up-and-coming actors, comedians, models, and singers. Brandy, the singer. They followed me during this whole *Halloween 6* [*Curse of Michael Myers*] fiasco. Watching it back now, seeing my younger self so fucking stressed out, anxious, upset, and confused and trying to put on a brave face . . . I don't know what the actual negotiations were between my agent and business affairs. I just know what they told me. And that was that business affairs said no, this is a scale character. She dies in the first act, and my agent said "Well, this is her third movie in the franchise and she did all of this stuff, and we're just asking for double scale essentially," which would have just compensated me for what I had put out of pocket. They just said no. I think at the time, when it happened, I thought, *They're gonna come back. How silly would it be for them to not come back?* I also didn't understand at the time that we should be fighting for that. Looking back on it, as a kid, I was putting on a brave face and trying to sort of hold strong in my conviction. It wasn't right that they would say something like that and that nobody from the people that I had grown up with essentially stepped in and said, "No, let's give it to her. We cannot do it without her."

Also, at the time, I was pretty big in my career. I had done some really big movies. So it wasn't like I had never done anything and was asking for some crazy amount of money. It was never that conversation. I didn't pass; they passed on me. There was no social media. I didn't have a computer, so I didn't really have a way to keep track of what was going on with the movie. I know my mom went and saw it. I didn't even see it. My mom went and saw it in the theater and walked out halfway through. I remember her calling me just saying, "Oh, it was garbage." But that was all. I knew that things were kind of changing a little bit with the film through the negotiations and me going to court. I know there were some script changes and some things that were talked about that were really weird. I know I didn't like the way that Jamie died, and I didn't understand whose baby it was. How is Jamie having Michael Myers's baby? Isn't that her uncle? I didn't get it. I still haven't seen the whole thing, unfortunately, but I've seen the first half of it. The only thing I regret is not working with Paul Rudd, because I just love him so much. I was a little bummed that I didn't get to work with him. Maybe they'll bring us back. Watching it I felt like that wasn't Jamie. I love J. C. Brandy [who played Jamie Lloyd in *Halloween: The Curse of Michael Myers*]; she is a friend of mine. She did a great job, and I feel bad for her that she got a lot of shit after the movie came out. It definitely wasn't the movie that I think we all had hoped that it was going to be. I've worked with Dan Farrands after that, and both he and I are like, "One day we're gonna redo *Halloween 6* [*The Curse of Michael Myers*] the way it should have been done." Maybe we'll get a chance. Who knows?

I know it cost me $3,000 to hire a lawyer and get emancipated. I remember specifically because when they offered scale, scale was half of what I paid to get emancipated. So we were just asking for double scale. We're not even asking for a lot. I just wanted to pay myself back what I had put out, and they said no. I'm pretty sure my agent at the time, my mom, and I were like, "Forget it. I'm not gonna do it." I was more like, Oh God, am I doing the right thing? I was scared and upset that this is what it had come to and thought maybe it would get turned around. I thought maybe Moustapha or Paul Freeman or somebody that was there would have the final say. I'm producing now. I'm directing now, and the movie that I'm about to do with Scout [Taylor-Compton], we are giving up our salaries to pay two actors that deserve more money because we're going to get more money when we sell our movie because of their name. So we're not taking anything, because it's not in the budget. So we're taking it from us to give to them without even a second to think about it. It's shocking to me that nobody on the production side was willing to step up at that time and say, "Come on, guys, you're talking about $1500." In one of the sequels, they show a little clip from *Halloween 4*. I believe it's *Halloween: The Curse of Michael Myers*, but I haven't seen it. I remember my agent calling, saying, "They wanna use a three-second clip, and they're gonna have to pay you. What do you want?" I said I want $3,000, and they gave it to me, for not being in the movie. But they wouldn't give me the $3,000 to be in the movie. So I got paid back anyway. but in a really fucked-up, roundabout way. I just thought, *Wow, I can't even believe this is the way that it all went down. That's crazy.*

AG: The trend of discarding leading ladies and final girls in horror franchises was problematic for a long time.

Danielle Harris: Because they didn't want to pay these women. They're gonna get people into the theater because she's there, then kill her off. It's not like any one of these actresses were ever asking for an enormous amount of money. We all knew what we were gonna get paid. I think I made $5,000 a week when I did *Halloween 4*. I remember thinking, *How can you guys come to me seven years later and offer me half of what you paid me for my first movie?* It makes no sense to me, but that's what they did. It's very strange. I get it; it's a business, but there's just something different about the horror community. The right hand doesn't know what the left hand is doing. It's very strange.

AG: Especially when you consider how passionate and devoted fans are.

Danielle Harris: One of the things that I do regret was talking about my lack of residuals in a documentary that I had done quite a few years ago. Scout and I always talk about it. I always felt like maybe there's some animosity towards me in the franchise from some higher-ups. I can't figure it out. I love making these movies, and again, I'm professional, and nobody has anything bad to say about me. I'm supportive, a fan girl all the way and big in the community. I just feel like there's something. I can't quite put my finger on it, but I should be sitting here being excited about the possibility of more *Halloween*, but there's just a little pit in my stomach that's like, "They're not gonna come to me, and I don't know what I did." One day maybe I'll figure it out. I always wonder if I did something that I don't know about that makes them mad at me. That's still the child in me that wonders that. The only thing that I could think of is that I talked openly about not getting paid any residuals. I just started getting residuals finally, I think three years ago.

AG: Let's talk about the Rob Zombie movies. You're ten years removed from everything with *Halloween: The Curse of Michael Myers*. You're going through this period of time of wondering why things worked out this way, the sense of rejection, and dealing with how poorly you were treated. Then along comes Rob Zombie. Tell me how that kind of played out.

Danielle Harris: I was at a convention, and a fan came up to me and said, "I hear they're remaking *Halloween*. They're remaking the original, and Rob Zombie is going to direct it." I was a fan of Rob Zombie's. I'd never met him before, but I was a fan of his movies. I love *Devil's Rejects* and loved *House of 1000 Corpses*. Then they said, "Yeah, and you're gonna be Laurie." I was like, "What? No, I haven't heard anything." Fans come up with the craziest rumors they heard on the internet. I'm like, "Yeah, it's not happening, guys." I left there and went and called my manager and said that I hear they're doing this remake. "Maybe I could do a fun little cameo or something? Could you find out who's casting it and see if there's anything in it for me?" So she called casting. My manager had a contact there, and she said, "Danielle would love to be part of this." Casting said, "Rob doesn't want anybody from any of the other *Halloween* movies involved. He just wants a clean slate." My manager kept pushing and said, "Let's just let her just come in and read for something." The breakdowns had come out, and there were the three girls. I was thirty playing opposite real seventeen-year-olds. My manager convinced them to bring me in just to audition.

Nobody knew that it was *Halloween*. I knew that it was *Halloween*. There were the three main characters, Linda, Laurie, and Annie. I wasn't going to do full nude, but I thought it would be an interesting career move if I did a topless scene for the first time in this movie. Maybe people in the horror world will stop seeing me as little Jamie Lloyd, and they'll see me as a woman now or as an adult now if I do this. So I went in and auditioned like everybody else. I signed in and went in and read for Annie. They asked at the end, on tape, if I was okay with nudity. I always try to go in as the character, so I always feel like I have a better chance of getting a job by being a little bit of a tough girl, a little bit rough around the edges. I am from New York, so a little bit of that personality I feel more comfortable with. So in typical Annie fashion, I said something on camera like, "Yeah, I'm okay with nudity. I mean, who wouldn't wanna see Jamie Lloyd's tits?" Something funny and sassy. I'm not 100 percent sure, but I heard that Rob was next door. I know that he has said to me that he's never in the room with people that are auditioning because he doesn't wanna be swayed one way or the other based on who they really are. The first time he's gonna be seeing them, he wants to see them on-screen the same way that someone in the audience would be seeing them, which is a really cool idea. He got my tape, and I kind of won him over. He was like, "I want her," and that's kind of how it happened. Then Weinstein signed off on me and Malek signed off on me. I didn't have a script or anything, but that took a couple of weeks. Then I got the script, read it, and thought, *Holy shit, Annie lives.* This is different than the original. Maybe I could do another one. I talked to Rob on the phone for the first time and was just really excited about everything and couldn't wait to be back. But I didn't feel like it was my movie. I 100 percent felt like, *I'm just here to pass the torch to Scout. This is really her movie. These movies are hers now, and I'm just here to facilitate the passing of the title over,* and I was happy to do it. That character was superfun. I just had a great time working on it and getting to come back for the second one and working with Brad Dourif. I also thought maybe if I had come back for *Halloween* 6 that I wouldn't have maybe come back for Rob Zombie's movies. Maybe that would have been done for me because I would have died on-screen. So maybe it would have been different because that wasn't me in *Halloween 6*, and people were still wanting to see a little bit more of where I was.

Everyone thinks Rob wanted me in the movie. No, he didn't want me at all. He wanted nobody. I had to audition and went in, and I was happy to. I don't know if you have seen the extras on the DVD, but they have our auditions on there, and it's so, so traumatizing to watch what you do in a room as an actor, so embarrassing. I'm surprised I got the job based on that, but I think Rob's got a pretty good eye for real people, which is why I like his work so much.

AG: I have heard nothing but good stories about Rob Zombie.

Danielle Harris: I feel bad for him. He dreamed of doing this movie, and I think his remake was so fucking good, and he just had such a horrible experience. It's a bummer that this franchise has left such a bad taste in his mouth. It's so sad. It didn't need to be that way.

AG: How would you describe the shoots? How was the atmosphere on set for both films?

Danielle Harris: A little bit chaotic, a lot going on. It was also weird for me to be in a *Halloween* movie that was like such a big production. Mine were like two- and three-million-dollar budget movies, and this one was like twenty million. It had been a good ten years since I had been on a production that size. So it was weird, but I just wanted to do a really good job. I knew I had an opportunity to do something really special. I'd only done *Urban Legends* between *Halloween 5* and Rob Zombie's *Halloween*, which is weird to think of because everybody still thinks that I'm so involved in this, but it only really started after Rob's *Halloween*, which kind of launched me into that world again.

AG: A lot has been said of what Rob endured from producers, external forces, the Weinsteins, etc. Everybody has their own recollections of that, but how much of that did the cast feel?

Danielle Harris: You could tell that he was stressed out. I didn't work a lot, so I didn't see a ton of it. I kinda just showed up, did my thing, and minded my business. I knew more when I went to do ADR and Rob was getting calls about stupid stuff, things he was saying at the time, and he was just venting. I think at that point he was done. But he kept it pretty close to the vest, at least in front of me. I didn't really know a lot that was going on, but I knew that it was a mess. I knew the second movie was more of a mess because I was wrapped and came back twice. They wrapped me twice, and then I would get a call. "We're gonna fly you out on Tuesday. We need you to work on Thursday." I'm like, "For what? I'm done. What am I doing?" "Oh, Rob has some stuff for you." One time I got on a plane; I think it was either Valentine's Day or my anniversary. It was something where I had to reschedule with my boyfriend at the time, and I flew to Atlanta for *Halloween II*. I got there, and I called them because nobody was there to pick me up. I called production. "Hey, guys, I'm here, and there's no one here to pick me up." Production was like, "Wait, you're here? What do you mean you're here?" They were like, "What are you doing here?" "What am I doing here? You sent a car to pick me up [to take her to the airport], and you booked my plane ticket. I didn't do any of this myself." So I literally got off the plane and turned around and went right back on and went back to LA that same day. Everything was all over the place. It was just a fucking mess. I remember Wayne Toth [special effects artist] in the car one morning was like, "So apparently I am slitting your throat today." I was like, "What?" He said, "I'm so glad I have all of this extra stuff on me because Rob wants to slit your throat." I was like, "For what? That's so weird." But we just trust Rob. Rob's like, "Go over there in that tent and just scream for like ten seconds." I have no idea what this is for, but whatever he tells me to do, I'll just do. He didn't want to come back [for the sequel], and then he came back [for the sequel] and there were a lot of moving parts. I just feel bad for him that he had to have a bad experience making something that he loves so much.

AG: What was it like for you to go from one end of the spectrum to the other in these films? In your first two films as a child, you're the sweet, young, innocent hero character. Then, as an adult, it's a combination of sex and violence. We see you in this vulnerable state. We see you as a more sexualized character. We also see you in some of the most brutal scenes in the entire franchise. It's quite a remarkable range.

Danielle Harris: That's where I was anyway at my age. I tried to young her up a little bit for the first one with Rob Zombie. I knew that it was time for me to do a role like that, and I was happy to get gritty and dirty. A lot of that stuff too was made up on the day. The original script for Annie in the first one was basically how Mya's character died in the second film. I was supposed to have sex. That boy was like eighteen, and I was thirty. I was like, "Oh, you're so young, and you're so cute." We did the scene, and Michael grabs my boyfriend and throws him off and comes after me. I had said to Tyler [Mane], "You better put pads on or something because I'm the sheriff's daughter. I'm gonna whip your ass." I just had this different sort of take on it, and I wanted to prove myself. I think all of those things were exciting for me as an actress. I knew there was gonna be a level of vulnerability by doing the nudity and the sex scenes that I had never experienced on set before. I hadn't done anything like that. So it was a way for me to prove to everyone that I was an adult and also sort of explore a different side of myself creatively.

I remember laying on the floor there after he cut me up, and I'm screaming. Malcolm's [McDowell] character comes in and Brad's

Danielle Harris covered in blood. Image courtesy of Phil Parmet

character comes in and I'm still laying there, and I remember that everybody was trying to cover me up with a towel or a sheet or whatever. I was like, "I just wanna be left alone. I just wanna be left here." It was fucking freezing, and my teeth are chattering in one of the scenes, and I thought, *Oh God, I'll use this. This is shock. I feel like my body is in shock, and this is what happened, and this feels really real, and it feels really good.* It was something that I could sink my teeth into. I wasn't afraid or hesitant to do any of that stuff. I was excited that somebody was giving me the opportunity.

AG: After everything you've been through with these films, it only feels right to end this conversation on a high note. You have this beautiful friendship with Scout that's turned into a successful podcast and continued working relationship. It's absolutely transcended *Halloween* at this point.

Danielle Harris: It's so crazy, right? COVID brought us together. I've obviously known her for a long time, and we were never close. She always tells that stupid story about how she wanted to be my friend so bad. She went over to my house, and I went out with my boyfriend and left her alone. I think I just never wanted to get in the way of her part of *Halloween*. I let her do her thing, and I did my thing. We had shared experiences. I got her into doing horror conventions. I was like, "There's this whole world you could live in, and it's pretty cool. You're gonna love it, and it could help you pay your bills when you're not getting jobs." I saw her grow up. I saw her go through her twenties and now her thirties. Her and I have a lot in common being child actors and growing up in the *Halloween* franchise. We both have sex- and love-addiction issues, and we both have father issues and a lot of familial complications. We didn't know it until we started to do our show. I've gotten to know her, and she's gotten to know me in a really deep, emotional way. I know she's not had the best luck with girlfriends, which I get. Girls are jealous of her. I've always been someone that wants to support other women, and she is the same way. We want everyone to succeed. We wanna lift each other up; we want to create opportunities to support one another and make fucking awesome movies. It's developed into this big sister/mom relationship, but yet I'm watching a version of myself and I'm seeing her grow.

I'm very protective over her and try to teach her as well about business stuff. She lets me handle the money stuff. We just went and opened a bank account the other day together, and she's like, "Girl, I haven't even done this with my husband." So we have a very strong bond, and we're very protective over one another and dependent on one another too. The only time I have those deep emotional conversations throughout my week are usually with her, and it's usually recorded. It's been cool to share it and to experience it at the same time that the fans are getting to hear us and getting to know us in that way no one really knew before. This has been an interesting ride for us, getting to share a very intimate side of who we are with people. Now we have people come and talk to us about everything. It's made our appearance much more interesting. There's also that fine line with the boundaries that are a little bit confusing to people. There's some characters that like these movies. Sometimes we kind of have to reel it in. We don't want people to come to us at a show and talk about something that's incredibly personal. It's better to send it and we'll read it. But I also feel like we're helping people in a way that we didn't really set out to. I always wanted to be either a homicide detective or a psychiatrist. My whole family was cops. I'm kind of doing both in a sort of weird way. I'm getting to experience true crime stuff and fake murders on set and then getting to help people and openly talk about my problems on a weekly basis with everybody. I hope that I stay friends with her forever.

It is just about the community. That's what keeps it going. I think that we just sort of dove into it. She's a little different because she still wants to do a lot of TV and films. I'm very happy in the horror community, working here and there, raising my kids and living a normal life in Texas, then getting to come on set and get to sink my teeth into these roles. Sometimes they're small, but I'm okay with that too. I don't always wanna be number one on the call sheet all the time. As long as I get to show up and sink my teeth into something, then I'm good.

-CHAPTER 11-
THE LEGACY OF *HALLOWEEN*

Halloween over the years has impacted the horror genre in ways John Carpenter and team likely never thought possible. The legacy of this film franchise is one of inspiration. The reach of Carpenter's 1978 indie film about babysitters being murdered and the twelve films that followed is massive, resonating with not just fans, but also filmmakers, critics, authors, and podcasters. Below some of the voices from this genre speak on what *Halloween* has meant to them. This is the legacy of Halloween:

Adam Marcus (Director, *Jason Goes to Hell, Secret Santa*): "I was eleven when I first saw *Halloween*, and it changed my life forever. Not only did it start my obsessive love of all things Carpenter, but it was, in a very deep way, the opening salvo to a life in horror. I was already a fan, but something about the way Carpenter told the story stayed with me. It was truly scary. And he didn't need buckets of blood to do it. In fact, it was almost as if he was saying blood would make it less scary. He spent so much time in the dark with his heroes, so much time creating tension and suspense, so little time bloodletting. He could just have someone sit up in the out-of-focus background of a shot and get the whole audience screaming. And that was the trick. Every slasher that copied him over the years didn't get that memo, but I did. I learned that what is unseen is what makes a movie scary. Best lesson any aspiring horror director could get."

The Strode house. Image courtesy of Ivan Bukta

Heather Wixson (Author, *In Search of Darkness/Monsters & Makeup & Effects Volume 1*): "There aren't a lot of horror fans who would ever declare *Halloween: Resurrection* as their favorite entry in the famed franchise, but that doesn't mean that it's a movie that shouldn't be celebrated in some capacity. Sure, the opening does the character of Laurie Strode dirty, but once you get past that and let the 'dangertainment' begin, *Halloween: Resurrection* is one of the few movies in the *Halloween* series that actually feels timely. In retrospect, having a reality show hosted in the home of a notorious serial killer seems like something that would be perfectly at home these days airing on the Discovery channel, ultimately making *Resurrection* a story that is, and was, two decades ahead of its time (not to mention Deckard's text prompts that help Sarah survive that Halloween night). As the horror genre was heading towards more serious and gruesome territory with the coming influx of American extremism horror projects in the following years, *Halloween: Resurrection* feels like a bit of a breath of fresh air for that era in modern horror and also gave us some wildly fun quotes to boot. After all, Michael Myers is a killer shark in baggy ass overalls, and Busta Rhymes was right to remind us of that fact in 2002."

Tony Timpone (Editor Emeritus, *Fangoria*): "Jamie Lee Curtis's performance in *Halloween* 2018 was pure, raw emotion. You felt her mental and physical pain. She deserved the Oscar for her work, more so for *Halloween* than *Everything Everywhere All at Once*."

Jeffrey Reddick (Creator of the *Final Destination* franchise): "*Halloween H20* was one of the strongest *Halloween* entries. Jamie Lee Curtis gave a tour de force performance that realistically captured Laurie Strode's trauma and her ability to overcome it by killing Michael Myers."

Patrick Bromley (Coauthor, *In Search of Darkness*): "Though it may sound blasphemous to say, *Halloween 4: The Return of Michael Myers* is my favorite of all the *Halloween* films. It has my favorite characters—I'm more invested in Jamie Lloyd [Danielle Harris] and Rachel [Ellie Cornell] and their relationship than anyone else in the franchise—and several of my favorite set pieces (rooftop chase!). Dwight H. Little, long one of my favorite filmmakers, recognizes that he's probably not going to outdo John Carpenter in technical craft (can anyone?), so instead he brings depth and, for lack of a better word, warmth. From the opening moments that perfectly capture October vibes to its shocking climax, this is the *Halloween* movie I return to most."

Phil Nobile Jr. (*Fangoria* Editor in Chief): "The Shape is a gas leak that kills the family of five down the street while they sleep. The Shape is the heavy quiet in the room where doctors tell you there's nothing they can do about the stage-four cancer taking away your partner a pound at a time. The Shape is the brutal, banal knowledge that the clock is ticking on your time on Earth and that the end is moving steadily and relentlessly in your direction" (quoted from *This Isn't a Man: The Shape of Halloween* with Noble's permission).

Matt Emert (Cohost, *Happy Horror Time* podcast): "I saw John Carpenter's *Halloween* for the first time when I was eleven years old. From its chilling score to that terrifying white mask to the various places the Shape appears watching and waiting to attack his victims, it had me mesmerized from start to finish. To this day, no other film has had that effect on me."

Ryan Showers (Host of the *Scream with Ryan Showers Podcast*): "*Halloween: H20* is my favorite *Halloween* film. As the host of a *Scream* podcast, the way *Halloween: H20* adopted the *Scream* formula and style is not only cinematically fulfilling but allows the franchise to skyrocket to the next level. *Halloween: H20* contains some of the—if not *the*—definitive best writing in the franchise. In particular, *H20* showcases the elite interpretation of Laurie Strode—the deep character arc, the superb performance by Jamie Lee Curtis—over the forty years of our time with the original final girl."

Anthony Brownlee (Executive Producer, *FredHeads*): "My personal experience with *Halloween* goes all the way back to the early nineties, when I saw *Halloween 4* for the first time at around age six or seven. That opening of *H4* was like no other. The *Halloween* scene that was portrayed over that score by Alan Howarth still haunts me to this day, and no other *Halloween* opening, in my mind, beats it. Obviously the original is a stamped classic, but *Halloween 4* had an undeniable charm to it. The scene of the false Michaels is horrific, not knowing which one is which, and the fact that he had now multiplied had my kid brain in shambles."

Sean Parker (Critic, 25YL, Horror Obsessive): "The enduring legacy of *Halloween* is one synonymous with suburban paranoia. People were fleeing rising crime rates in the cities and moving to the suburbs, promoted as the statistical "safe spaces," and commuting back to the cities for work—the American dream of white picket fences, summer BBQs, and the reliant comfort in believing parents were protecting their families. But as summer ends and October 31 dawns on Haddonfield, Carpenter dismantles the illusion of safety effortlessly, turning that American dream into a walking, stalking masked nightmare. Whether it's Laurie, Jamie, or even the kids with masks in Season of the Witch, the bogey man comes for the middle-class family, often leaving me to wonder if the home security system boom of the 1980s isn't partially due to the fear instilled by Michael Myers."

Alison Star Locke (Director, *The Apology*): "I hate to be basic, but for me, the original *Halloween* is still far and away my favorite. Debra Hill's notoriously humane, grounded production style. John

Fixing Michael's mask. Image courtesy of Phil Parmet

Carpenter's music and framing and tension. Laurie pounding on the door and no one helps her. The porch light being turned off. Curtis's frantic, grounded, very real teenager performance. The head tilt in the kitchen. But as formidable and fascinating as Michael Myers is, the most resonant story of the series for me is women having to smarten up and fight for themselves, of living under constant fear of a male attacker and how you face that, and that violence has a legacy to it. . . . I love that each filmmaker has had their own unique take. I love the griminess and poverty of Rob Zombie's *Halloween*. Seeing Sheri Moon Zombie trying to be there for her little boy in prison after he went on a killing spree that included her own daughter was a real tribute to a mother trying to endure and how impossible that can feel at times. I also really love David Gordon Green and company's first *Halloween*. The tragedy of what that trauma did to Laurie Strode and how family trauma is thus passed along to the next generations of women felt so cathartic. Trying to constantly gauge how vigilant or calm you should be with your children is one of life's big parenthood questions, and the extra layer of mother/daughter relationship only compounds that. Knowing that women face this extra threat at all times, albeit here in the form of a supernaturalesque killing machine, makes a hell of a metaphor. I adored the great Judy Greer as Laurie's daughter, Karen, and really related to her wishing she could live a safe, relaxed life but then being faced with yet again, nope, you have to be vigilant. One of my favorite moments in all of the movies is in the basement where Karen fakes being a helpless victim so she can get the good shot at Michael. Boss move—her mother taught her well."

Richard Newby (Author, *We Make Monsters Here*): "I often wonder why I'm so drawn to the *Halloween* installments more than any other horror franchise, particularly when those initial sensations wrought by the on-screen horror have subsided. I think in the end it comes down to a mystery raised in *Halloween Kills*: what was Michael staring at out of the window of his room as a child? It's not really much of a mystery at all. He was staring at Haddonfield. He was staring at us, the evils we unleashed reflected back and consumed by him. And as evil surely changes shape over the decades, so does the Shape, the horrors of each generation given form and purpose within the body and mind of a young boy trapped within the frame of a monster."

Jason Zinoman (*New York Times* Critic at Large; Author, *Shock Value: How a Few Eccentric Outsiders Gave Us Nightmares, Conquered Hollywood, and Invented Modern Horror*): *Halloween* is "one of the more enduring and innovative horror movies ever made. The reason can be boiled down to a few brilliant elements. First, there's the music. . . . The stripped-down notes and propulsive, unstoppable 5/4 meter lodged in the minds of viewers. The music in *Jaws* told you something was coming. The music in *Halloween* made it clear it was never going away. Then there is the bravura opening tracking shot, the most influential in the history of the horror film. . . . Carpenter did care about genre conventions but he had no interest in exploring politics in his action and horror movies—and there has never been a portrait of a serial killer less interested in psychology. And that gets to the great innovation of *Halloween*: Michael Myers himself. Since he has been imitated so often, it's easy to forget that he was actually a rather radical, even experimental character, an entirely new kind of monster" (quoted from *Shock Value* with Zinoman's permission).

ACKNOWLEDGMENTS

To my wife, Tracey: Thank you for pushing me to do this, helping me narrow down my ideas, dealing with my highs and lows, tolerating the late nights, rewatching these films with me over and over, and listening to my 2:00 a.m. rants and revelations. In short, I never would have done this (or finished it) without you. I love you. Let's go ghost hunting, babe.

To my sons, Brayden and Jack: I hope this book shows you that dreams are always worth chasing, that hard work yields results, and that it's never too late to get started. Pursue your passions, my sons.

Jack Grevas dressed as Michael Myers, from author's personal collection

To Scott and David for taking a chance on me and giving me enough time to go big here. I've learned a lot from working with David throughout the editing process—invaluable lessons that have made me a much better writer.

To Ivan Bukta for all the location photos. Ivan's pictures took the book up a level and provided me with a lot of inspiration and momentum, especially thematically.

To Matt and Melanie for not only the cover, but also many wonderful creative conversations and support.

To my parents for their encouragement and support.

To Dwight Little and Danielle Harris for believing in me and this project enough to help me line up interviews. This book is significantly better because of you two vouching for me and my work.

To GK and Chris the Brain: I may not have finished college, but you guys gave me my start. None of this happens without the real-world journalism experience I gained working for you.

To the Horror Movie Night crew at Steve Taylor's apartment every Wednesday and the CDX20 crew: Wil Don, Blackjack Carson, Chris, Johnny, Casey, Phil, Magan Faile, Jurassica Pop, Jimi, Dantana, Natalie, Randy, Steve, and so many more. Great movies. Great music. Great people. Great memories.

Lastly, I want to acknowledge two people who aren't here anymore. My stepmom, Marty Helms, and my cousin Jeff Tucker. Marty pushed me to write from a young age and read every word I wrote before she passed. Jeff introduced me to all things horror at a young age. I wouldn't love this genre the way I do if it weren't for my cousin and the time we spent together as kids. Love and miss you both.

–ABOUT THE AUTHOR–

Andrew Grevas is an author and journalist based out of Cincinnati, where he lives with his wife and younger son. Andrew is the founder of websites such as 25YL and Horror Obsessive and has assisted with the launch of websites that focus on television and film as a whole. Prior to that, Andrew worked in the wild world of professional wrestling, honing his journalism skills both on camera and off, working as a broadcaster, a columnist, and a writer for live event programs.

Andrew's lifelong fascination with all things spooky likely stems from watching Mark Frost and David Lynch's *Twin Peaks* at the tender age of five with his mother as it originally aired. His obsession with long-form storytelling and the artistry of filmmaking began at a young age, setting him on a path of analyzing the work he found intriguing (or scary) through both the written word and interviews with artists and performers.

MORE TO READ AT TUCKERDSPRESS.COM

MORE TO READ AT TUCKERDSPRESS.COM